ZEEBRUGGE

ZEEBRUGGE

The Greatest Raid of All

CHRISTOPHER SANDFORD

CASEMATE
Oxford & Philadelphia

Published in Great Britain and the United States of America in 2018 by
CASEMATE PUBLISHERS
The Old Music Hall, 106–108 Cowley Road, Oxford OX4 1JE, UK
and
1950 Lawrence Road, Havertown, PA 19083, USA

Hardcover Edition: ISBN 978-1-61200-504-1
Digital Edition: ISBN 978-1-61200-505-8

A CIP record for this book is available from the British Library

For a complete list of Casemate titles, please contact:

CASEMATE PUBLISHERS (US)
Telephone (610) 853-9131
Fax (610) 853-9146
Email: casemate@casematepublishers.com
www.casematepublishers.com

CASEMATE PUBLISHERS (UK)
Telephone (01865) 241249
Email: casemate-uk@casematepublishers.co.uk
www.casematepublishers.co.uk

For my father Sefton Sandford (1925–2012), a great navy man

Who durst be so bold with a few crooked boards nailed together, a stick standing upright, and a rag tied to it, to adventure into the ocean?

THOMAS FULLER

Bravery never goes out of fashion.

WILLIAM MAKEPEACE THACKERAY

We reached Dunkirk at 3am, where we put up. A very bloody sight.

SUB-LIEUTENANT EDWARD BERTHON, RN, A SURVIVOR

Contents

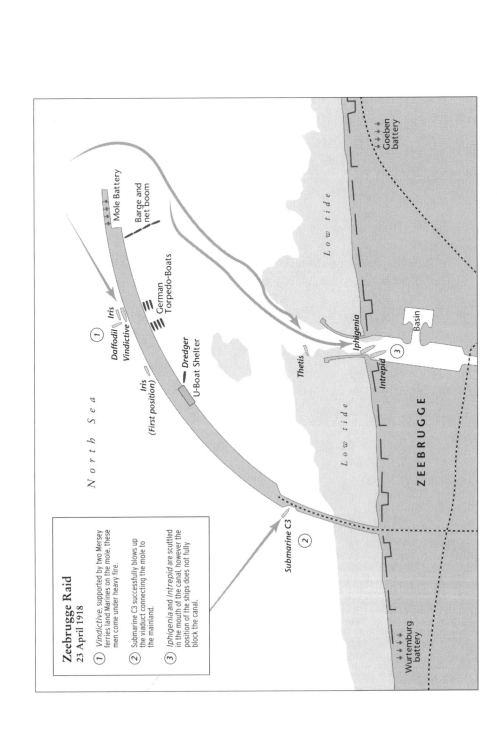

Zeebrugge Raid
23 April 1918

① *Vindictive*, supported by two Mersey ferries land Marines on the mole, these men come under heavy fire.

② Submarine C3 successfully blows up the viaduct connecting the mole to the mainland.

③ *Iphigenia* and *Intrepid* are scuttled in the mouth of the canal, however the position of the ships does not fully block the canal.

North Sea

Mole Battery

Barge and net boom

German Torpedo-Boats

Daffodil *Iris*
Vindictive

Iris
(First position)

Dredger
U-Boat Shelter

Low tide

Thetis

Iphigenia

Intrepid

Basin

③

Low tide

Submarine C3

②

ZEEBRUGGE

Low tide

Goeben battery

Wurtemburg battery

Acknowledgments

This is not a comprehensive list or account of each and every one of the brave individuals who took part in the British raids on the Flanders coast of April and May 1918. No slight is intended on any name that might be missing, and anyone interested in reading more about the subject will find some suggestions in the bibliography at the back of the book. Every effort has nonetheless been made to portray the events exactly as they occurred, and to record as accurately as possible the recollections of the men who lived them. I only wish I could blame someone listed below for the shortcomings of the text. They are mine alone.

The book began life late one wet Saturday evening in April 1968, when I was an 11-year-old schoolboy and my father Sefton was a captain in the Royal Navy. Together with my mother we were living in a thatched cottage in Marlow-on-Thames, a bucolic spot that perhaps lacked some of the racy intrigue of our next family home: Moscow, then in the depths of the Cold War, where my father was about to serve as British naval attaché. On the evening in question we were sitting around our coffin-sized radiogram listening to the news about strikes and currency crises at home, and mass shootings and race riots in America, when out of the announcer's patter a new programme cut through the gloom by combining breathless, Dick Barton-type narration with equally vivid sound effects in a feature to mark the fiftieth anniversary of the Zeebrugge Raid. I remember hearing the name 'Richard Sandford' mentioned, followed in turn by the noise of an enjoyably shrill simulated explosion. When the broadcast ended my father went on to explain how we were related to this heroic individual, and at that moment somewhere deep inside my titanically vain younger self the gnarled middle-aged author awoke with a start. I regret that it's taken me a further fifty years to see the project through, and that my father, to whom the book is dedicated, didn't live to see this small fulfillment of our mutual fascination with the events of St. George's Day 1918.

For archive material, input or advice I should thank, professionally: AbeBooks; Alibris; *America*; *American Renaissance*; Francesca Anyon; Lucy Arnold; Barrow Submariners Association; Bookfinder; Jessica Borg; Britannia Royal Naval College, Dartmouth; British Library; British Newspaper Archive; Brocks Fireworks; Brotherton Library, Leeds; Miles Wynn Cato; *Chronicles*; Commander Robert Dunn, RN; General Register Office; Eric Grove; Sarah Gunn; Hampshire Record Office;

Christine Harper; *Hedgehog Review*; David Henderson; Hillingdon Libraries; Laura Hilton-Smith; the History Press; Keith Hollick; Imperial War Museum; Charles Keyes; King's College Library, London; Barbara Levy; Library of Congress; Clare Litt; Colin McKenzie; George Malcolmson; William Meredith; the Ministry of Defence; John Moore; National Maritime Museum; National Museums Liverpool; National Museum, Royal Navy; *National Review*; Jenni Orme; Steff Palmer; Richard Porter; Tim Reidy; Renton Library; Royal Marines Museum, Eastney; Royal Museums, Greenwich; Royal Naval Historical Branch; Royal Navy Officers' Club, Portsmouth; Royal Navy Submarine Museum; *Russian Life*; David Rymill; Martin Salmon; Daniel Sandford; Seaside Library, Oregon; *Seattle Times*; Ruth Sheppard; Andrew Stuart; *Touchstone*; Remi Turner; Mark Ulrich; UK Maritime Archives and Library; UK National Archives; University of Leeds Library Special Collections; University of Montana; University of Puget Sound; Vital Records; William Wagner; Dominic Walsh; Western Front Association; Wirral Archives Service; Captain Jolyon Woodard, RN, and Jenny Wraight. My particular thanks to Robin B. James for the index.

And personally: Lisa Armstead; Reverend Maynard Atik; Pete Barnes; the late Ryan Boone; Rocco Bowen; Robert and Hilary Bruce; Jon Burke; Don Carson; Changelink; Hunter Chatriand; Common Ground; Christina Coulter; Tim Cox; Andrew Craig; the late Deb K. Das; the Davenport; Monty Dennison; Micky Dolenz; the Dowdall family; John and Barbara Dungee; Reverend Joanne Enquist; Malcolm Galfe; the Gay Hussar; Gethsemane Lutheran Church; the late Don Gordon; James Graham; the late Tom Graveney; Norman Greenbaum; Jeff and Rita Griffin; Grumbles; Steve and Jo Hackett; Hampton Tutors; Hermino; Alex Holmes; the Hotel Vancouver; Jo Jacobius; Julian James; Lincoln Kamell; Terry Lambert; Belinda Lawson; Eugene Lemcio; the Lorimer family; Robert Dean Lurie; Les McBride; Heather and Mason McEachran; Charles McIntosh; the Macri family; Lee Mattson; Jim Meyersahm; Missoula Doubletree; the Morgans; John and Colleen Murray; Greg Nowak; Chuck Ogmund; Phil Oppenheim; Valya Page; Robin Parish; Owen Paterson; Steele Paulich; Peter Perchard; Chris Pickrell; the Prins family; Scott P. Richert; Ailsa Rushbrooke; St. Matthew's, Renton; Susan Sandford; Sandy Cove Inn; Peter Scaramanga; Seattle C.C.; C.D. Smith Construction; Dorothy Smith; Fred and Cindy Smith; the late Reverend Harry Smith; Marty Smith; Debbie Standish; the Stanley family; Jack Surendranath; Belinda and Ian Taylor; the late Mary Tyvand; Diana Villar; Karin Wieland; Soleil Wieland; Debbie Wild; the Willis Fleming family; Karla Winch; Aaron Wolf; the Woons; Doris and Felicia Zhu, and Zoo Town Surfers.

My deepest thanks, as always, to Karen and Nicholas Sandford.

CHAPTER I

The Sea Churned Red

The night was pitch black, though with silvery flashes of lightning sometimes pulsing over the inky water and silhouetting the shore to the west. It soon became a matter of increasingly miserable weather, and even more miserable visibility, for the British naval force making its way out to sea off the coast of Scotland. Persistent rain squalls soaked the convoy of 30 warships of various classes and sizes, along with their dozen accompanying support vessels. A petty officer on the cruiser HMS *Courageous* complained that 'nothing could be kept dry on board' and if an enemy attack had occurred 'they could have been on us before we saw them, so thick was the mist and low cloud'. Years later, he compared the whole exercise to 'rid[ing] on the Ghost Train at a seaside resort – you'd be bumping along, turning blind corners, braced for a collision, and then suddenly there'd be this blinding sheet of light, with huge shapes rising up all around you, and then total darkness again. I have never been so terrified in all my life'.

It was the night of Thursday, 31 January 1918, and the British ships were on their way from their home base in Rosyth to take part in Operation EC1, a fleet exercise due to begin early the following morning off Scapa Flow in the Orkney Islands. The force was under the overall control of 47-year-old Vice-Admiral David Beatty, commander-in-chief of the Grand Fleet, whose reputation for audacity at sea was matched both by his colourful personal appearance, illustrated by his rakishly tilted cap and non-regulation three-button 'monkey jacket', as well as his increasingly complex domestic life, which by now included an affair with the wife of a senior colleague who also happened to be naval equerry to the king. Beatty was widely thought to have distinguished himself twenty months earlier at the Battle of Jutland, where he is remembered for his comment that 'there seems to be something wrong with our bloody ships today' after two of his squadron had exploded. He later remarked that 'a display of leadership was essential' under the circumstances.

As well as *Courageous*, Operation EC1 included no fewer than seven other battlecruisers with their destroyer escorts, three cruisers and, bringing up the rear, two flotillas of submarines, each led by a light cruiser. The whole force was to proceed in a single line down the Firth of Forth and out into the North Sea, where it would rendezvous with other Royal Navy detachments before steaming north to Orkney. It was a large-scale and complicated enough manoeuvre to undertake at the best of times, requiring the highest standards of seamanship, quite apart from the twin challenges posed by the threat of marauding enemy U-boats and the abysmal weather. Although conditions were relatively calm when the main force left Rosyth shortly after dusk on the 31st, a steady drizzle and sea mist soon set in. As the *Courageous* petty officer recalled many years later: 'In those days, navigation was almost unchanged since Nelson's time, and we had to grope our way in the dark. There was no radar, and no signalling was allowed. Looking back, they were terrible conditions.' On went the litany:

> Per orders, each ship in the line showed only a dim blue light to the one behind it, while maintaining strict radio silence. So now imagine you're travelling on a motorway in the fog with no headlights, and thirty other cars are right behind you with nobody knowing for sure where anyone else is, or whether there's someone waiting up ahead to ambush you. Nobody got a wink of sleep that night, not just the lookouts, and you didn't dare go below to rest and wash your face – no hot food or drink – and all this time in a great state of mental anxiety.

That was certainly the case among the crews of the nine steam-propelled K-class submarines accompanying the fleet that night. Dirty, cramped and notoriously prone to break down, these particular vessels had earned the nickname of 'Kalamity class' since first entering service in 1916. Of the 17 K submarines built, six were eventually lost in accidents. 'That was their reputation in a nutshell,' one survivor wrote. Just two months before Operation EC1 got underway, the submarine *K1* had collided with her sister *K4* while on patrol off the coast of Denmark. Her commander had then scuttled her to avoid capture.

The whole concept of British underwater naval strategy remained in its infancy at the outbreak of the European war in August 1914, and even then only proceeded in the face of the hostility of most of the service's more traditionally minded officers. While serving as First Sea Lord in 1910–11, Admiral of the Fleet Sir Arthur Wilson, VC – known to his subordinates, generally affectionately, as 'Old 'ard 'art' – had judged the submarine to be 'Underhand, unfair and damned un-English'. The sort of men who volunteered for K-class duty in the years 1916–18 (when the boats themselves were still given only numbers, rather than the dignity of actual names) were widely seen as somewhat eccentric, bearded figures who operated in damp, claustrophobic quarters that smelled of tar and corticene, and whose preferred dress of sweaters and oilskins contrasted with their upstairs colleagues' pressed dress uniforms and decorations. At an unwieldy 339 feet long, the K boat was difficult to steer, and normally required fully 30 minutes to submerge to its maximum depth of 200 feet. Even then, there were frequently problems in doing so. In one early sea trial with Prince George – the future King George VI – aboard as an observer, *K3* had lost control and buried herself nose first in a sandbar while her propellers continued to wildly scythe the air above. The commander of the boat later informed an Admiralty court martial that he had not been aware of his exact position at the time because 'rats had eaten my charts'.

Each K submarine was equipped with eight 18-inch torpedo tubes, four in the bow and four on the beam, with a spare pair located on a swivel mounting on the superstructure, though the last proved all too liable to jam or backfire in heavy seas. In 15 years of service, only one K-class vessel ever directly engaged an enemy target, when on 16 June 1917 *K7* fired five torpedoes at a passing U-boat. Only one of the five hit its mark, and even that failed to explode.

In fairness, the K submarines were not quite a full-scale disaster of design. With a top speed of 24 knots, and eight knots when submerged, barring technical mishaps they were capable of comfortably matching or outrunning most of their potential attackers. At least in theory, under emergency conditions a K boat could secure her main engines, shift to battery power and execute a crash-dive in just three minutes, though few of the crews attempting this particular manoeuvre later spoke of the experience fondly. Within the confines of being thrown together in a steel-enclosed tube roughly the length of a football field, the ship's company of around six officers and 53 ratings was at least relatively comfortable while at sea: there was a proper deckhouse, built over the conning tower rather than the canvas awning fitted in previous British submarines; they were also the first vessels of their kind to be equipped with a diesel generator to charge the batteries, an advanced ventilation system (though they could still be stiflingly hot), a comparatively large mess room for the ratings, and even a small, carpeted officers' lounge which included an iron bathtub discreetly tucked away behind a screen in the corner. On paper, the K boats gave the Royal Navy a submarine force of the most advanced type, and one which should have been a match for its German opponents.

In practice, this was not always the case. All 17 of the completed K boats had serious operational issues. As we've seen, collisions, explosions, torpedo failures and groundings were common. One K submarine sprang a leak while at anchor at Gareloch in the west of Scotland, flooded her batteries, and came close to asphyxiating her crew with chlorine gas. In January 1917, her sister boat *K13* sank in the same location when seawater entered her engine room while she was preparing to dive; 34 crew members and civilian dockyard workers perished as a result. The wreck was eventually salvaged and recommissioned, without significant design changes, as *K22*, just in time for her to take part in Operation EC1 six months later. Meanwhile, *K5* would suffer repeated mechanical breakdowns during her four years of service, only to be lost with all 57 hands during a mock battle held after the war in the Bay of Biscay. Just a few weeks after this tragedy, *K15* sank at her mooring in Portsmouth when her diving vents opened without warning. The K boats often leaked, and in the words of the Admiralty a number 'submerged prematurely, producing losses'.

The most common complaint about the K class as a whole was that the submarines had 'too many damned holes' – the various hatches, valves, vents, hull penetrations, intakes and tubes made them excessively vulnerable when starting a dive, and even while operating on the surface the boats had an unfortunate tendency to ship water through their funnels and flood their boiler rooms, leaving them adrift on the open sea. They were simply unable to function at anything close to their peak efficiency except under ideal weather conditions and with unlimited time for their various diving and surfacing procedures, not circumstances likely to obtain in the typical north European waters of the war years 1916–18.

In September 1910, the Admiralty had appointed as its inspecting captain of submarines a 37-year-old Indian army general's son named Roger John Brownlow Keyes. A supremely self-confident individual, even at that relatively early stage in his career, he had remarked shortly after taking up his duties that the Germans deserved 'a thorough hiding'. Having joined the service as a 12-year-old cadet on the training ship HMS *Britannia*, Keyes had gone on to distinguish himself by leading a series of daringly irregular raids to harry the Chinese troops during the British intervention in the Boxer Rebellion of 1899–1901. In July 1900, he'd personally destroyed the heavily defended Chinese fort at Hsi-cheng while at the head of a landing party of 32 sailors armed with pistols, cutlasses and coshes. After the raiders had put the fort's garrison to flight, Keyes had stayed behind to methodically lay an explosive charge directly under the building's ammunition depot. Lighting the fuse, he then walked unhurriedly back down an otherwise deserted towpath to his waiting ship, HMS *Fame*, which was tied up on a nearby river. Keyes's biographer wrote of the ensuing events: 'The magazine went up with a roar that shook the countryside. Two of the landing-party were injured by the falling masonry. But these were the only casualties, and the *Fame* returned home without further incident.'

Slim and pale, with a clipped speaking style, rather over-prominent ears, and a permanently crooked left forearm as a result of a childhood accident, psychologists would later speculate whether these physical shortcomings had somehow driven Keyes on to almost suicidal acts of personal valour. To a naval colleague named Edward Renouf, 'He clearly fancied himself as a man of action, divorced from the routine world, free to concentrate on the sort of piratical missions that appealed to his jolly midshipman's personality.' In fact, Keyes was in some ways the beau ideal of the British fighting man of the period. 'His natural temper [was] both stoic and combative,' George VI later said of him. A newly arrived officer on Keyes's post-China command HMS *Venus* remembered being brought up short by a colleague for wondering if 'the old man' really deserved his heroic reputation. 'Captain Keyes,' he was told, 'is the one man in the Royal Navy who the men will follow into the jaws of hell … He is audacity personified.' That had concluded the exchange. As the navy's inspector of submarines, Keyes had come to envision a 'line abreast of high-speed submersibles that would work ahead of a main strike force – one that would engage the enemy even before the latter knew it was in a fight'. This fundamental shift in strategy from one that saw the submarine as an essentially defensive asset, conducting offshore patrols or leading occasional feints into the North Sea, hoping to draw the enemy out, to one that emphasised the submarine's hostile, first-strike potential would be a significant factor when it came to the Admiralty's decision to commission the K-class flotilla just a few years later.

✳

The men of K force were not the only ones with misgivings as they put to sea at the start of Operation EC1 on that dark January night in 1918. Commodore Ernest Leir, on the bridge of the cruiser HMS *Ithuriel*, would also remember looking back uneasily over his shoulder and seeing only 'the dimmest of lights, haloed like street lamps in a thick London fog' as the convoy reached open water and increased speed to 22 knots. Leir added that there had been a 'lot of dust and pieces flying around' as his 1,700-ton ship's steam turbines began to quicken, and that even so *Ithuriel* had soon lost sight of her guide *Courageous*, though she was only a minute's sailing time behind her. *Ithuriel* herself lay at the head of a mile-long convoy of five submarines – *K11*, *K12*, *K14*, *K17* and *K22*, the former *K13*. To their rear came the battle cruisers *Australia*, *New Zealand*, *Indomitable* and *Inflexible*, followed in turn by the light cruiser *Fearless* and four more submarines, *K3*, *K4*, *K6* and *K7*. Several smaller surface boats bobbed and swerved between them, and the heavy rain squalls as night descended, accentuated by banks of patchy fog, led Commodore Leir to think of the whole exercise in terms of 'juddering along a very bumpy, insufficiently lit road, towards an unseen and ill-defined destination'. Behind the last of the submarines bulked a flotilla of three battleships accompanied by their screening destroyers. 'The lights up ahead,' wrote a sailor on *Indomitable*, 'were so dim that it became obvious to every man of us that the utmost vigilance was required, not only to dodge the enemy but to avoid collision with our own side.'

These were prescient words. As *Ithuriel* and her submarine flotilla left the estuary and headed northeast on a course that took them close to the small, uninhabited Isle of May, some five miles off the Scottish coast, a lookout reported seeing a cluster of lights off the starboard beam, apparently closing in on their position. The sudden appearance of traffic ahead of him, combined with his natural fears of possible U-boat activity in the area, seems to have come as an unpleasant shock to Commodore Leir, who ordered a sharp turn to port to avoid a collision with the mysterious shapes that lay about a mile and a half distant. It's now thought that these were nothing more sinister than a convoy of British minesweeping trawlers, oblivious to the fleet manoeuvres, and that the two groups of ships would have gone on to pass by without incident had each simply maintained its course. In theory, at least, Operation EC1 had been devised as a series of carefully coordinated advances from one neatly drawn map grid to another, 'with adequate separation maintained at all times in the light of visibility and [sea] conditions'. But in practice it also involved sending a large, mixed-class fleet into some of the busiest shipping lanes in the world, sailing at close quarters and at high speed in the dark. Given the K boats' known technical deficiencies and tendency to break down at inopportune moments, it might now reasonably be thought that the potential for disaster had existed from the time the move order had first been drafted on 28 January, and then been communicated down the line two days later. 'It may have sounded like a good idea on paper,' one submariner wrote, 'but to me it was just a stupid order coming from men sitting on their backsides in front of the fireplace at the Admiralty. My mates and I all thought something would go wrong.'

It did: the moment the unidentified lights appeared in the haze about two minutes' sailing time ahead of *Ithuriel* was the beginning of a chain reaction of misadventures that later became known as the 'Battle of May Island'.

The first intimation of real trouble ahead came when the officer of the watch on *K14* saw the vague shape of *K11* swing to port ahead of him, and communicated this fact to his senior colleague, Commander Thomas Harbottle. 'Then the game began [as] our helm jammed tight from being put hard over at 20 knots,' a crew member wrote. 'We pushed on into the blackness, but now in a circular motion, tak[ing] us far out of our rightful position in the dance … Soon the hissing and grinding of the engines was terrific, and bitter words were exchanged among those in the deckhouse attempting to alleviate the problem.'

With little more to do than frantically spin the wheel from port to starboard and back again, 'cursing richly' as he did so, Commander Harbottle ordered that *K14* turn on her main navigation lights 'so that some damn fool doesn't run us down in the dark'. A moment or two later, the boat's helm righted itself and she again appeared to be alone on the sea. Harbottle then ordered that *K14* turn back to starboard and without further ado resume her place in the line behind *K11*. But before she could do so a voice from the conning tower called out 'Ship astern!' and simultaneous with the last syllable 'there was a fearful thud and a roar like that of an exploding volcano'. *K14* had begun her turn just in time to be rammed by the last submarine in the line, the refurbished *K13*, now designated as *K22*, which was travelling at some 21 knots at the time of the collision. She hit *K14* squarely on the rear port side, immediately behind a loaded torpedo compartment. Both boats stopped dead in the water while the rest of the flotilla, unaware of the unfolding drama behind them, carried on into the night. According to the subsequent report there was a 'great mass of twisted steelwork in *K14*'s midsection' and she appeared to be 'going down slowly by the bow'. Water had burst into the boat's living quarters at the point of impact and drowned two of her crew members. 'In light of these circumstances,' the report continued, '*K22* broke radio silence long enough to report to *Ithuriel* that there had been an incident in the dark behind her,' and that *K14* was crippled and sinking as a result.

Meanwhile, Commander Harbottle sent out a rapidly repeated SOS on his Aldis lamp, while another *K14* crew member stood by astern with a Very pistol in hand, ready to warn off any traffic coming up behind them.

Twelve minutes later the lookouts of the floundering *K14* and *K22* observed a number of grey shapes steaming out of the night and bearing down ominously on their position. This was the 2nd Battle Squadron of eight combined cruisers and destroyers, travelling at 18 knots on their way to their preassigned rendezvous with the other units of Operation EC1 in the North Sea. They appeared to be moving in two groups, four ships leading four more, steering east by northeast and coming straight towards the stricken submarines. Seven of the eight ships passed safely by, but the battlecruiser *Inflexible* hit *K22* a hard glancing blow. The force of the impact bent the first 30 feet of *K22*'s bows at right angles like a can being ripped open before going on to tear off her ballast and fuel tanks. For the second time in a quarter of an hour there was 'an ear-splitting, stupefying din, [with] lights suddenly switched on and flashing madly fore and aft, [and] a jet of steam driven into the sky'. The disabled *K22* immediately began to list to port and then to sink down into the water, until only the submarine's bridge showed above the waves.

Two minutes earlier, on the bridge of HMS *Ithuriel*, Commodore Leir had at last successfully picked up one of the flickering lantern signals from *K14* to say that she had been struck by *K22,* and could a surface ship please now come to their mutual assistance. At 8.11 p.m. Leir ordered his flotilla to turn around to go to the aid of the two submarines. At that point he still knew nothing of the subsequent collision between *K22* and HMS *Inflexible*. Leir completed his turn at 8.18 p.m. and was surprised on doing so to see the 20,000-ton battlecruiser HMAS *Australia* coming straight towards him out of the sea mist at a speed of 20 knots. Rapid evasive manoeuvring meant that the two ships passed narrowly by each other, suffering only a violent wash as they did so. *Australia* then nearly hit the submarine *K12*, slicing by her port side with only three feet to spare.

Having completed her turn, *Ithuriel* continued her zigzagging progress towards the stricken *K14*, in the process managing to lose contact with all three of the submarines that were meant to follow her. In the subsequent confusion *K17* collided with the scout cruiser HMS *Fearless*. The impact was enough to impale the conning tower of the submarine on the larger ship's bows before she was thrown loose to flounder in a morass of churning seawater, escaping oil and wreckage. The steel skin of her starboard forward compartment lay peeled back like tinfoil. Nine minutes after the collision, *K17* slid below the surface and sank. All 56 members of her crew managed to jump into the freezing water, where in time they were cut down by the seven ships of the 5th Battle Squadron passing through the area, oblivious to what had happened there. Only nine men out of the submarine's company survived this second ordeal, and one of these died of his injuries shortly afterwards.

Meanwhile, *K12*, having barely missed HMAS *Australia*, was struggling to come about and restore something of the symmetry of the line that was supposed to form up behind *Ithuriel*, a process one of her men (like other Operation EC1 survivors, resorting to latter-day forms of transport for an analogy) compared to 'putting six high-speed aircraft one in front of the other in the middle of a raging storm at 30,000 feet'. It was a difficult manoeuvre to execute at the best of times, let alone in the conditions that prevailed off the Isle of May on the night of 31 January. 'As we came round,' *K12*'s Lieutenant-Commander John Bower recalled, 'it suddenly appeared we were on a crash course with another submarine which had been in the flotilla behind *Fearless*.' This turned out to be *K6*, which altered course to port just in time to avoid a head-on collision. 'In only a few seconds, this boat, even at close quarters only visible in glimpses, had disappeared into the night, and we breathed a sigh of relief that the worst seemed to be over.'

The officer on watch on *K6* who took the last-minute evasive action to prevent her hitting *K12* was a 26-year-old bishop's son named Lieutenant Richard Douglas Sandford. An ungainly child, Sandford had since acquired austere good looks, with receding dark hair and a trim, compact build that defined him as a submariner, a sportsman and something of a playboy. When off duty he often rather curiously favoured an ensemble of grey shorts and a matching grey jersey, which gave him the look of an overgrown schoolboy. Unmarried, he enjoyed church music, cricket and an occasional glass of gin. Some of the younger men on *K6* knew him fondly as 'Uncle Baldy'. One of those who used the term was a 17-year-old midshipman called Louis Battenberg, who went on to be known to the world as Earl Mountbatten.

Although Sandford was able to successfully avoid ramming *K12* in the mounting chaos off the Isle of May, his hard turn to port had taken him out of the line supposedly following HMS *Fearless*. As he came about, he now saw a single white light ahead, about 200 yards directly in front of him. Without further delay, and 'employing the bluntest of terms', Sandford duly alerted his commanding officer, Commodore Geoffrey Layton, who appeared post-haste on the bridge of *K6*. Within moments, both men realised to their horror that the light Sandford had seen belonged to a darkly silhouetted submarine which lay broadside across their path. It was their sister ship *K4*, which had gone off course and come to a stop close to the spot where *K17* had sunk only a few minutes earlier. Layton ordered full steam astern, but *K6* still met *K4* with a 'hideous, ramming blow which nearly cut her in half'. Sandford's official log entry of the incident is a model of restraint: '... 8.34 p.m. Altered course to port to avoid green light bearing one (1) point on Port Bow. 8.35 Reduced speed to slow both engines. 8.36 Collided with another submarine. 8.36 Full astern both. 8.39 Stop both. Navigation lights [and] searchlight switched on.'

As they collided the two submarines were briefly locked into one mangled body, which 'rose up grotesquely' for an instant and then 'crashed down into the water where they began to sink rapidly'. At the last second, *K6*'s wildly flailing propellers wrenched her free of the mortally wounded *K4* and within a few feet of yet another submarine, *K7*, which cut past them in the gloom before just as quickly disappearing into a swirling pall of grey smoke. None of *K4*'s 59 crew survived her sinking.

It did not help the overall chaos off the Isle of May that whether through ignorance, indecision or lingering concerns about security, there was still no general radio alarm about the positions of the stricken ships and their survivors. At around 8.15 p.m. the destroyer HMS *Venetia* had at least managed to locate the distressed *K14*, and now lay alongside her with a searchlight trained on the submarine's freakishly twisted midsection. Even so, four more surface ships passed by 'terrifyingly close, their wash breaking over *K14*'s sinking bridge' and apparently knocking one man overboard from *Venetia*'s aft deck.

Worse was to follow when two minutes later the full force of the 5th Battle Squadron surged out of the night, tearing past the submarine *K3* – one of the few of her group so far undamaged – and heading straight into the path of *K7*, which had taken up position close to the spot where *Fearless* had rammed *K17* in order to help recover any survivors. The column of seven speeding ships cut down no fewer than 48 of the shipwrecked men struggling helplessly in the water. This was the most destructive single episode of the night's tragedy, and the scene lingered long in the memories of those who witnessed it. 'In less than two minutes,' one of *K7*'s crew remembered, 'the heavy ships ran past, one after another, churning the sea dark red, until the cries of those in their path and the fearful clamour of engines was replaced by a terrible silence.'

In *K6*, Lieutenant Sandford was able to report to his captain that their boat still appeared to be seaworthy, and for some time after that they joined in the search for any further survivors from the night's collisions. None was found. *K6* and *K7* then took up position alongside the damaged *Fearless* to steam slowly back to home port. The confused remnants of Operation EC1 followed at intervals during the night. 'It was a veritable charnel-house,' Sandford recorded of the returning convoy as it finally straggled back to base. In less than two hours, the Royal Navy had lost two submarines, a further four had been damaged, and the cruiser *Fearless* effectively been put out of action, all without a single shot being fired by the enemy.

Arguing in an overnight cable to the war cabinet in London that the disaster raised 'serious questions about how sensitive information may be disseminated when national morale is at stake', the Admiralty successfully hushed up the news of Operation EC1, at least for public consumption, and little of it appeared even in official circles. A top-secret 'Naval Weekly Appreciation' paper tabled at Downing Street on 2 February 1918 noted only:

On Jan 28th, the torpedo gunboat 'Hazard' was sunk at Portsmouth as the result of a collision with a hospital transport ... On Jan 30th the special service vessel 'Wellholme' was sunk by gunfire by an enemy ship, 20 miles south of Portland Bill ... On Jan 31st in the North Sea, Submarine K17 collided with HMS 'Fearless', and sank. About the same time, Submarines K4 and K6 were also in collision. Five officers and 43 men were lost from K17 and five officers and 50 men from K4.

That concluded the formal political discussion of the matter. It took a further 84 years for a commemorative plaque to be erected on a cairn in Anstruther, the nearest Scottish port to the scene of the tragedy, though even that would fail to mention the cause of the loss of life. Divers have since discovered the wrecks of the two sunken submarines, which lie just northeast of the Isle of May, about 100 metres apart and 50 metres down, on a site now designated an official war grave.

The few injured men who survived the ordeal were taken to a military hospital in Rosyth. Richard Sandford perhaps spoke for many of those who emerged from the exercise when he said that 'I stopped being a child' that night 'and came face to face with the reality of the world.' Apart from the physical injuries, there's evidence that some of those who took part in Operation EC1 suffered from what we would now call post-traumatic stress disorder. One man from *K7* who had seen the carnage caused by the 5th Battle Squadron running down the survivors of *K17* is said to have been 'not right in the head ... He was taken to a hospital, [but] is supposed to have become deranged and wandered away ... since which his friends have heard nothing from him'.

Commodore Leir of HMS *Ithuriel* was one of 19 officers who faced trial by court martial as a result of their role in Operation EC1. He was charged with 'negligently or by default losing [sight of] submarine K7' which was relatively mild compared with some of the other indictments handed down to his co-defendants. These included drunkenness, willful disobedience and 'gross neglect of duty, result[ing] in damage to His Majesty's property'. Leir himself was acquitted. He remained in the navy until 1931, and returned to serve with distinction in the Second World War before retiring in 1943, aged 60, for the final time. Nine years later, Leir was convicted by a civilian jury of having assaulted the elderly rector of Ditcheat in Somerset after taking offence at the clergyman's sermon one Sunday. He was fined £20 and ordered to pay the costs of the prosecution.

Although Ernest Leir was absolved of blame by the 1918 court martial, 16 of his brother officers were found guilty of charges under the Naval Discipline Act. They faced sentences ranging from summary dismissal, or forfeiture of promotion, down to the more modest penalty of transfer to another branch of the service. Coincidentally or not, several of their former ships were soon also discarded, and within only three years HMS *Ithuriel*, *Fearless* and *Inflexible* had all been broken up and sold for scrap. There were those who continued to think that the men at the top had sent up 'a smokescreen of lies' about the whole affair, and that a disproportionate share of the blame had fallen on their junior subordinates. To such critics, the secret inquiry conducted by 51-year-old Rear Admiral William Goodenough, CB, seemed only to emphasise the inaptness of that officer's surname. It not only again exonerated Commodore Leir but failed to so much as mention those of Leir's superior officers responsible for the executive planning of Operation EC1, such as Admiral Sir Hugh Evan-Thomas, overall commander of the 5th Battle Squadron, or his friend Vice-Admiral Beatty of the Grand Fleet.

In time there was to be some muted but persistent criticism of those who had pushed for the introduction of the critically flawed K-class boats in the first place, a list that prominently included Roger Keyes. Although Keyes had been nowhere near the Isle of May on the night of 31 January, his original proposal that the navy move swiftly to commission a fleet of 'fast, large, steam-turbine submersibles [and] that these be deployed in advance of the main fleet' had arguably contributed to the fatal haste with which the K boats had been brought into service. He was always attracted by the possibility of adopting any weapons or tactics that took the fight to the enemy. As the official naval historian wrote of his role in 1910–12: 'The post of Inspector Submarines was originally instituted as an administrative appointment, but under Commodore Keyes it tended to become an active command.'

Meanwhile, of Lieutenant Richard Sandford, the officer of the watch on board *K6* at the time she struck her sister ship *K4* on the night of 31 January 1918, an official note of censure on his service record read: 'Sandford [was] informed by Adm. Beatty that blame attributable to him for not at once appreciating the necessity of getting clear and for not taking action to do so on hearing the sirens ahead of him.' This was a serious enough rebuke for any ambitious young officer, quite apart from the moral responsibility he might have felt for the deaths of 59 of his fellow British servicemen.

Curiously, just over ten weeks later Keyes and Sandford would be at the forefront of a daring seaborne operation that led many to invoke the name of Nelson, and of which Winston Churchill came to reflect: 'It may well rank as the finest feat of arms in the Great War, and certainly as an episode unsurpassed in the history of the Royal Navy.'

This is the story of that small but fanatical force of British sailors and marines who set out in April 1918, bound for its spectacularly violent collision with the enemy. Its destination was Zeebrugge.

CHAPTER 2

Total War

Even in the early morning gloom and wrapped in a heavy overcoat, Ted Palmer could instantly recognise the man who came out of the dripping London rain for his first day's work in a new office as being a 'Parisian dresser' and at least by reputation already known as his department's most 'active, intelligent, brilliantly deductive and reasoning brain' – which meant, 'more properly, a true Sherlock Holmes'. Palmer eagerly shook his new colleague's hand and welcomed him inside to the sparsely furnished upstairs room where he would spend much of the next three years. It was Monday, 7 September 1914, and some 400 miles away a million Allied soldiers were then in the process of desperately pushing their shoulders against a front line being battered by the advancing German army on the outskirts of Paris. To Ted Palmer, 'It truly did seem that, in a ghastly way, the war would actually be over by Christmas.'

Palmer himself was a 28-year-old Welsh research physicist attached to the British Admiralty, and more particularly to OB (Old Building) 40, the cryptography department concerned with cracking the German military and diplomatic codes. Sometimes called 'Room 40', in reality it was a maze of interconnecting 'cubby-holes, dens and barrack-like typing pools' of various shapes and sizes, and at peak capacity it employed some 800 wireless operators and 90 other specialists. In February 1917 the boffins at Room 40 were to play a significant role in determining the final outcome of the war when they successfully decoded the 'Zimmerman Telegram' in which the German government had sought to encourage Mexico to attack the United States, a key part of US president Woodrow Wilson's decision to enter hostilities on the Allied side.

The 'Sherlock Holmes' figure emerging out of the Whitehall rain that September morning was 59-year-old (James) Alfred Ewing, a silver-haired Scot who had served as the first professor of engineering at University College in his native Dundee, before going on to take up a series of teaching posts at Cambridge and, in April 1903, to assume the newly created role of Director of Naval Education (DNE) at Greenwich. It was said of Ewing that he was 'careful at all times of his appearance ... his suits were mostly grey, added to which he generally wore – whatever the fashion – a white piqué stripe to his waistcoat, a mauve shirt, a white butterfly collar and a dark blue bow tie with white spots'. To this ensemble the newly arrived DNE often added an ivory-topped walking stick, which he would sometimes flourish in a colleague's face for added conversational emphasis.

Physically, Ewing was something of a macaw in the rookery of British naval intelligence. Mentally, he was probably the most eminent of the various intellectuals and academics to pass through Room 40 during the course of the war, a list that also included a 'siren-voiced' Presbyterian minister and biblical-authority-turned-code-breaker named William Montgomery; the more diffident Nigel de Grey, an Eton-educated book editor so mild-mannered he was popularly known as 'the door mouse' but who liked nothing better than to 'casually deconstruct' seemingly impossible ciphers for his own relaxation; Dillwyn 'Dilly' Knox, a classics scholar and papyrologist who once absentmindedly forgot to invite two of his brothers to his own wedding, and who was said to have done some of his best wartime work while lying in the bathtub he had installed in his Admiralty office; and Alastair Denniston, a former Scottish Olympic field-hockey player and a world-renowned expert on German literature who would still be working as a British intelligence analyst in the Second World War.

Presiding over this group from November 1914, and matching them all for personal idiosyncrasy, was the 44-year-old Director of Admiralty Intelligence, Captain Reginald Hall, widely known as 'Blinker' due to a pronounced facial twitch said to have caused one of his eyes to 'flash like a navy signal lamp', a feature he combined with a penetrating gaze, luxuriantly bushy eyebrows and a set of conspicuously false teeth and, according to the US ambassador to London in a cable home to President Wilson, 'The one genius the war has developed ... Neither in fiction nor in fact can you find any such man to match him'. The Government Code School established in August 1939 at Bletchley Park was the direct successor to this team of brilliant and often eccentric civilian scholars, lawyers, publishers and theologians assembled 25 years earlier at the Admiralty building in Whitehall.

Alfred Ewing's arrival in Room 40 that dark September morning in 1914 happened to coincide with a notable stroke of luck for the Allied cause. Just ten days earlier, the German light cruiser *Magdeborg* had run aground off the coast of Estonia and been boarded by marines from a pair of patrolling Russian frigates. Fifteen German crew members died in the ensuing skirmish. Among the corpses recovered by the Russians was that of a drowned wireless operator still clutching a German naval signal book and its current encryption key in his hand. In time these 'sea-stained priceless documents', as Winston Churchill called them, landed on Ewing's desk at the Admiralty. The latter became so engrossed in decoding them that after three consecutive days and nights at his desk he had to be ordered home to rest.

The British then had the further good fortune to recover a second set of top-secret charts and codes from the hold of a stricken enemy destroyer that a passing Harwich fishing trawler came across in the North Sea. These, too, quickly found their way to

Ewing and his staff. The German high command soon realised that the British were reading their signals as a result, but evidently believed that the decoded information would already be outdated by the time the enemy came to act on it, or else that they had only to continually change their encryption keys to be safe. Such thinking fatally underestimated Ewing and his team's energy and resourcefulness. 'As the amount of raw data reaching Room 40 expanded, the time taken to analyse it contracted,' the American ambassador wrote. At around teatime six or seven days a week, Ewing would sit at his desk and rapidly sift and collate the day's intercepts, attach to them his crisply worded remarks, seal everything in a red envelope, and then hand this to an Admiralty messenger to carry the short distance down Whitehall to Downing Street.

For all these British successes, German U-boats continued to pose a threat to Allied maritime supremacy until quite literally the last days of the war. An early example of what Admiral John Jellicoe, Beatty's predecessor as commander of the Grand Fleet, would call 'the one great peril to the supply of these islands' when reflecting on how close Britain had come to being starved into submission – 'If the Huns had had half a dozen men of the stamp of our submarine commanders, we should now be a German colony,' he later noted – came on 5 September 1914, when *U-21* sank the scout cruiser HMS *Pathfinder* off the Isle of May with the loss of 252 of her 270 crew.

The 20-year-old Aldous Huxley was staying nearby, and wrote to his father of the aftermath of the tragedy:

> The St. Abbs' lifeboat came in with the most appalling accounts of the scene. There was not a piece of wood, they said, big enough to float a man – and over acres the sea was covered with fragments – human and otherwise. They brought back a sailor's cap with half a man's head inside it. The explosion must have been frightful. It is thought to be a German submarine that did it, or possibly a torpedo fired from one of the refitted German trawlers which cruise all round painted with British port letters and flying the British flag.

Later that same month, *U-9* sank three British armoured cruisers in a single action before going on to dispatch the cruiser HMS *Hawke* as she stopped to collect her mail from a supply ship off the coast of Aberdeen. A total of 1,983 British personnel died as a result of these four incidents. There were no German losses. 'It is quite within the bounds of possibility,' Jellicoe, not one of life's natural optimists, told the cabinet on 30 October 1914, 'that half our battle-fleet might be disabled by under-water attack before the British guns opened fire at all.' We will return to the U-boats' destructive military and commerce-raiding potential as these developed during the course of the war. By January 1918 they were sufficiently potent to persuade the Admiralty planners to commission the 'suicidal' final assault on Zeebrugge.

This still-open gateway port had come to the Allies' attention as early as October 1914, when the British army had successfully landed two divisions of some 28,000 men at Zeebrugge before deploying them on the Western Front. As part of the transport operation, Roger Keyes (by now a naval aide to the king, while retaining executive control of the submarine service) had organised a combined surface and underwater force to defend the sea approaches to the Belgian coast. In the event, there had been no enemy interference. Characteristically, Keyes had decided to personally accompany this escort, and disembarked on the Zeebrugge 'Mole' – a vast, curving wall jutting out into the North Sea to screen the harbour like a protective concrete claw – early in the morning of 6 October. He'd later taken the opportunity to draw a sketch map of the area which was still on his office desk nearly four years later. Keyes's first biographer wrote:

> Following the disembarkation of infantry and artillery, the 2nd Cavalry division began their landing; and to Keyes's delight, for no one was fonder of a good horse, the quay was soon crowded with a representative collection of the finest hunters in England, and a concourse of thoroughbred polo ponies who would earn their wartime keep by carrying officers' mess kits. Later that day he stood on the raised platform of the Mole viaduct and watched the Household Cavalry moving off to battle.

Keyes's next significant intervention in the war came the following December when he led a force of eight submarines and two destroyers hurriedly sent to intercept a German convoy that had appeared out of the early morning mist and begun to shell the English seaport towns of Scarborough, Hartlepool and Whitby, at a cost of some 550 civilian casualties. In the panic and shock that ensued, 'streams of people were seen moving out of the town, so hurried in their flight that in some instances they ran along in their stockinged feet,' the *Scarborough Mercury* reported. At least three decrypts passed on by Room 40 between 14 and 16 December had warned of the Germans' plans, but had seemingly been lost or overlooked until the actual bombardment began. Thanks to the deteriorating weather and further indecision in Whitehall, the enemy raiders had then escaped largely unscathed. A message specifically ordering Keyes to torpedo the retreating ships failed to reach him until too late.

It still remains arguable whether the Germans' naval assault on the British mainland materially advanced their nation's war aims. But it undeniably helped to solidify Allied public opinion in its condemnation. In January 1915 the raid became part of a British propaganda campaign, 'Remember Scarborough', used on army recruitment posters. Editorials in neutral America similarly deplored the attack. 'Civilized behavior has completely collapsed,' the New York *Independent* was left to remark.

Meanwhile, the first battle of Ypres (22 October–22 November 1914) had effectively established the stalemate that would characterise the Western Front for much of the next four years, with both sides adopting deep, defensive positions along a line that extended some 350 miles from the Channel to the Swiss border. Although Allied troops would continue to hold a small 10-x-25-mile sector of northwestern Belgium for the remainder of the war, the initial German thrust had quickly overrun most of the Flanders coastline. As a result, the harbour at Zeebrugge where only weeks earlier Roger Keyes had stood admiring the assembled cavalry now became one of a series of ominously well-positioned, interlocking bases for enemy destroyers and submarines. A plan for an Allied attack on the area reached the desk of 74-year-old 'Jackie' Fisher, a veteran of the Crimean war and now recalled as First Sea Lord, as early as 26 January 1915. He quickly rejected it, though as a sop to public opinion he went on to order a squadron of battlecruisers to be deployed off the English coastline close to where the 'baby-killer' German navy (as the press now dubbed it) had terrorised the streets of Scarborough.

In February, the Germans in turn announced their policy of unrestricted U-boat activity in the waters around the British Isles, where 'every naval and merchant vessel encountered will be destroyed'. All the 19th-century conventions of first allowing an enemy ship's crew to take to the lifeboats before sinking her were to be dispensed with, even if this policy 'might result in the imperilment of noncombatant personnel' – as it notoriously did in the case of the liner RMS *Lusitania*, sunk by *U-20* on 7 May 1915 off the southern coast of Ireland with a loss of 1,200 lives.

In time, Room 40 was able to provide certain technical details of the U-boat *Kapersnest* – or 'Pirates' Lair' – based around the Belgian coastal towns of Ostend, Blankenberghe and Zeebrugge. 'None of these redoubts [were] natural harbours,' Alfred Ewing reported, 'although their mischief-making potential [as] military centres capable of inflicting material loss on our side, and securing propaganda gains on the other' was significant. All three of the ports had been cut out of the coastline by excavation and dredging, and a network of canals connected them to the inland base of Bruges. Ewing likened this situation to that of a 'nest of buried vipers, allowed to wriggle free down a warren of tunnels to inflict havoc upon the outside world'.

The most significant of these routes was the newly opened channel linking Zeebrugge and Bruges. It was eight miles long, almost perfectly straight throughout, and could accommodate traffic up to and including a 5,000-ton armoured cruiser. As a result, Zeebrugge would come to serve as the gateway for the Imperial Navy ships and submarines sent to prosecute their policy of unrestricted warfare against Allied shipping. Even in what the German kaiser called an 'uncooperative' environment such as that of an inland Belgian market town, where silting constantly encroached on the local waterways, 'the area still had the greatest hold on our interest'. By April 1915, Bruges was home to a flotilla of 17 smaller UB- and UC-type U-boats; in October 1917 the unit was split into two groups with a total of 29 U-boats; and by January 1918 there was a force of 36 mixed-class submarines regularly using Zeebrugge as their port of exit for operations in the North Sea and English Channel, although the Royal Navy periodically reduced this figure to around thirty.

The U-boats were housed in a series of open-sided shelters with wooden or, later, concrete foundations that were generally impervious to the kind of bombs light enough to be dropped by hand from the cockpit of a biplane. Given the weapons technology of the time, the *kapersnest* at Bruges would clearly not easily be destroyed from the air. The proposal that reached Admiral Fisher's desk in January 1915 called for 'a diminution … of [the] enemy's warfaring potential by denying him access to the sea at Zeebrugge' – what Winston Churchill called, in a perhaps characteristic metaphor, 'stopping up the bottle with a cork' – and was essentially the same one the Admiralty planners returned to three years later.

Meanwhile, the British were involved in the two most significant, if at best inconclusive, of their set-piece wartime naval operations. The first of these opened on 18 March 1915, when a fleet of 19 British and French battleships, with a supporting force of cruisers and destroyers, began a heavy bombardment of Turkish shore batteries at the barely mile-wide entrance to the Dardanelles. Intended to force a passage for the rapid Allied occupation of Constantinople and thus drive the Ottoman empire from the war, it did not go entirely as planned: the British naval commander suffered a nervous collapse on the eve of the engagement, and under his hurriedly promoted deputy the Allies lost some 700 lives, with three battleships sunk and several others crippled.

The 42-year-old Roger Keyes was in the thick of the action as commander of a minesweeping squadron sent to clear a way for the main strike force but this, too, seems to have critically underestimated the enemy defences. In the face of these, the naval offensive was abandoned two days later. Admiral Fisher then resigned as First Sea Lord, having promised to do so on what *The Times* called a 'not infrequent basis' since his first coming to office. Keyes himself was appointed a Companion of the Order of St. Michael and St. George and awarded the DSO as a result of his work in recovering British troops from the débâcle of the Dardanelles. The Turkish war minister Enver Pasha would not unreasonably depict the events of 18 March 1915 as a great victory for his country, where the rout of the British navy is commemorated to this day.

The Battle of Jutland of 31 May–1 June 1916 already commands a wide literature. In what amounted to a role reversal of the usual national stereotypes, the British tactics were constrained by a series of Grand Fleet Battle Directives that laid out in advance everything from the precise intervals and intensity of gunnery salvoes to be fired at the enemy to the acceptable limit of undress for engine-room stokers in the heat of battle, while the equivalent German orders were brief and allowed considerable leeway to individual commanders. Beatty's own flagship HMS *Lion* soon presented an appalling sight. A heavy shell fired by the German battlecruiser *Lützow* took the roof off one of her port gun turrets, killing or injuring everyone inside, and started a fire that ignited the eight full propellant charges in the turret's loading chamber. The area dripped blood throughout the next ten hours of intermittent action, with the bodies of several men trapped in the wreckage; a further catastrophic explosion was avoided only by the heroism of Major Francis Harvey, the mortally wounded turret commander, both of whose legs were severed, who managed to flood the magazine sufficiently to douse the fire.

The conventional wisdom of Jutland is that while the British lost more ships than the enemy, and more than twice the total tonnage, the German fleet was disinclined to ever again challenge the Royal Navy for command of the North Sea. 'The claims of both combatants to outright victory ultimately proved hollow,' Churchill wrote, 'and it would be unwise to portray [Jutland] as having significantly altered the course of the war in either direction.' The mutual naval blockades continued as before. Neither side again risked its capital ships in a showdown battle. On the whole, this was a less decisive outcome to the action than the German kaiser had proclaimed when visiting his fleet as it lay at anchor at Wilhelmshaven three days after returning from Jutland. Described by the American naval historian Arthur Marder as 'almost hysterical in his theatrical display of emotion', the kaiser had embraced his admirals and liberally distributed Iron Crosses before shouting to the assembled crews: 'The journey I have made today means very much to me. The English were beaten. The spell of Trafalgar has been broken. You have started a new chapter in world history.'

In time, the German war office's confidential report on Jutland struck a less sanguine note in assessing the balance of naval power. Citing the enemy's 'great material superiority', it told the kaiser that 'Even the most successful outcome of a future fleet action will not force England to make peace,' before concluding: 'A victorious end to the war can only be achieved through the defeat of British economic life – that is, by using the U-boats against British trade.'

The day after the kaiser's visit to Wilhelmshaven, the British secretary of state for war, Lord Kitchener, was dead. Having survived front-line action in both the turn-of-the-century invasion of Sudan and the Boer War, before going on to serve as commander of the army in India, he was drowned when en route to a goodwill visit to Russia on the cruiser HMS *Hampshire*. The ship struck a mine laid by the newly launched German submarine *U-75* and sank west of the Orkney Islands – a 'ghastly reaffirmation of the destructive force of underwater warfare,' Roger Keyes wrote. Of *Hampshire*'s crew of 651, just 12 survived. Kitchener, who was 65 at the time of his death, was last seen immediately after the explosion walking unhurriedly up the ship's quarterdeck to the bridge. His body was never recovered.

Less than a month later, the protracted bloodbath began around the river Somme, a name inaptly derived from the Celtic word for 'tranquility'. It's a frequently repeated fact that there were close to 60,000 British casualties on the first day of the battle, a third of them killed, and that a further 140 days of attritional fighting followed. Total German losses in the action, if it can reasonably be called that, are the subject of dispute, but may have reached 650,000 in the period 1 July–18 November 1916. Since many of those lost were simply pulverised by explosions or ground underfoot into the mud, the real number will never be accurately known.

The German chief of naval operations Adolf von Trotha later described a meeting with the army head of staff Erich von Ludendorff that took place in December at Ludendorff's headquarters at Pless in modern-day Poland:

After dinner, the general took me into his room and rang up the German high command in France. The telephone had a loudspeaker and the commander at the other end described the situation as very bad. The Somme battle had claimed all our efforts and we had put our last reserves in the line. Ludendorff then said to me that … the new unrestricted U-boat war, moderated after the [loss of the *Lusitania*] must now be implemented.

It was against this backdrop that on 8 January 1917 the kaiser summoned his joint chiefs of staff to announce that he had 'come round to the idea that total U-boat warfare was now called for, and he [was] definitely in favour of it even if the chancellor, concerned about the possible reaction of the American president, was not.' The new attack orders issued to U-boat commanders that month advised them that hospital ships, as well as those belonging to the US-funded Belgian Relief Commission, were to be spared, but that even then individual captains should know that 'if, in spite of the exercise of due care, mistakes were made', they would not be held responsible.

As a result of this newly intensified campaign of trade warfare, U-boats sank 527,000 tons of merchant shipping in the waters around the British Isles in February 1917. The figures in March and April rose to 566,000 tons and a near-catastrophic 869,000 tons respectively. In light of this, it seemed to many of those responsible for the British war effort that the renewed German submarine menace might in fact succeed where more traditional tactics had failed. 'The shipping situation is by far the most serious question of the day,' wrote Admiral Jellicoe – a spare, ascetic figure who reminded many of a Victorian schoolmaster – in January 1917, a month after the fall of the Asquith government, in part because of its inadequate response to the 'nearly unchecked U-boat marauding off these shores … I almost fear it is nearly too late to retrieve it. Drastic measures should have been taken months ago to stop unnecessary imports, ration the country and build ships.'

In a minute to the new premier David Lloyd George, Jellicoe added on 21 February 1917, 'The position is exceedingly grave.' Very soon, he feared, the government would have 'to determine how long we can continue to carry on the war if the losses of merchant shipping continue at the present rate.' Voluntary rationing was introduced to Britain that same month, with compulsory measures following at stages between November 1917 and February 1918, as the nation's supply of wheat fell to just six weeks' worth. Roughly a third of all British-bound mercantile shipping was sunk during 1917. In the period from 30 April to 10 July of that year, the Germans destroyed over two million tons of urgently needed food and matériel. If those figures had kept up, Lloyd George admitted, the British people would have been starving 'in appreciable numbers' by March 1918.

The German public in turn enthusiastically supported the policy of resumed all-out submarine raiding, not because they had become proponents of total war per se but because they were hungry. The third winter of the war was known in Germany as the turnip winter, because that unappealing root vegetable now became a depressingly familiar staple of people's diet. If you were unfortunate enough to live in Berlin in the latter half of the Great War, with no access to the black market, you got by on just two eggs a month and similarly meagre rations of meat and bread. In the winter of 1917 the potato crop failed, leading to food riots and to the appearance of dishes such as cooked rat and boiled crow on many dinner tables.

In time the Reich capital would become the scene of almost medieval squalor, as Alexandra Richie writes in her book *Faust's Metropolis*:

> Old horses, donkeys and even circus elephants were used to pull coal carts … Black crosses and the names of those who had died a 'hero's death' filled the newspapers and the lists of casualties which appeared daily at the War Ministry in the Dorutheenstrasse grew longer and longer. [The artist] Georg Grosz wrote: 'The Berlin to which I came was a cold and grey city … I drew men drunk, men vomiting, men with clenched fists cursing the moon, men playing cards on the coffins of the dead. I drew soldiers without noses; war cripples with crab-like limbs of steel; two medical orderlies tying a violent infantryman up in a horse blanket; a one-armed soldier using his good hand to salute a heavily bemedalled lady who had just passed him a biscuit; a colonel, his fly open, embracing a nurse; a hospital orderly emptying a bucket full of pieces of human flesh down a pit. I drew a skeleton dressed up as a recruit taking his medical.'

It was in this atmosphere that the German people had begun to ask why, if their nation truly possessed a machine that could break the Allied blockade of their homeland and bring the enemy to its knees, was this weapon not now being employed in the most aggressive and indiscriminate way, whatever the possible views of President Wilson on the subject? Certainly the initial results of the newly expanded U-boat campaign in terms of material losses on the British side were all that the kaiser and his war planners could have wished for. But the resumption of 'wholesale interdiction of inimical sea traffic', as the orders put it, soon claimed collateral damage as well. On 12 March 1917, a German U-boat thought to have been either *U-38* or *U-39* opened fire on the US steamer *Algonquin* as she lay about 60 miles off the coast of southwest England. The submarine's shells failed to sink the unarmed ship, so men from the U-boat carrying bombs boarded the *Algonquin*, lit the fuses, and blew her up. The shipwrecked American crew members escaped and reached Penzance after 27 hours adrift in open boats. Four days later, three US merchant vessels, the *Illinois*, *City of Memphis* and *Vigilancia*, were torpedoed without warning in the Atlantic shipping lanes; a total of 16 men perished. On 2 April, with American resentment against Germany swelling, President Wilson summoned Congress to a special session to hear 'a communication concerning grave matters of national policy'. Four days later, Wilson announced that a state of war existed between the United States and Germany.

The new U-boat campaign was a shock in that, whatever its strategic merits, it seemed to many in Britain to sever Germany's last ties with civilised behaviour. It also continued to destroy British imports at an unsustainable rate. A system of Anglo-American convoys was then instituted in July 1917, after Lloyd George – or so he later claimed in his memoirs – personally 'galvanised the Admiralty' into taking the necessary action to 'save the country from certain strangulation'. The concept of sending large numbers of merchant vessels across the Atlantic under naval escort was not entirely new, however, and nor was it an overnight success. Allied shipping losses continued largely unabated until at least November 1917, by which time the Royal Navy would also come to call on the tactical resources both of the new 'Allied Submarine Detection Investigation Committee' (or ASDIC, later SONAR) and the added protection afforded by the sort of crude but increasingly effective air cover provided by the likes of airships, seaplanes and towed kite balloons.

Between September 1914 and October 1918, running as a through line to British anti-submarine strategy, the Dover Patrol sought to contain if not actively to eliminate the U-boat hunting grounds. Initially a rather ramshackle unit composed of a few retirement-age cruisers and monitors, it grew to employ an impressive flotilla of destroyers, minesweepers, drifters, trawlers and even commandeered civilian yachts and motor launches all dedicated to the protection of the southern North Sea and Dover straits.

By 1 January 1918, the Patrol had become an enterprise comprising over 300 vessels, two discrete seaplane units, a squadron of airships and its own advanced base at Dunkirk. It was widely judged successful as a reconnaissance force, if not one that conspicuously took the war to the enemy. At 7 o'clock that same wet New Year's morning, 45-year-old Roger Keyes, newly promoted vice-admiral, arrived to take command of operations at Dover. The day after hoisting his flag he summoned all the principal officers of the Patrol to announce that he proposed to make certain changes to the overall anti-submarine tactics adopted over the course of the last three and a half years, and that on the whole these would now be of a more proactive nature. Coloured star shells soon streaked up into the night sky, and an offshore flare barrier regularly lit the Dover approaches. 'He immediately,' wrote Winston Churchill in *The World Crisis*, 'redoubled the patrols; and by night the [straits] became as bright as Piccadilly. The German destroyers attempted to break down the patrols by sudden raids. They were repulsed.'

Keyes informed his commanders that the Patrol would be divided into two constituent parts: an essentially defensive force to 'deny the sea lanes to enemy craft' and a more actively combative one charged with 'rooting out the evil from its lair'. In the two years before Keyes's arrival, the Dover Patrol had destroyed a total of two U-boats and captured a third which had blown itself up on one of its own mines. The average for the period January–March 1918 was six enemy submarines sunk each month. Since nothing in the land war then suggested that a British victory, or even her national survival, was assured, it was perhaps no wonder that Churchill, then Lloyd George's minister of munitions, later thought these figures represented 'an immense service rendered to the final outcome'.

Though 'quietly satisfied' with the progress made during the first weeks of his new command, Keyes himself did not want a false sense of security to develop.

As he later acknowledged, the Allies would continue to wrestle with the U-boat threat to their economic welfare right up until the end of the war. It's true that British-bound monthly shipping losses, though still 'burdensome' as the cabinet put it, gradually fell from their extreme levels of spring 1917 as the first regular system of Atlantic convoys went into effect later in the summer. But it's also true that the submarine menace in and around the North Sea and Channel, still thought by many to prefigure a full-scale land invasion of the British Isles, was enough for Admiral Jellicoe, writing a month after the American entry into the war, to advise the cabinet: 'We are carrying on … as if we had the absolute command of the sea. We have not … Disaster is certain to follow, and *our present policy is heading straight for disaster.*'

On 8 June 1917, Jellicoe went on to share with the cabinet his misgivings about the relative speeds of the latest class of U-boat and that of their prey. 'The preponderance of vulnerability,' he wrote, 'is in vessels of below 12 knots nominal speed.' The First Sea Lord attached figures which showed that 92.6 per cent of all ships torpedoed or otherwise destroyed while en route to British ports had been in 'the slower and heavier category'. He concluded: 'In view of the increasing submerged speed of enemy submarines it is prima facie sound to build [merchant] ships of a higher speed even at the expense of a reduced cargo capacity.'

This was obviously a long-term proposition at best, and in the meantime the British countered the German tactics by adopting their own policy of disrupting commercial traffic suspected of running guns or food to the enemy. On 29 June 1917, Jellicoe wrote in a memorandum to the cabinet, 'The Royal Navy submarine "E41", which had been engaged in mine-laying off the Frisian coast, had sighted two German merchant ships, [and] had dispatched one of them. This had been done under Admiralty orders to sink at sight any vessel in those waters presumed to be German.' Later that month, Jellicoe reported that 'our Air Squadron at Dunkirk had carried out an effective bombing raid on Bruges harbour, causing considerable damage to the shipping there'. On 24 August, Jellicoe's deputy reported in cabinet: 'An attack by motor-boats was carried out at Zeebrugge, torpedoes being fired inside the Mole. All torpedoes were observed to explode. All boats returned.'

Although the cabinet expressed the hope that 'further such assaults' would restore the 'inviolability of waters around the home coast', later in the summer Jellicoe reported that U-boat activity in the Channel 'continu[ed] to gain in stridency' and thus 'exert great pressure, constantly brought to bear, on import cargo for our home use'. This remained his essentially sombre fallback position on the state of maritime affairs right up until the moment he was relieved of duty on Christmas Eve 1917. From the previous summer onwards, the cabinet secretary had adopted the shorthand formula of noting merely, 'The First Lord made his usual statement of shipping losses' to convey Jellicoe's relentless hammering of the civilian authorities on the need to 'urgently restore our marine supremacy, especially in securing the main commercial routes from underwater attack'. Sometimes the old Grand Fleet commander seemed to accuse the politicians of willfully ignoring the nation's peril. 'The whole of our war experience has shown that a fair measure of protection to shipping can only be guaranteed by a system of individual escort of at least two fast patrol craft, or by arranging for ships to sail in groups with an escort on practically the same basis,' Jellicoe told the prime minister in an action memo of 1 July 1917. 'There is, unfortunately, *no desire or possibility of the number of such craft ever reaching the required figure*, and palliative means must continue, combined with a vigorous offensive against any submarine that gives us a chance of attacking her.'

Among such initiatives to be considered over the years was the idea of a concerted seaborne raid on the U-boat bases in Belgium, a proposal first tentatively raised in December 1914 but which took on a new momentum only after the appointment of the monocle-wearing, Dardanelles veteran Admiral Rosslyn 'Rosy' Wemyss as First Sea Lord three years later. Possibly the most ambitious of the earlier plans to neutralise Zeebrugge following its occupation by the Germans in November 1914 was one to bombard the harbour with a massive, 150-ton, 70-foot-long artillery piece. The supergun was to have been assembled in Dover and then shipped across the straits on a specially constructed raft to the port of Westende. There, British marines would somehow drag the weapon on its 18-wheeled carriage through the town's cobbled streets and install it in an upstairs room of the Palace Hotel, where it would be trained on the lock gates at Zeebrugge 30 miles to the east.

This particular plan appeared to present 'more of a problem' to Admiral Fisher than an opportunity. It was quietly shelved when it was pointed out that significant numbers of British land troops would be required to secure the area around Westende from counterattack by the German army in Flanders. 'Such an initiative might prove problematic,' the cabinet noted, in the 'prevailing environment' of the Western Front in late 1914, where both sides were already abandoning any vestiges of mobile warfare and instead adopting deep, entrenched positions for the foreseeable future. As a result, the British would be forced to settle for a policy of harassment, rather than capture, of the North Sea ports. A rather optimistic headline in the London press in that first Christmas of the war read: 'Battleships wreck German submarine base at Zeebrugge. Hindenburg's army in retreat. German failure in Poland. Belgian ports successfully razed by British warships.'

While the supergun proposal was still petering out in January 1915, the Admiralty began to discuss other, less troop-intensive schemes for nullifying the threat of the Belgian ports. One idea was for a small Flemish-speaking group of British special forces drawn from the Royal Marines to land at night somewhere on the deserted coast between Blankenberghe and Zeebrugge. From there they would insinuate themselves into the local community by posing as fishmongers 'and spend time in reconnaissance of the harbour defences, [if] practical rendering these inoperative' by laying a series of time-delay mines. The men were then to retire as swiftly as they could in a small boat to be out of range before the German guns went up in flames.

When the day came, however, the troops were put ashore by the Royal Navy on the outer edge of a large sandbank and found themselves having to wade through waist-high mud and silt in order to reach dry land. One man nearly drowned before, by now soaked to the skin and freezing in their light civilian disguises, the group staggered up a hill and collapsed in the supposedly deserted farm building at Donkerklok, about three miles west of Zeebrugge, where they were meant to retrieve a cache of food, clothes and munitions. Something had gone awry, however, because all the marines found waiting for them was an elderly Belgian farm labourer asleep in a cot, who had opened his eyes at the strangers' arrival and shouted loudly at them to leave. After an uncomfortable day spent hiding in the nearby woods, late the next night the men had been forced to wade back out through the sandbank, at the edge of which a small skiff carried them to a waiting Royal Navy submarine stationed near a light-buoy in the channel. They had had nothing to eat for 36 hours, and the man who had stumbled and nearly drowned on their first disembarkation was found to have a broken leg. The plan for a commando-style raid on Zeebrugge was then indefinitely postponed, though the time the troops had spent in the area was not to be entirely wasted. They brought back with them a sketch map of the coastline immediately west of Zeebrugge, which was 'bristling with heavy and medium guns overlooking the sea in every direction'.

Later in 1915, 58-year-old Admiral Lewis Bayly, newly appointed commander of the Channel Fleet, came up with an audacious plan to attack the lightly populated German island of Borkum, close to the enemy home port of Wilhelmshaven (and the location of early Nazi guided-rocket tests twenty years later). The idea was to 'dispatch a force of warships under cover of smoke-screen, with minesweepers going ahead, [and] and then to land two brigades of marines and soldiers on the northwestern coast', from where they would proceed to 'harry the enemy defences and if the strategic situation was satisfactory, attack the German ships at anchor in order to sink these or force them to sea'. In the end the idea of sending 10,000 British troops into the heart of enemy territory was abandoned as impractical, but Bayly then modified his plan to involve similar mass landings at Ostend and Zeebrugge. This, too, was listed as 'non-viable' by the Admiralty director of operations, and the war cabinet vetoed it in November 1915.

Undaunted, 45-year-old Commodore Reginald Tyrwhitt, in charge of the Harwich fleet and another of what Churchill called those 'firebrand young officers [whose] intention and instinct was not to prolong, but appreciably shorten' the war, tabled an alternative plan of attack on the German U-boat bases. This proposal called for an explosive-laden British battleship to force its way into Zeebrugge harbour under a smokescreen of poison gas, then to ram the lock gates linking the port to the submarine pens at Bruges, and finally to scuttle herself in the channel. 'Properly executed,' Tyrwhitt wrote, 'this action [would] deny the enemy submersibles access to the sea for many months to come.' Again, however, more cautious political minds prevailed. 'The Director of Military Operations reported his concerns that a change of wind might subject [Zeebrugge's] civilian population to the noxious effluvia,' it was noted in cabinet.

Nonetheless, the proposals about how best to prevent Germany's U-boats from entering or leaving their Flanders bases continued to come thick and fast – given a new urgency by the events of 26/27 October 1916 when 23 enemy ships slipped out of Zeebrugge by night, sailed to the edge of the underwater steel-netting defences, or 'barrage', outside Dover and proceeded to sink the Royal Navy destroyer *Flirt*, as well as several transport vessels, drifters and trawlers, at a cost of 45 British lives. Asked for a report on the disaster, 53-year-old Vice-Admiral Reginald Bacon, Keyes's predecessor at Dover, and unlike him not a proponent of the policy of illuminating the local sea approaches after dark, was unapologetic. 'It is as easy to stop a raid of express engines with all lights out at Clapham Junction,' he told the Admiralty, 'as to stop a raid of 33-knot destroyers on a night as black as Erebus, in waters as wide as the Channel.'

By December 1916, the problem of the Flanders naval bases was sufficient for the chief of Imperial General Staff to write to Lloyd George 'to further apprise [him] of the submarine menace, and of the need for action against Ostend and Zeebrugge'. At a cabinet meeting the following January, Admiral Jellicoe stated 'that the Board desired to take up eight coasting steamers to be fitted out as decoy vessels to engage German submarines [off] the line Zeebrugge–Bruges–Ostend … the employment of such vessels having been found, on the whole, to be the most effective method of dealing with submarines.' The next month, Admiral Bacon of the Dover Patrol was back with a scheme to send a fleet of coastal motor boats to fire torpedoes at the Zeebrugge lock gates, before Admiral Tyrwhitt in turn submitted a more ambitious plan – perhaps unnecessarily dubbed 'Operation Hush' – for a combined land–sea attack on the Belgian ports, which would then be reoccupied and converted into a staging post for a 'mass [Allied] assault on Antwerp, and a redoubled offensive against the enemy's northern flank in Flanders'.

On the cold Sunday morning of 21 January 1917, Alfred Ewing of Room 40 sent a handwritten note to the former First Sea Lord and now senior adviser to the navy's director of operations, 'Old 'ard 'art' Sir Arthur Wilson. Wilson in turn took it post-haste to the current First Lord, his friend John Jellicoe, who happened to be in bed with a heavy cold in his flat attached to the Admiralty. Ewing had intercepted a German naval signal which revealed that an enemy destroyer group was about to set out to reinforce the garrisons at Ostend and Zeebrugge. It was another case where the British intelligence-gathering capacity outstripped the resulting performance of her men at arms. Two days later, detachments from Harwich Force and the Dover

Patrol were duly waiting when the German ships appeared out of the pre-dawn fog off the Dutch island of Schouwen. The British cruisers opened fire but, as at Jutland, the enemy deftly reversed course and promptly vanished into the murk, a manoeuvre they had often practised in training exercises over the years. They had turned 16 assorted warships about in just three minutes. It was not quite a perfect retreat, however; in the confusion of night, the German torpedo boat *V69* collided with her sister *G41*, jamming the former's steering. The British force moved in to shell the stricken *V69*, managing to kill her commander and several of her crew but failing to sink the ship itself. A retiring German destroyer then fired a torpedo into the hull of HMS *Simoon*, which went down with the loss of 47 lives. 'An unsatisfactory resolution,' Admiral Wilson was left to conclude.

Two nights later, three Zeebrugge-based German destroyers sailed unmolested up the coast of East Anglia, briefly exchanged attack signals and in a near-replay of the Scarborough episode began to shell the small Suffolk town of Southwold. A local solicitor and Home Front organiser named Ernest Cooper wrote in his diary:

> I had been in bed about ten minutes when there was a double explosion … I jumped out of bed but in a moment came crashes of gunfire, very fast and loud, and I told the Missis to hurry and get the baby down as the Germans were upon us. In five minutes they put 68 shells and two starshells into us … So far as I saw the townspeople behaved extremely well, there was no panic, the special constables were out but very few others and most folks seem to have gone to bed again quietly. Some of the papers called it a comic bombardment, but to those who were in it there was nothing funny or silly but a very present danger.

Although no British lives were lost in the attack, it again focused official minds on the need to neutralise Zeebrugge not only as a safe haven for enemy U-boats but as a base of operations for their surface ships when they came to violate the British mainland.

A week later, Germany reopened unlimited submarine warfare in the North Sea and English Channel. 'Every resource [was] now required in the struggle against this menace,' Jellicoe wrote in a minute for the war cabinet. Part of the British counter-measures took the form of strategic adjustments to the Dover Patrol, and part a more technical course. On 8 March 1917, the cabinet noted: 'The First Lord stated that he had just learned from a good source that the United States Government had not yet completed their investigations of Mr. Edison's reported submarine detector, though [they were] hopeful of success.' Two weeks later, Jellicoe reported that 'the enemy [has] concentrated some 30 destroyers at Zeebrugge, and such a concentration must be for the purpose of covering a landing on the Belgian shore, or raids in the Channel, or to attack [our] convoys and their escorts'.

In the early hours of 12 May 1917, three Royal Navy monitors lying ten miles off the Belgian coast opened fire on Zeebrugge, while British and German aircraft were soon engaged overhead. The British later claimed five enemy planes shot down, but the naval exercise failed; although the cabinet heard that '15 rounds had landed on or near the lock gates on the western side, and four rounds on the eastern', Zeebrugge remained open to enemy sea traffic. 'Our success might have been greater but for difficulties in range-finding,' Jellicoe was forced to admit, as reports came in to suggest that the majority of British shells had fallen harmlessly on the nearby sand dunes. Whatever the outcome, however, this was more like the sort of 'bolder stake, upon a more ambitious throw,' as he put it, to appeal to the new prime minister sitting behind his desk in Downing Street. Now he wanted more of the same. 'I was dissatisfied that our Navy with all its tremendous power could do so little against the Belgian harbours,' Lloyd George later wrote. Jellicoe responded in cabinet that 'Zeebrugge [was] defended by navigational conditions … You could not render the port so unpleasant that ships could not use it. Our grand fleet could not go nearer to Zeebrugge than 18,000 yards range; and if monitors, which were unarmed, closed to that range, they would be sunk'.

Just six days after the failed attempt to effectively pulverise Zeebrugge from the sea, Commodore Tyrwhitt again sent up a paper which called for a special-operations force to land on the Belgian coast by night, destroy as many of the lock gates and canal entrances as possible, disable any German destroyers that might be lying nearby and then retire. Looking back at the profusion of Zeebrugge proposals today, it sometimes seems surprising to learn that the Admiralty ever had time to discuss anything else. Tyrwhitt's scheme became known in official circles as the 'dicing' plan, as in 'dicing with death', and, although praised in cabinet as 'bold and imaginative', for the present nothing more came of it. 'In all the world there is no desolation more complete than the Whitehall meeting,' Tyrwhitt later wrote.

> Brilliant as our rulers are, they are not men with whom anyone could ever have a normal conversation. As a rule, either they talked and everyone else present listened, or the others talked and the ministers sat lost in thought, only to then repeat their original position on the issue under debate.

Nor was there now any realistic chance that the First Sea Lord might vary his usual foreboding message to the cabinet. Later that summer Jellicoe told ministers that unless the Germans were soon 'thoroughly exterminated in [their] nest at Zeebrugge', the Allies would be unable to continue the war in 1918 through sheer lack of supplies. The problem lay in successfully evicting the enemy from their heavily entrenched position nearly a hundred miles from the nearest British staging port, particularly when long-range bombardment had failed in the recent past. Merely to again pound Zeebrugge from the sea was 'an operation which I am sure that no responsible naval officer would recommend, and it is, indeed, hardly practicable,' Jellicoe wrote in a memorandum. 'We might practise such an attack many times, but chaos [is] destined to reign in practice.'

A straightforward land assault 'might nonetheless be feasible,' Jellicoe allowed, but even this was conditional on British troops breaking out of their positions around the Ypres salient and converging 'in a smoothly interlocking combined assault involv[ing] ships, tanks and artillery' on the Belgian ports. Instead of this carefully coordinated eastward push, the third battle of Ypres, as it was officially known and seldom called – the soldiers used the familiar name Passchendaele – proved the culmination of horror. Although the Allies eventually deepened the salient by some five miles, they suffered around 300,000 casualties in doing so. After that there would be no further thought given to the possibly already quixotic-sounding proposal of sending front-line troops to assist in the invasion and occupation of a well-fortified enemy harbour and its inland submarine pens.

By December 1917, the indefatigable Tyrwhitt had radically modified his plan in order to take better account of the prevailing ground conditions. Like Churchill's 'stopping up the bottle with a cork', he now called for a specially fitted blockship to cut its way through the outlying minefields and shifting sands at Zeebrugge and, directed by wireless from circling aircraft, to sink itself broadside across the mouth of the main canal 'while subsidiary exercises take place against enemy troops and shore defences'.

The increasing British determination to strike at the heart of the enemy submarine sanctuary on the Flanders coast met with an accelerating programme of creative and often richly eccentric naval special operations as a whole. Perhaps the most visually dramatic of the countermeasures introduced in the campaign to hunt down enemy raiders were the 'Q' or 'mystery' boats phased into service in 1915–16. These were disguised cargo vessels, colliers and coasters which cruised the main shipping lanes manned by civilian crews and flying the red (merchant navy) ensign. But, as Churchill approvingly wrote, they also carried guns 'which by a pantomime trick of trap doors and shutters could suddenly come into action'. Their commanders' orders were to attack and destroy any enemy ships they encountered without further ado.

The deception scored an early success in March 1916 when the submarine *U-68* came across the apparently defenceless trawler HMS *Farnborough* (Q5) off the southwest coast of Ireland. The submarine at first fired a torpedo at its prey, narrowly missing her, and then surfaced in order to strafe the British craft at her leisure. According to *Farnborough's* commander, Gordon Campbell, at that stage 'I blew my whistle … At that signal the white ensign ran [up] the masthead, the wheel-house and side ports came down with a clatter, the hen coop collapsed; and in a matter of seconds three 12-pounder guns, the Maxim, and rifles were firing as hard as they could.' As *U-68* began to sink, Campbell steered *Farnborough* overhead and dropped a depth charge that blew the bow of the submarine out of the water. All 38 German crew members perished.

By mid-1917 what some saw as a distinctly un-British 'wiliness' or 'treachery' – and others heralded as a positive national genius for deception – increasingly came to bear in the Admiralty's thinking on anti-U-boat strategy and counterattack measures.

Churchill later wrote of his thrill at sitting next to the director of Naval Intelligence in the back of a car being driven through the Fife countryside towards Rosyth:

> At last the road went winding downwards round a purple hill, and before us far below gleamed a bay of blue water in which rode at anchor, outlined in miniature as in a plan, the twenty Dreadnoughts and Super-Dreadnoughts on which the command of the seas depended. Around them and darting about between them were many scores of small craft. The vessels themselves were painted for the first time in the queer mottled fashion which marked the early beginnings of the science of Camouflage. 'What would the German emperor give,' I said to my companions, 'to see this?'

Along with the navy's adoption of mottled or dispersive disguise, there was the pioneering work of the Admiralty Board of Invention and Research based at Stratford in east London. Chaired by the former First Sea Lord, Jackie Fisher, the board employed over 250 scientists, who in time not only produced or refined the first practical underwater-detection devices such as hydrophones and sonar, but also evaluated some 40,000 invention proposals submitted by members of the public with a view to applying them to naval warfare. One of the leading lights at Stratford from January 1915 was an irrepressible, peppery figure named Frank Brock, the 26-year-old son of the head of the family fireworks firm, who developed a new and improved smokescreen, or 'artificial fog' as he preferred to call it, which could effectively cloak a warship roughly the size of London's Tower Bridge as it bore in on the enemy. Brock soon added to this breakthrough other, more directly offensive weapons such as phosphorus grenades, portable flamethrowers and mobile rockets. Many of these new-fangled armaments were crude by modern standards, and some caught fire or exploded prematurely in action, but by April 1918 they all added to what Brock enthusiastically called the 'surprise value' of the British attack on Zeebrugge.

For men like Room 40's 'Blinker' Hall and Alfred Ewing it was not enough to develop deceptive new tactics or futuristic weapons. The fortunes of war would favour those who were best able to intercept and decipher the enemy's secret military traffic. By January 1918 the Admiralty maintained a dozen regional listening stations dotted around Britain and Ireland to collect U-boat signals and in turn pass these to Whitehall. Since the cabinet's priority remained to keep the existence of Room 40 secret, they were frequently forced to refrain from sharing the intelligence gathered with individual naval commanders. It's been estimated that the Admiralty decrypted around 15,000 enemy messages during the four years of war, a rate of roughly ten a day. The British self-restraint was remarkably effective: even after Room 40 took possession of the impounded luggage of Wilhelm Wassmuss, a German agent in Tehran, and discovered that this contained the enemy's entire diplomatic codebook, Berlin seemingly had no idea that their communications were being read quite as promiscuously as they were.

From around Christmas 1917, the British even began to periodically transmit fake intelligence to German U-boats – warning them of nonexistent anti-submarine defences in the Channel, for instance – though for obvious reasons such 'black' signals were only ever sparingly used. Along with the innovations in camouflage and technology, this limited but carefully calibrated disinformation campaign also became part both of the plan of attack at Zeebrugge, and the larger British strategy for breaking the Germans' stranglehold, as it then seemed, on sea communications as a whole.

✳

Roger Keyes was not one to worry unduly about the future course of the war any more than he was likely to minimise his own possible contribution to its final outcome. As commander-in-chief, Dover, he was in his element. 'There is no doubt that he [had] great ability as an organiser and leader, flawed by a certain impatience with any official impediment or delay,' Winston Churchill would say of this 'thoroughly British man of action'. Like Churchill himself, Keyes combined a remarkable capacity for detail with an instinctive love of special-forces raiding parties, moonlit amphibian landings, saboteur attacks and anything else that smacked of unorthodox warfare. Striking behind the enemy lines was 'always a means to inflict considerable damage – if not knock him out altogether,' he later wrote.

Nonetheless, when Keyes first turned his attention from the routine patrol of the Dover straits to the more 'assertive' matter of attacking the German naval refuge at Zeebrugge, even he acknowledged the presence of certain 'incalculable hazards [of] navigation, logistics and weather – not the least being the need to take a fleet across the straits under cover of dark, on a date when high tide would occur, with no moon, and successfully infiltrate a fortified citadel zealously watched by men and guns'. A few days after he took up the discarded Operation Hush and proposed a modified version of it designed to 'storm the enemy redoubts [and] immobilise the submarines that would be resting or refitting there', Keyes privately admitted that he felt so pressured by his job and various Whitehall conflicts that he was 'far too often' awakened by bad dreams or found it impossible to sleep.

And the challenges that arose from this new plan also often resembled a nightmare, particularly when it came to the unique combination of natural and manmade obstacles confronting any Zeebrugge attacker. 'Batteries were placed on both sides of the canal entrance,' wrote 36-year-old Commander Alfred Carpenter, who had studied the Flanders ports as part of the Admiralty plans division, and was soon to have the opportunity to apply the lessons he learned there.

'The guns ranged from 4-inch to 12-inch,' Carpenter noted.

Barbed-wire entanglements were erected along the shore line; trenches, containing machine guns, were dug close behind them … A battery of six or seven guns was situated at [the] end of the mile-and-a-half-long Zeebrugge Mole, which itself undulated in height. They fired a shell of approximately 100 pounds in weight. It was believed that these guns could either be trained out to sea or be turned to fire towards the shore. The access to the canal was further protected by entrenched infantry … Entry into the harbour could be made only through a narrow gap in these defences, within point-blank range of the artillery on the Mole and of any destroyers lying alongside the quay.

But even the heavy pounding of the assorted German guns would likely be only a curtain-raiser to the risks inherent in successfully storming Zeebrugge. Keyes had been present in April 1915 when the first Allied troops landed on the Gallipoli peninsula. 'Attack the enemy with the bayonet and utterly destroy him,' the Turkish operational command had read. 'We shall not retire one step, for if we do, our religion, or country, and our nation will perish.' Many of the subsequent individual Allied landings had 'abandoned the logic of their own orders, which called for a steady, parade-ground advance,' the official American observer wrote, 'and instead collapsed amid scenes of almost prehistoric barbarity.' Of the first 209 mainly Irish soldiers to disembark from the SS *River Clyde*, a converted collier, just 21 reached the beach alive.

'It was all too literally a shambles,' Keyes was later to admit to his friend and colleague Edward Renouf, as the landings had proceeded amid maniacal Turkish resistance and, what was worse, only the 'tepid fighting spirit' of the Allied commanders. Of a visit to General Birdwood, in charge of the Australian and New Zealand army corps at Gallipoli, Keyes wrote:

He told me of all his disappointments and cruel losses. How I hate it, and I feel all the time that we could stop it and win this great prize … My [men] go up the Straits with an even-money chance of never coming back, but they have the only thing that matters – the spirit that will risk everything to win their great reward … I was sure a most glorious page [would] be added to our Naval History.

Three years later, thinking of the proposal to send troops ashore under similar conditions at Zeebrugge, Keyes told Renouf that he sometimes had a dream in which the sea seemed to be boiling red.

CHAPTER 3

'A Daring and Arduous Stunt'

Men of action are surprisingly often drawn to the occult. There was a worldwide surge of interest in the paranormal in the immediate aftermath of the American civil war, during the course of which even Abraham Lincoln had held a regular series of candlelit séances in the White House, by no means the last time a sitting US president was to dabble in the supernatural. In later years both Douglas Haig, commander of the British expeditionary force on the Western Front, and his American counterpart John Pershing were known to consult the cards before deciding on a major strategic initiative. The overlap between psychic belief and traditional military procedure was extensive in the Great War, and a report published by the spiritualist researcher Charles Richet in the January 1917 *Bulletin des armées de la République* listed 'many thousands' of tales from 'all ranks … both the ignorant and the intellectual … of prophetic dreams, presentiments, telepathy and troubling metaphysical occurrences' in the trenches. The particular legend that a sword-wielding angel had appeared in the field to protect the British troops during the August 1914 battle of Mons also enjoyed a certain currency among senior officers, perhaps anxious for any available proof of the action of divine providence on the Allied side.

In the Second World War, General George 'Old Blood and Guts' Patton would periodically take time off from attacking the Germans to visit the scene of some ancient European battle and unerringly describe the events that had taken place there – a part of his belief that he had once been a Roman legionary, an English knight and a Napoleonic marshal, among several other historical incarnations. Even the austere figure of Air Chief Marshal Hugh Dowding, who revelled in the wartime nickname 'Stuffy', became an advocate of spiritualism, writing of his dreams of meeting dead 'RAF boys' in his sleep – spirits who flew fighters from ghostly mountaintop runways made of light – and going on to become an active member of the Fairy Investigation Society. In retirement, Dowding once wrote to the Ministry of Defence to inquire if they would like to establish an annual award in his name to the serviceman who did most to advance the cause of research into the world of 'miniature life' and at the same time 'protect the welfare of the vegetable kingdom'. The offer was rejected.

So it was unusual, but not unprecedented, when on the bank holiday of 25 August 1917, at a naval garden party at Aberdour House in Fife, 44-year-old Rear Admiral Roger Keyes, recently appointed second-in-command of the navy's ten-ship 4th Battle Squadron, should have broken off from his exchanges of pleasantries with other senior officers and their wives in order to join the queue to consult a woman described in a contemporary account as 'tall and thin, [with] fiery black eyes and a long Athenian nose, clad in a silk coat studded with tiny silver stars, and with a knotted scarf embroidered in many colours, [while] on her bosom reposed a bouquet of fresh-plucked twigs and berries', perched awaiting her customers at a stall under a tree. There among the patriotic flags and bunting, the organisers of the fête had arranged for a local fortune teller to entertain their guests.

'The lady only gave most people a few minutes,' Keyes recalled,

> but insisted on keeping me for at least half an hour … She said I was shortly to leave the fleet and go south by train to take up a completely new life. I said that was out of the question … She replied, 'Nevertheless it is true.' She then asked me if I went up very high. I said, 'Possibly 70 or 80 feet (the height of my upper bridge), but why?' She said she thought it was higher than that; I would be in great danger, not while I was at a great height, but when I was coming down. She then asked me if I would mind her telling my fortune by cards – she had great faith in them. She got quite excited and said all she had seen in my hand was written in the deck.

Although Keyes seems not to have been fully convinced by this consultation with a seer who also worked part-time behind the counter at the nearby Dalgety Bay fish bar, it's nonetheless true that just a few days later he found himself 'swaying distinctly' aloft when a sudden wind blew up while he was standing in an observation balloon tethered some 800 feet above HMS *Colossus*, and that a possible disaster had been averted only by the action of a quick-thinking sailor who had seized the balloon's mooring rope as it then slithered across the deck; and also that not long afterwards, much to his surprise, Keyes found himself summoned by train to London to take up the position of Director of Naval Plans.

At the time Keyes assumed his new duties in September 1917, the convoy system and other recently adopted defensive measures had slowly begun to mitigate Allied shipping losses. But the prospect of continued U-boat marauding remained 'quite real enough,' Lloyd George later wrote in his memoirs. Watching the British losses mount earlier in the year, the PM would write that he had looked into the 'fear-dimmed eyes of our Mall admirals' and seen only 'stunned pessimism'. Later historians have tended to find fault with this account, and in time Keyes would give some backing to that judgement. Nonetheless, the loss curve continued: 470,000 tons of Allied matériel went to the bottom in October 1917. The figure fell in November to 305,000 tons, but rose again in December to 445,000 tons, roughly a third of it thanks to the Flanders U-boats, whose captains' preference for old-fashioned signalling by flag or lantern, rather than wireless, made them especially problematic to Allied intelligence.

Continuing his wry appraisal of the war from his home in Southwold, Ernest Cooper wrote in his diary that Christmas: 'Very few here are in their usual health, I have probably lost about two stones in weight owing to worry and rations but do not feel much the worse for it at present, altho' I dread another cold winter like last …'

And just a few days later: 'The Huns bombarded Yarmouth from the sea again, putting in 50 to 60 shells in 7 minutes, killing seven and wounding many more … The next night set in the sharpest frost known here since 1894–5, I had 4 pipes burst and 140 houses in the town suffered in the same way …'

Natural unrest at the continuing German naval activity around the English east coast was sharpened by rumours that the enemy was again fortifying its Flanders bases with a view to launching a last-ditch amphibian invasion of the British Isles. Not untypical was the cabinet meeting of 1 October 1917 which discussed six separate submarine encounters over the previous week, and concluded: 'In extension of War Council 241, Minute 10, the First Sea Lord reported that attacks on the Zeebrugge lock gates had occurred.'

As we've seen, the idea of ambushing the enemy U-boats in their bases and undermining their sea operations in general had been debated in various forms almost from the start of the war, and a cabinet meeting held as early as 22 December 1914 had referred to 'the desirability of put[ting] pressure on anchorage facilities in Belgium.' There had been a significant step forward on 21 November 1916 when the War Committee first discussed a specific plan to 'disallow the Germans access to [the] sea at Zeebrugge'. Many of the early proposals to do so had foundered on the issue of Admiral Jellicoe's misgivings about coordinating a possible joint operation involving the navy first bombarding the Flanders coast and then putting men and artillery ashore there, while land forces broke through from Ypres. Jellicoe soon found arguments to justify his views convincing himself that the Germans were not such fools as to fail to anticipate such a raid. Surely no one in their right mind would house fully a third of their submarine fleet in a base immediately across the water from the enemy homeland without first building up significant shore defences, possibly including the willingness to release supplies of some fearful poison gas to repel any invader? Alternatively, Jellicoe saw the Germans as having somehow tapped the British military telegraph, just as applied the other way round: hence the enemy would be waiting when the British ships appeared from over the horizon at the gates of Zeebrugge. 'At all costs, we must be careful to avoid springing a trap,' Jellicoe wrote.

It did not take long following the battle of Jutland for the British public to take the side of one or other of their executive commanders in the engagement in seeking to explain the at best only partly satisfactory outcome of the action. In time a tentative consensus came to propose that the dashing, 45-year-old David Beatty had practically won the day before the faint-hearted, 56-year-old John Jellicoe had fatally hesitated and let the enemy escape into the night. It was a caricature of the two men – one Beatty himself failed to actively discourage – but not wholly without a grain of truth. Once this legend was established, it was easy to continue in the same belief about the personal characteristics of the men successively directing Britain's naval operations once Beatty replaced Jellicoe as commander-in-chief of the Grand Fleet in December 1916. A certain renewed impetus began almost immediately for a direct assault on the enemy sea bases in Flanders. 'The port of Zeebrugge,' wrote Beatty in May 1917, 'is so narrow that blocking it is eminently practical. A blockship built of concrete … would have many chances in her favour of reaching the entrance to the locks.'

By 13 November the plan had passed from the Admiralty drawing board onto the war cabinet table in Downing Street. It envisaged the main thrust of the attack being delivered by a British cruiser that would appear out of the night, tie up to the Zeebrugge Mole and put men ashore there, beginning an infantry battle that would act as a diversion while a blockship positioned herself in the canal mouth roughly half a mile to the south. Beatty appended his initials to what became known rather prosaically as Operation 'Z' (later 'ZO') on 3 December 1917. Roger Keyes also soon satisfied himself that this 'bold but simple' approach might succeed in 'severely limit[ing] the usefulness of the line Zeebrugge–Ostend to the enemy', although some question remained about whether to try and cripple the main Zeebrugge lock gates by ramming them or instead seal them off by means of a strategically sunk concrete ship.

'It may be regarded as a hazardous enterprise,' Keyes was left to admit in a memorandum to the Admiralty. He knew very well that all previous such operations had foundered because of tactical anxieties and personal rivalries. 'But I feel very strongly that we shall not be asking the personnel engaged to take any greater risk than the infantry and tank crews are subjected to on every occasion on which an attack is delivered on shore.' Keyes's later proposal that two explosive-laden British submarines be used to further harry the enemy defences by deliberately ramming the Zeebrugge Mole viaduct and blowing themselves up there at the height of the mêlée provided Beatty with exactly what he had been reaching for, the element of 'diverse surprise' missing in previous plans. 'The scheme involves numerous different challenges to the enemy's capacity to concentrate his resources on our attack,' he later wrote.

Such was the plan on paper, and it was typical of Keyes – purposeful, bold, and neat. He had one further request. The old mariner chafed at the idea that the navy would merely supply the transport to reach Zeebrugge, and then rely on soldiers to actually storm the Mole. 'Sailors and marines [are] quite capable of executing this particular aspect of the exercise [and] would indeed be greatly offended not to do so,' he argued in a memo sent direct to the Admiralty board. The Admiralty concurred and, on 2 January 1918, Keyes, now newly installed at Dover, put in a first formal request for volunteers.

The final agreed mission these men flocked to join in the early weeks of 1918 was relatively simple in concept. A mixed fleet would sail from the southern coast of England before breaking into two separate battle groups. An inshore squadron of two cement-laden blockships, seven destroyers and 18 light craft would turn for Ostend, where the enemy would simultaneously come under fire from the siege guns of the Royal Marine Artillery in Flanders. While the barrage continued, the blockships would make use of a series of marker buoys to thread their way into the narrow mouth of the Bruges–Ostend canal and there sink themselves – an enterprise that would 'require some small feat [of] navigation,' Keyes allowed, though one 'readily attainable [if] normal order prevails'.

Meanwhile, a larger force would attack the Germans 15 miles up the coast at Zeebrugge. Although this was a more ambitious venture involving the landing of storming parties, the distinct prospect of ensuing fierce man-to-man combat and such spectacular adjuncts to the main action as the detonation of the breakwater's steel viaduct – thus preventing German reinforcements reaching the Mole during the battle – the essence of the plan was again to scuttle ships in such a way as to deny the enemy access to the open sea. There would be 'formidable obstacles' to achieving this, Keyes acknowledged, though the penalty for inaction would be equally severe. It was officially estimated that U-boats based at Bruges had been responsible for the loss of 2,512 Allied vessels of one type or another in the period 1 November 1914–31 December 1917, a rate of more than two ships a day. 'By reason of its position and relative security, Flanders has constituted a continual and ever-increasing menace to the sea communications of our Army and the seaborne trade and food supplies of the United Kingdom,' Keyes wrote in an official minute on the expedition.

Although 'straightforward in concept,' as Keyes put it, in operational terms the project was confronted with several challenges, not least the need to keep a total invasion force containing some 1,600 men and 85 ships secret from the enemy. There would be roughly two months of intensive training involved, and this in turn necessarily brought with it restrictions that proved 'mightily tiresome' to at least one participant. Private James Feeney of 7 Platoon, Royal Marines, later wrote in his diary of being confined for several days and nights below decks on the battleship HMS *Hindustan*: 'No room. Don't like ship life. No room to even change your mind,' he noted.'*

There may also have been a degree of wishful thinking on the part of those who planned the finer detail of Operation ZO. The bottling up of an enemy harbour in

---

* Pt. Feeney nonetheless retained a certain quiet stoicism in the face of these hardships, and reacted with equanimity when he and his shipmates finally learned of their destination. 'We are to land on the Mole and destroy all we can in the space of time that the wind and tide will allow,' he wrote. 'The general opinion here at the moment is that it will be either completely successful or we shall be all wiped out.' Feeney survived the action and later retired to his native Ireland.

wartime was neither a new nor a consistently successful idea. As Keyes himself later admitted, 'the precedent for this sort of incursion [was] only partly encouraging.' Even the immortal Admiral Nelson had once failed in his attempt to storm the Spanish-held port of Tenerife, losing several hundred men and his right arm in the process. More recently, Lieutenant Richmond P. Hobson of the US Navy had embarked on a similar amphibian raid, complete with blockships, in order to seal up the enemy fleet in their base at Santiago, Cuba, in June 1898. 'It was not a total success,' Hobson was left to admit, during a subsequent period spent as a Spanish prisoner of war. Keyes himself made no bones about the very real risks of the present mission when he came to interview the first batch of officer candidates who assembled in front of him in the wardroom of *Hindustan* while she lay at anchor in Chatham. 'With one exception only,' he later wrote,

> they appeared to be simply delighted and most grateful for the honour I had done them in offering them such a wonderful prospect. Then I got them an outline of the plan, and said that although I would make every endeavour to save them after they had sunk the ships, I felt that it was a very remote hope. They took everything for granted, asked few questions, if any, and went away apparently full of joy and gratitude.

What made the men's prospects so forlorn was not only the natural and manmade fortifications of the enemy bases they were to storm, but the need to 'coordinate several different marine and land exercises [into] one seamless whole' or, having 'stirred the wasps' nest from three or four directions at once, to then successfully withdraw amid the ensuing furor,' as Keyes put it. Zeebrugge, in particular, was a defenders' market. The ten miles of coastline to either side of the harbour were screened by a total of 232 guns, of which more than half were of the 'heavy' type – six inch and above – or one major artillery piece for roughly every 150 yards of ground. There were also 128 emplaced machine-gun nests, and up to thirty assorted lookout units equipped with powerful searchlights in the same general vicinity. Some of the largest German batteries fired six-foot shells each weighing a ton and capable of travelling up to 50,000 yards, or some 28 miles. It was further believed that there were between 600 and 700 men garrisoned in barracks or huts built on or near the Zeebrugge Mole itself, with the prospect of thousands more able to reinforce them at a few minutes' notice.

Formidable as they were, these were far from the only hazards facing any would-be intruder to the area. The outlying sea channels were also liberally strewn with mines. Due to inefficient and inadequate dredging operations, heavy silt had built up on either side of the narrow passage leading from the harbour's entrance at the eastern end of the Mole to the site where the blockships would be sunk – 'a problem of some complexity under idyllic sailing conditions, which these were not,' it was noted. The Germans had placed booms variously consisting of rock-filled barrages and impenetrable steel-mesh nets around the approaches to the 350-foot-wide channel that marked the only viable point of access to the mouth of the Bruges canal itself. As mentioned, there were also the not-insignificant challenges of steering a large armada across a channel constantly patrolled by enemy submarines and out into a system of notoriously fickle tidal streams of wildly varying depths, and to do so without lights or directional signals of any kind. The fleet exercise off the Isle of May had clearly shown the risks inherent in operating under broadly similar conditions, with five collisions occurring between eight vessels and 104 men lost without a single shot fired in anger. Even if all the interlocking parts of the Zeebrugge operation went exactly to plan, Keyes admitted, there would still be only limited time to evacuate the area and turn the strike force back for home before daylight brought the ships within range of the heavy-calibre shore batteries. Since it would be necessary to leave the Mole by no later than 1.30 a.m. to be clear of the danger zone, and for similar reasons it was impossible to arrive there much before midnight, a 'certain degree of celerity of action would be needed throughout the proceedings,' the plan stated.

The actual assault on the steeply raised, fortified Mole was a 'peculiar challenge,' Keyes acknowledged, perhaps thinking back to his experience 18 years earlier at the high-walled riverside Chinese fort, but one it was 'rather essential' to meet.

'Near the northeastern extremity of this great sea wall certain guns have been located,' he wrote.

> It is considered that these guns form a serious obstacle to the safe passage of our block-ships which will have to pass within one cable [200 yards] of these guns.
>
> The batteries are believed to consist of 3–4 heavy guns firing to the eastward, i.e. parallel to the line of the Mole, and 4 or 5 smaller anti-aircraft guns whose arc of training is uncertain.
>
> It is therefore very desirable to obtain temporary possession of this end of the Mole before the block-ships meet with any opposition therefrom.
>
> The seamen storming parties will be trained in securing their ship alongside the Mole, in working the disembarkation ladders, in the use of Stokes guns and in demolition work.
>
> The [Royal Marine] personnel are being trained in the use of flammenwerfers, machine guns, and howitzers.

Keyes also knew his naval history, and acknowledged that there was 'a precedent for some concern' when it came to the withdrawal phase of the Zeebrugge operation. In May 1798, a British expedition under the command of Captain Home Popham had landed at Ostend and proceeded to destroy the town's sluice gates and flood much of the surrounding countryside then in French possession. At that point a violent gale had blown up which prevented the reembarkation of the British troops, with the result that 115 of the invaders were killed and ten times that number taken prisoner. The weather would also be a concern to the modern-day attackers. The raid had to occur on a moonless night, be timed to coincide with a high tide, and required a westerly wind strong enough to blow Frank Brock's artificial fog over the approaching fleet, but light enough so that the accompanying small craft not be swamped by any sudden swells.

Sea conditions would also play a significant part in the land-assault element of Operation ZO. The troopship put alongside the Zeebrugge Mole needed 'an adequate degree of stability so that landing ramps could deploy to efficiently put the men ashore', in the words of the official Admiralty directive. The 'efficiently' part proved easier ordered than done. In the event, the sailors and marines who stormed Zeebrugge would have to climb out along wooden gangways that were little more than planks, rising up and crashing down with the rocking of the ship, and do so while each carrying around 60 pounds worth of assorted bombs, ammunition belts, Lewis guns and other equipment – roughly the weight of a typical five- to six-year-old child of the 21st century, and just as irksome. It's perhaps not surprising that while many career officers stepped forward when Keyes first appealed for volunteers, others in the ranks were less rosy about their prospects of survival. As Lieutenant-Commander Ronald Boddie of the Apollo-class cruiser-turned-blockship HMS *Thetis* wrote, there was a 'distinctly prickly' element among the 'otherwise generally willing' response to the mission.

> In February 1918, the Admiralty called for a limited number of volunteers for 'a dangerous venture' from the Grand Fleet. The volunteers were to be unmarried, and of V.G. [very good] character. No other particulars were given … The other squadrons except the Americans were to contribute equally.
>
> To my astonishment, the [nature of] the venture discouraged the men from volunteering, and I had great difficulty in persuading and cajoling 6 eligible but rather indifferent men to accompany me.

The individual who would come to personally organise and execute the whole enterprise could be similarly obdurate and congenial: 'a man with a nice smile and iron teeth,' it was said of Roger Keyes during his time as commander-in-chief, Dover. On his sunny days he was a benign and avuncular senior officer with a talent for mimicry, known to write lighthearted and sentimental verse – 'as good a friend as he was bad an enemy,' his younger colleague Edward Renouf remembered. Keyes could also be witheringly blunt if the situation demanded it. Following an inadequately opposed U-boat attack off Dover on the night of 14 February 1918, which left 76 British officers and men dead and eight merchant ships on navy service at the bottom, Keyes ordered an immediate court martial of those responsible. This was done, and the young commanding officer of the patrol boat *Amazon* received a formal reprimand as a result. According to the naval writer Barrie Pitt, 'Keyes, his blood up, exploded to the Admiralty at the incredibly leniency of the sentence, and the Admiralty agreeing with him, the young man was in turn relieved of his command and given clearly to understand that his career was finished.' The sorry tale was not quite over, however. Keyes evidently reconsidered matters, because early in March he quietly reversed himself and called in the disgraced party for an interview. 'I attributed his failure to lack of experience rather than want of courage,' Keyes later wrote, 'and I felt so sorry that so young a man should have his future in the Navy damned at the outset of his career that I sent for him and offered him an appointment on the [Zeebrugge operation], which he gladly accepted.'

This particular officer never forgot that Keyes had ultimately stuck by him after his fall from grace, when he could as easily have thrown him to the dogs and ended his career forever. He later wrote that 'the Admiral could blow hot and cold, [but] I chiefly remember both his loyalty, and the personal kindness of his family' – Lady Eva, née Bowlby, whom Keyes had married in 1906, and their three daughters and two sons, including the future Lieutenant-Colonel Geoffrey Keyes, VC, who would be killed in action at the age of 24 while leading what proved to be a suicidal raid on General Rommel's Afrika Korps headquarters in the Libyan desert, a feat of arms in no way diminished by the subsequent revelation that Keyes had almost certainly been accidentally shot by one of his own men.

In general, this was not a family given to an excessively cautious or personally diffident approach to life's challenges. 'Both father and son were the embodiment of patriotism and bravery – "Whatever it takes to get the job done," I heard Geoffrey remark calmly before wading out into a crocodile-infested river under enemy sniper fire,' Edward Renouf later recalled.

Admiral Keyes retained his own uncompromising attitude to the art of warfare even when brought out of retirement at the age of 67 to become Britain's first Director of Combined Operations in June 1940. 'The chiefs of staff will certainly postpone victory as long as they are guided by the advice of committees of comparatively junior officers, without practical combat experience ... Their chief object seems to be to array all the difficulties and dangers of any offensive operation within our powers,' he would soon be writing to his friend the prime minister, one of many such complaints over the next 16 months. In October 1941, Winston Churchill finally succumbed to those same bureaucratic voices of reason and Keyes was relieved of his post.

In his search for a suitable officer to command the main assault vessel at Zeebrugge, Keyes's eye soon fell on his kindred spirit Alfred Francis Carpenter, who had for several months past been performing 'valuable if unexciting' staff work under his direction in the Plans Division of the Admiralty. Lean and ascetic, with rubbery, expressive features not unlike those of the actor Martin Clunes, the London-born Carpenter had served as a young sub-lieutenant during the Boxer Rebellion. Aged barely 19, he wrote a rather precocious letter home about the justness of the British cause, which ended: 'We should distinguish – logically, historically and morally – from an act of material gain and one undertaken to restore God's order in the world.' Carpenter was not merely a student of war, however. In June 1900 he would also be intimately involved in a daring, commando-like raid when whaleboats launched by the destroyer HMS *Whiting* went ashore at night in order to lay explosives around a Chinese fort near the modern coastal city of Tianjin. Like all the best such sorties, it had nearly come to grief. The defenders had been alerted by the noise of the landing and in the subsequent firefight Carpenter had shot back with one hand while using the other to drag a wounded colleague back to the boats, which had then just escaped the attentions of the awakened heavy shore artillery. Clearly, this was a man after Roger Keyes's heart. Commander Carpenter, who had gone on to distinguish himself as a navigating officer, would take charge of the hurriedly refitted HMS *Vindictive* at Zeebrugge, with orders to position the 350-foot-long, nearly 6,000-ton cruiser alongside the Mole and hold her steady there for up to an hour and a half while being continually pounded by German shells and machine-gun fire. 'It was an uninviting prospect, which I gladly accepted,' he recalled.

Keyes wrote to Admiral Beatty from Dover on 10 February 1918:

> Carpenter will travel up with this letter tomorrow. [He] will be able to give you all the information you will require on the Plan, including the total number of officers and men who will be engaged. I don't want to be grasping and greedy, [but] of course the more that can be lent from the Grand Fleet the happier and more confident I shall be, for they will come down so full of fire and the spirit of the Fleet that nothing will stop them.

Keyes's sanguine mood darkened appreciably when, just four days later, a German destroyer flotilla under the command of Captain Oskar Heinecke successfully plundered the Dover straits with the significant British losses noted. Disgracefully, the enemy had then 'escaped without being brought to action by our monitor or the destroyers on patrol,' Keyes wrote. Just 24 hours after this débâcle, a German submarine had then slipped into the Channel unopposed, dropped some mines, and fired 22 shells into Dover town centre before stealing back into the night. A 13-year-old girl named Gertrude Boorman was killed by the bombardment as she lay asleep in bed, and her 15-year-old brother William was crippled by a shell splinter to his leg. Eight days later, Keyes presented his final draft of Operation ZO to the new First Sea Lord, Admiral 'Rosy' Wemyss, and his colleagues in Whitehall. Wemyss recalled:

> At a meeting of the Naval Lords in my room I put forward to them what it was proposed to do, and Admiral Keyes unfolded his detailed plan. Luckily there was no dissentient voice and I therefore was spared the difficulty of carrying out this operation against their wishes, which I had made up my mind to do in case of their disapproval.

As we've seen, Keyes wisely chose to adopt the volunteer principle when it came to manning the total of three sacrificial blockships – HMS *Iphigenia, Intrepid* and *Thetis* – finally selected to scuttle themselves at the mouth of the Bruges canal. Following individual interviews, it was decided the ships would be commanded respectively by 25-year-old Lieutenant Ivan Franks, a veteran of the Q-boat operations; Lieutenant Stuart Bonham Carter, 28, a keen all-round sportsman who had once taken a cricket bat into action with him while serving as turret officer on the battleship *Emperor of India*, the better to 'biff' any hostile German crew members he might encounter when patrolling the North Sea; and Commander Ralph Sneyd, DSO, 35, who despite being the one holdout to the otherwise general acclaim that had greeted Keyes's initial wardroom briefing on HMS *Hindustan*, went on to be commended for his extreme personal gallantry at Zeebrugge. In the words of the official citation, 'This officer blew the charges to make salvage of his vessel impractical, and, himself wounded, [did] not abandon his ship until he could be of no further assistance in attaining the objective.'

In Keyes's view, men such as Franks, Bonham Carter and Sneyd faced risks to their survival and that of their crews that matched anything encountered in the horrors of the trenches. 'For the most part, they nonetheless accepted their roles as though stepping forward to receive a jackpot won at the roulette table,' he wrote admiringly. From the ranks of the Royal Marines, meanwhile, came the likes of 27-year-old Sergeant Norman Finch, an ordinarily cheerful and mild-mannered Birmingham native who went into battle armed with a club engraved with the words 'Forget me not' at its business end, and who despite being severely wounded would continue to harass the German defenders on the Zeebrugge Mole with a combination of two-pound 'pom pom' shells and rich Black Country invective; his adjutant Captain Arthur Chater, who wrote in his diary on 8 February 1918, 'When the details of the operation were explained to me, I was thrilled by having been selected to take part in it'; and the young private soldier William Hopewell, who said simply, 'I volunteered for this particular job because I lost two brothers at the front in six months and I wanted to get my own back.'

Elsewhere, the division between elective and compulsory participation in Operation ZO was not always quite so clear-cut. Of the former school, 42-year-old Commander Patrick Edwards, RNVR, already a veteran of both the Gallipoli and Somme campaigns, wrote of his commission to join the storming party on HMS *Vindictive*:

> I was full of it. I thought [the plan] was quite hopeless, but, oh my goodness, it was quite gloriously hopeless. It was desperate; but I realised our position and the frightful losses the U-boats were inflicting on our shipping were also desperate ... I went off to my cabin that night, but I could not sleep. How lucky I was to be in it.

By contrast, some of the ordinary seamen and marines enlisted for the mission seemed to suggest less of a voluntary process and more one of straightforward recruitment. Petty Officer William O'Hara had served on the dreadnought HMS *Conqueror* at the battle of Jutland, but by his account had done little since then but 'occasionally move the ship to and fro' between Dover and Portsmouth. 'Service in the Grand Fleet in the war was dull,' he wrote in 1931. 'I was young and wanted to see [action]; therefore, when I was sent for in February 1918, and told I was chosen for special service duty I was very pleased indeed.'

O'Hara was typical of the men who were simply assigned to the Zeebrugge raid and who cheerfully fell in with the plan despite all the risks. Another such conscript was 29-year-old Leading Deckhand James Smith, who had worked as a baker and served as secretary of the Wesleyan Church in his native Burnley before going off to sea in August 1916. Eighteen months later, Smith and his fellow crew members on Motor Launch (ML) *262* 'were informed [we] had been detailed to take part in a special mission – a particularly hazardous affair in which it was expected that 75 per cent of ships and men would be lost.' O'Hara later remarked that he too had been 'very happy to be loaned out' for the job.

One of those who actively tendered his services for the Zeebrugge raid was 30-year-old Lieutenant-Commander Francis Hugh Sandford, who had been attached to the submarine depot ship HMS *Arrogant* on the Dover Patrol when Keyes casually inquired if he might be interested in 'a do' to take place on the Belgian coast. He was. Sandford, the sixth of seven sons of the late archdeacon of Exeter, was that relatively rare career naval officer (almost unknown today) whose fundamental approach to his duties was equal parts boffin and buccaneer. 'Frank was a most peculiar fellow,' said Edward Renouf. 'One moment he was reading Tolstoy and quoting the Greek poets, and the next he would be discussing the best way to blow up an enemy port.'

Horrified by his experience of naval munitions while serving on the Trafalgar-era frigate-turned-training ship HMS *Vernon* before the war, Sandford had set about improving the performance of British mines and torpedoes to something like the standard of their German equivalents. The result was his co-invention of an oscillating mine that could be deployed from a surface craft or a submerged torpedo tube, and in theory find its way to its target under the action of a small, electrically-driven propeller without the need for mooring cables. Although 'teething issues remained,' Admiral Beatty later wrote of this development, 'it was to bring our navy's capability in the area within hail of our enemy's.'

Sandford was not only concerned with the scientific or technical aspect of warfare, however. In February 1915, he led a demolition party from HMS *Irresistible* to successfully storm the Turkish gun positions at Sedd-el-Bahr on the southern tip of the Gallipoli peninsula. Four weeks later, Sandford again volunteered for a raid organised by Admiral Keyes on the nearby enemy minefields, hazardous enough for the civilian crews of the British minesweepers commandeered for the occasion to have rapidly turned about and fled the scene. Three Allied ships were sunk in the subsequent action, which contained numerous instances of outstanding individual bravery but left its author ruing the missed opportunity for a total breakthrough.

'I saw Sandford on the morning of the 19th March,' wrote Keyes, 'almost in rags, with clothes and skin discoloured by the fumes of a high explosive shell, and was immensely impressed by his gallant, light-hearted bearing.'

Three months later, Sandford was blinded in the right eye when a mine he was attempting to lay in the Gulf of Smyrna instead exploded in his face. He came home, spent a month in hospital, collected a DSO for his work in Gallipoli, and eventually joined the Dover Patrol in January 1918. One evening Keyes called Sandford in to his office, briskly mapped out the details of the Zeebrugge operation, using some cups and saucers on his desk to represent the enemy defences, and asked him if he had any particular thoughts about the most efficient means to demolish a 300-yard-long viaduct supported by steel pilings and strong enough to bear the weight of a seaside passenger train-turned-goods wagon regularly passing overhead to carry supplies to the German troops garrisoned further along the Mole. Since this particular causeway linked the sea wall to the shore, its removal would 'rather serve to limit the enemy's ability to reinforce the scene of the party,' in Keyes's measured words.

At that Sandford went away and conducted experiments with unmanned rafts loaded with delayed-action charges, abandoned these as unreliable, and in time reported back that the only way forward in his opinion was to fit out an old submarine (or two submarines, in case one broke down or in some other way became 'suddenly degraded' in his enigmatic phrase) with high explosive and to manually steer this at high speed into the target. Keyes nodded his assent, and inquired merely if Sandford happened to know of any young, unmarried submarine officer who might be amenable to taking on what seemed to them both to effectively be a suicide mission. It was now the third week of February 1918, less than a month after the shambles of Operation EC1. 'Yes, I do,' said Sandford.

The result was a signal that went out from Keyes's office on 22 February, requesting that two unattached officers report to him for interview in Dover. The first to appear was 25-year-old Lieutenant Aubrey Cecil Newbold, who listened to the proposal that he pack the 1905-era submarine *C1* with dynamite and then ram this into the Zeebrugge harbour viaduct, before in theory escaping into the surrounding mêlée in a motorised dinghy, with what Keyes called 'mounting enthusiasm' at the prospect. The same terse qualities that made Newbold so decisive and widely admired an officer came into play here, as he searched for the words with most telling effect. '*Sir*,' he said at length, snapping out a salute, and that concluded the commission. Newbold went post-haste to Portsmouth to begin two months of intensive preparation and training for his role in the operation.

The other individual to be summoned for duty was Francis Sandford's younger brother Richard.

This latter officer was still stinging from Admiral Beatty's rebuke following the ill-fated exercise off the Isle of May, and later remarked that he had wanted to 'efface the humiliation' of that disaster. Born in Exmouth on 11 May 1891, the youngest of the nine children of the Venerable Ernest Grey Sandford and his wife Ethel, Richard had enjoyed a rather perfunctory education at Clifton College in Bristol before joining the navy as a 12-year-old cadet at the training establishment HMS *Britannia*. Promoted to midshipman in September 1908, he had served on the pre-dreadnought battleship *Hibernia* based at the Nore on the Thames estuary, and taken a series of other 'unexacting home commissions,' as he called them, before volunteering for submarine duty in 1913. Awarded his submariner's engine-room certificate on 4 August 1914, the same day on which Britain declared war on Germany, Sandford, now a lieutenant, joined his brother in the crew of HMS *Arrogant* on the Dover Patrol. From there he transferred in January 1917 to the submarine *K6* as first lieutenant, with the unhappy result noted.

At the end of February 1918, Sandford, now in official disfavour, was appointed to command the 12-year-old *C3*, based at Portsmouth. Though not quite the final dregs of the submarine service, nor was this semi-obsolete and notoriously leaky boat a conspicuous step in the direction of the 26-year-old officer's professional rehabilitation. Sandford was 'thoroughly brassed off,' he admitted in a family letter, with little to do but 'endlessly order the scrubbing of the tub's sides, etc' as she lay at anchor in Camber Quay under the shadow of the town's Anglican cathedral. 'Boredom [was] always the enemy,' he added. To divert himself one day, Sandford went out in a rubber dinghy to a secluded spot off Portsmouth Point and experimented with the effects of amatol high-explosive, primed with a time fuse, sent 'scudding on a float like a hand-propelled torpedo' towards a contraption made of old bicycle tyres and wooden potato crates. A 'most gratifying' result had ensued. Like his elder brother, Richard always took a keen pleasure in blowing things up.

On or around 1 March 1918 Admiral Keyes called in Lieutenant Sandford, who 'agreed with alacrity' to participate in the Zeebrugge operation. The admiral asked in closing what steps the young submariner proposed to take to save himself and his five-man crew from being blown up along with their vessel at the point of impact with the viaduct. Sandford replied evenly that the ship's company would be quite easily able to take to a life raft while gyroscopic control steered *C3* the last hundred yards or so to her target – 'but,' Keyes later recorded when reviewing the events of 22/23 April, 'I do not believe that he or his brother ever intended to make use of the [auto-pilot], and they only installed it to save me from a subsequent charge of having condemned six men to practically certain death.'

This did not stop the Sandford brothers from commandeering a £14,000 (now £350,000) production-model Broom power boat to 'test' as a possible escape vessel, only one of several such high-speed sea trials they conducted around the Solent during March. The one-eyed Francis reluctantly agreed that he would be unable to go aboard either *C1* or *C3* during the raid itself, but he nonetheless proposed to follow the submarines into battle and personally rescue their crews after they had successfully demolished the viaduct. 'I can think of no one I have ever met who carried enterprising initiative further than this most gallant and gifted officer,' wrote Keyes after the event, while acknowledging: 'It was a long time before my office was free of bills and other correspondence connected with the Sandfords' activities.'

While the Sandford brothers were still busy terrorising the English south coast, the various navy and marine contingents attached to Operation ZO were assembling at training depots in Chatham, Portsmouth, Plymouth, Dover, Rochester, Deal and in a few cases as far afield as Scapa Flow. Despite the generally contented mood among the volunteers, it would be wrong to suggest that there was a universal spirit of enthusiasm or even detectable optimism about a mission where roughly one out of every three men was expected to be killed or wounded. Some of the participants may have signed up less from unbounded zeal for the raid itself and more as a temporary relief from lives necessarily spent in a confined space for weeks or months on end, with not enough to do and in conditions that were rarely dangerous but often tedious and uncomfortable. Even then, it wasn't always a case of the Zeebrugge recruits to a man cheerfully embracing all the hazards and privations of their training. At Deal, discipline evidently broke down among the 1st Battalion, Royal Marine Light Infantry (RMLI), where the official war diary rather cryptically notes, 'Btn. Exercise on the Lynch. No. 7 Platoon failed to fall in as ordered.' The record shows that four officers from that particular unit were replaced as a result, and a one-word entry stamped into another officer's file: 'Rebuked'.

Later in March 1918, a total of 18 men spread across the Portsmouth, Plymouth and Chatham training depots were similarly punished for being absent without leave. Lieutenant-Commander Boddie in turn recalled that some of the naval stokers who mustered on the mission's parent ship HMS *Hindustan*, still ignorant of their final objective, 'were disappointed when they were drafted to the lousy looking blockships to handle coal, raise steam, and clean up unwanted rubble and cement … Their messes aboard were overcrowded and uncomfortable. They had gathered the impression that they were going to France, and would see some fighting. It was necessary to eliminate a few of the more troublesome, after which a sort of restless peace reigned.' Petty Officer Harry Adams, for his part, was 'happy to volunteer' for the cause from his 'dreary' berth on HMS *Royal Sovereign*, but also found the advance training 'a pain … we were never allowed any shore leave, [but] I did hear that some of the lads in a certain lorry held up the driver with a revolver that they might stop to purchase mouth-organs.'

While the human beings endlessly rehearsed for their roles in the operation, their transport and equipment were also being prepared for battle. The dockyard engineers at Chatham worked around the clock to refit the three obsolete cruisers – *Thetis* (laid down in 1889), *Iphigenia* (1890) and *Intrepid* (1891) – to be beached at Zeebrugge, and the two – *Sirius* (1889) and *Brilliant* (1890) – destined for Ostend. The essential balancing act was to make all five blockships light enough to allow them to pass safely over the treacherous outlying sandbanks and shoals off the Belgian coast, but heavy enough so that once sunk they could not be easily moved. Since the British flotilla would presumably come under intense enemy fire while on its final approach to its targets, the blockships' forward gun turrets and other exposed positions were reinforced with half-inch steel armour. Each vessel was strategically loaded with around 1,500 tons of assorted cement, concrete and rubble, while anything copper or brass (commodities the Germans then urgently needed) was removed. All five ships were fitted with duplicate controls, and equipped with industrial-strength smoke canisters. In order to make the approaching squadron less conspicuous, their masts were removed and they were painted a specially scruffy shade of grey. Deep inside each of the five ships' hulls nine explosive charges were wired to twin sets of firing pins placed in separate control panels, since – as Admiral Keyes delicately put it – 'the command of these craft might well pass rapidly.'

Elsewhere in Chatham, the task of converting the 20-year-old, Arrogant-class cruiser *Vindictive* into something resembling a medieval raiding galleon decked out with a variety of boarding ramps, grappling irons and bomb-lobbing catapults, crossed with dystopian, futuristic touches such as an intimidating 11-inch forward howitzer and a battery of mortar and grenade launchers, girders, trusses, chutes and flame-spewing pipes and hoses, exercised 42-year-old Lieutenant-Commander Robert Rosoman and a team of 98 civilian and naval volunteers, each sworn to secrecy, throughout late February and early March.

Sergeant Harry Wright from No. 10 Platoon, RMLI, later recalled his shock when he and his men first came to board their ship to Zeebrugge:

> On getting alongside *Vindictive* we were astonished to see how she was fitted up. There was a splendid deck built on the port side with ramps leading to it from the lower deck to starboard. On the port side were 14 huge gangways pointing out to sea, and tricked up with ropes and pulleys ready for dropping … Sandbag revetments were built around the fore bridge and other vital parts. In addition, there were two very powerful flame-throwers and a number of machine guns. As regards ammunition, the *Vindictive* was a floating arsenal, for there were shells of all sizes, ready fused, lying about everywhere.

In addition to these modifications and armaments, *Vindictive*'s mainmast was removed and a large part of it fitted horizontally across the deck, extending several feet over the port bow, to act as a kind of buffer when the ship met the Zeebrugge Mole on that side. 'Admirable and extensive' as these various alterations were, Alfred Carpenter was forced to conclude that, taken as a whole, 'in any classical sense, the ship barely deserved the term "seaworthy".'

In a somehow superbly British improvisation, meanwhile, two squat-nosed Mersey ferryboats, the *Iris 11* and *Daffodil*, were quietly withdrawn from service and sent to Portsmouth to be fitted out for front-line duty at Zeebrugge. As well as carrying troops, their role in the mission would be to bodily pin *Vindictive* against the Mole and, should the larger ship be sunk, 'to bring away such of her assets and crews as may possibly survive', in the words of the Admiralty directive. There were some spirited attempts to make jokes about these particular ferries – the sailor, for instance, cheerfully asking to see tickets as her passengers first came aboard – but nothing funny about their ultimate fate.

Meanwhile the Mole itself, or at least a strip of the gently rolling nearby downs taped out to loosely resemble it, was being attacked on a nightly basis in the otherwise peaceful countryside between Deal and Dover. 'For about a month a stiff course of training was carried out,' Lieutenant F. J. Hore of the 4th Battalion, RMLI, later told the press.

> After [dark] smoke floats, red, white, and green Very lights, short lights, dummy bombs, rockets, flares, and torches, were all used in practice, and so realistic was the training that the Btn. fully and ably responded to the great expectations and hopes of its Commander and Officers during the final engagement.

Although no one questioned the bravery of this particular unit's performance under fire, advance intelligence and many other aspects of the preparations for Operation ZO would later be subjected to a withering critique by War Office analysts. With the best will in the world, jogging amiably around in gym shoes up and down the suburban Dover hills under simulated shellfire was at best a pale imitation of actual battle conditions as they all too soon presented themselves on the Zeebrugge Mole. Amid what Lieutenant Hore called 'all the fine manly zeal' that characterised the various war games of late February and March 1918, no one seems to have given much thought to the practical challenges of landing some 250 marines at night on a steeply raked, enemy-held breakwater of over a mile in length, with only the most basic wooden ramps – many of them soon to be shot away – available for disembarkation. As Sergeant Wright was later to observe of this critical phase of the operation: 'We were continually swept by machine gun fire from the sea end of the Mole, hence the heavy casualties amongst the officers and ratings trying to fix the grappling irons … From the ship to the rail was simply a death walk.'

Meanwhile, elsewhere in Dover a team of three officers and 62 men from the Royal Naval Air Service billeted in a spartan dockyard workshop with a skull-and-crossbones sign hanging over the door were busy developing what their chief Wing Commander Frank Brock called the 'artificial fog [and] other visual treats' of the raid. As we've seen, Brock was the son of the head of the well-known family fireworks firm, where he himself had worked until June 1914, at which point he disguised himself as an 'ordinary wayfarer' and set off on a fortnight's walking tour of Germany 'to get a better look at her defences'. Commissioned into the Royal Artillery in the month war was declared, he'd transferred to the Royal Navy, and from there to the naval air service in early 1915. Although Brock rose steadily through the ranks, this sort of step-by-step advancement grew progressively less appealing to his flamboyant personality. A few weeks short of his 30th birthday at the time he asked (or more accurately, demanded) to join the Zeebrugge raid, he already had a long and colourful personal history with pyrotechnics of one sort or another, beginning from the day when as a teenager he blew up a stove in his Dulwich College form room. Solidly built with crisp black hair, a keen rugby player and cricketer, Brock was described in a friend's diary as 'courteous, with very good manners – a salty tongue in private

– and the most pleasant public personality, a "true English gentleman" who acted at all times with the utmost decorum and restraint until the moment came to blow someone or something up'.

Despite the occasional failed experiment (such as the time Brock 'miscounted' his chemicals and detonated an 'entire fifth of November display' inside a small Nissen hut as a result), he was also regarded as 'superbly well organised and controlled – a creature of habit'. Brock invariably appeared for work each morning with a to-do list attached to a clipboard. He followed the schedule scrupulously, ticking off each item as it was completed. Although in robust health, Brock was slightly hard of hearing – perhaps a legacy of all the explosions over the years – and he found the acoustics of his tin-roofed Dover workshop difficult. His colleagues learned to raise their voices, speak deliberately and look directly at him when they had something to say. Brock's own voice was 'surprisingly soft among all the shouted orders and grumbles of the men,' it was said. 'But perhaps this was only some kind of trick because you found yourself listening to him much more closely, afraid you would miss something.'

'I've never done a job with live explosives before,' a nervous recruit remarked to him on his first day at Dover.

'I've never done one without,' Brock replied.

Plotted on paper, Brock's assorted chemical 'treats' formed a bewildering pattern of tangled, intersecting lines, multicoloured blobs and intricate circuit diagrams that reminded one observer of an 'especially messy map of the London Underground Railway, which several bottles of ink had been liberally spilled over'. But the apparent chaos concealed a singleness of purpose that never for a moment lost sight of the objective, 'the trapping of the Hun in his lair'.

Commander Carpenter of the *Vindictive* often visited Brock and his men in their dockyard hut, and in his superbly controlled phrase,

> Their output, both in quality and quantity, was most satisfactory in spite of the many handicaps with which such innovations have to contend … No matter what our requirements were Brock was undefeated. He had travelled much and could tell you all that was worth knowing of any land from Patagonia to Spitzbergen. He was no mean authority on old prints and books, was also a keen philatelist, and was blessed with a remarkable memory. Wherever he went he carried with him a pocket edition of the New Testament, which was his favourite possession … His geniality and humour were hard to beat. But of all his qualities, optimism perhaps held first place.

Or at least it generally did: having once broken a workshop mirror and been facetiously told that he could expect seven years bad luck as a result, Brock replied matter-of-factly, 'I'm not going to live that long, chum.'

At the same time, 800 miles to the north in Scapa Flow, 25-year-old Lieutenant Cecil Courtenay Dickinson was cheerfully putting a landing party of some 50 Royal Navy bluejackets through its paces. Petty Officer Adams remembered of this process:

The [Lieutenant] gave you all the confidence in the world – 'secure' in short, a grand character, splendid leader, the kind one would serve under, go anywhere with, under any and all circumstances … Sometimes we would shoot at targets, seals, hares, practically aim at anything to help make you a good shot … Other days, we would land for an all-day paper chase over the hills. Plenty of boat pulling, physical jerks, etc, in fact anything that could be thought of to get a man really fit … On our final day, I remember pulling back from one of the islands, in a filthy rough sea, wet through, perished to the bone, hands too numb almost to hang on to the [oars], and we started to sing 'When you come to the end of a "perfect day"' – how typically, sarcastically true of that breed of Matloe. But the song did its job, and although undignified and 'un-Navalish', Lieutenant Dickinson let us get on with it, to get it off our chests – and bawl our lungs out at each roll or dip of our cutter. He seemed to understand it did us good. That was one of the outstanding qualities. He knew men.

Thirty-four-year-old Captain Henry Halahan, a pipe-smoking, family man from Surrey who had been in uniform ever since the Boer War would train and ultimately lead the storming party who sailed for Zeebrugge on HMS *Vindictive*. Keyes had asked him for the names of any possible candidates for the outfit, and at the end of the list he wrote: 'May I say that if the operation for which you said you might want some of my men is eventually undertaken, I should very much like to take part in it. I would willingly accept the same conditions, viz, that I should not expect to come back.' This latter assurance was duly read out when the remains of Captain Halahan were committed to the sea a tragically brief time later.

When Lieutenant-Commander William Bury, an engineering specialist, reported to Chatham, he found 'many divergent moods' among those assembled for the operation. Several of the enlisted men 'more or less happily adopted nicknames for themselves, such as The Suicide Club or The Death or Glory Boys.' Though still not aware of their final destination, the men had been told to prepare for 'furious fighting, likely in some cases to be hand-to-hand combat' and were understandably curious for more details. 'There was by no means a mutinous atmosphere about,' Bury reported, 'but a certain feeling of apprehension and testiness can reasonably be said to have asserted itself.' Writing home a few days later, by contrast, he recalled many of the officers reporting to Chatham being personally briefed by Admiral Keyes 'who immediately told us all details, and filled us with enthusiasm in his extraordinary quiet way [and] left us with a strong sense of assurance. Being the senior engineering officer of the lot, I got the *Vindictive* …'

In all some 3,000 men, whether combatant or ancillary, had by now begun to variously rehearse, equip or service the planned raids on Zeebrugge and Ostend. Less than a tenth of them knew the specific details of their mission. Most of the uniformed contingent, around 70 per cent, were navy, and a further 20 per cent were marines – with a dozen or so 'supernumerary staff' as they were called, really meaning Frank Brock and some of his handpicked air service colleagues, as well as a deep-chested individual in his mid-50s known only as Len, sent on secondment from the family fireworks firm to advise on more specialised technical matters, but whose chief role seems to have been to inflict an endless series of practical jokes on the men, such as genially offering around a plate of 'rock-cakes' one teatime that were, in fact, rocks, daintily covered with icing.

The civilian workforce also included over a hundred ship's carpenters, such as 32-year-old Jim Hirst, a lanky, slow-speaking married man with a congenitally deformed foot who shuffled in to the Chatham dockyard at five o'clock each morning, six days a week. One of Hirst's duties that March was to help reinforce HMS *Vindictive*'s conning tower in the belief that this would become the ship's command post if her bridge were disabled. Some attention was also paid in the area of what the Admiralty called *Vindictive*'s 'supplementary ordnance', which basically meant fitting weapons on the cruiser's deck for close-range infantry fighting.

In all, there was a 'fair amount of old-fashioned naval spit and shine' about the arrangements, Hirst later remembered. When it came to screening the ship's upper areas from possible enemy artillery fire, 'We were told to bring up sandbags and pack them in tight,' a gesture he recalled thinking 'quite useless for stopping anything much more than a lady's pistol bullet.' To protect the two flamethrower huts built fore and aft of the ship's false deck, 'We threw down some half-a-dozen very old and tired bed mattresses, which would have put up some fight against a popgun but not a well-aimed howitzer.' The spirit of improvisation extended elsewhere on *Vindictive*. While the marines continued to practise on a strip of nearby hillside believed to resemble the Zeebrugge Mole, Commander Carpenter thought to commission a scale model of the actual Mole and its outlying defences. Built of plasticine, it was mounted on a cardboard tray which he kept tucked behind some decanters in a locked cupboard in his cabin. From time to time, selected officers were invited in to inspect this and be quietly told, 'Gentlemen, this is the place where we will do battle.'

Early in March, Winston Churchill, still notionally minister of munitions, but given to bursts of what his son Randolph later called 'particular zeal and almost delirious excitement' whenever clandestine naval operations were involved, visited some of the Zeebrugge crews in training on the Kent downs, and later inspected the 4th Battalion, RMLI, as it formed up on the North Barracks parade ground in Deal. According to Private Ernest 'Beau' Tracey, Churchill told them: 'You are going on a daring and arduous stunt from which none of you may return, but every endeavour will be made to bring back as many of you as possible.'

At that there had been 'some slight stirring' in the ranks, Tracey remembered, before Churchill continued, 'Should any of you, for any reason whatsoever, desire not to go, you may on dismissal go to your company office, hand in your name and not a word will be said.' None of the parade took him up on his offer. Two days later, King George himself visited Deal, where he came across the fresh-faced Lance-Corporal George Calverley, who had finally managed to enlist after being repeatedly sent home earlier in the war as being underage. 'I was standing in the supernumerary rank, two paces behind my section,' Calverley remembered. 'The king had a very gruff voice. He looked at me for a couple of seconds and as he passed on I heard him remark to the accompanying General about someone being very young, and I assumed that it was me he was referring to.'

Ten miles away at Dover, Frank Brock's experiments with a patented flameless smokescreen designed to cover the British task force as it approached shore had hit a snag. Brock had had the inspired idea of injecting a noxious chemical mixture into specially heated chambers built into the various assault ships and the smaller accompanying craft. Mixed with water, the reaction would produce a thick, grey fog which would then surge upwards through the container and be dispersed by strategically positioned industrial fans. The problem was that the basic formula required large quantities of chlorosulphuric acid, a key ingredient in the manufacture of the artificial sweeteners then coming into their own on many British kitchen tables as a popular sugar substitute.

The result was a war cabinet order that diverted 63 tons of saccharin from its intended commercial destination, and instead sent it to Brock's hut at Dover. Although he eventually made good use of it, his initial progress was slow. 'Brock means well, I believe,' Keyes reported in a note to Admiral Beatty, 'and has been invaluable in providing the latest trench warfare devices and special rockets and flares. But I am afraid he is unreliable and he has certainly let me down in the matter of smoke.'

Captain Ralph Collins, commander of the eleven-strong motor-launch flotilla to accompany the invasion fleet, similarly wrote:

> The [preparations] nearly drove me off my head … The smoke expert Brock, an excellent chap, promised all manner of things in getting the boats ready but was always miles late, the boats were just ready in time but no drill had been carried out, and to overcome this I gave the individual [commanding officers] lectures on the subject and hoped for the best.

Keyes also had to face two 'quite unusually onerous tests' among his numerous other professional duties early that spring. The first was the need to constantly assess all the various factors involving tide and weather conditions, the state of the moon, and the readiness or otherwise of the men and ships forming the main attack group, then to decide on the most suitable date for the operation to go ahead, and to do all this without computer models, or satellite images, or any of the other benefits of modern technology. Keyes had originally wanted to set out for what he called the 'Great Landing' sometime in the middle of March. The continuing challenges of refitting HMS *Vindictive* and the blockships, and of accommodating Brock's technical needs, pushed this back to a period between 9–13 April. Keyes himself had meant to personally accompany the task force on board *Vindictive*, but on further reflection chose not to spend the night in question tied up on the side of the Zeebrugge Mole, and instead to fly his flag on the newly commissioned destroyer HMS *Warwick*, which would lay off just outside the harbour, and monitor developments from there.

'The C.O. was a warrior,' Edward Renouf remembered, 'and was not about to sit in Dover and follow events by moving coloured pins around on a map.'

Keyes's other priority was to quietly ensure that there would be enough medical resources available to treat the high number of casualties expected at Zeebrugge. Thirty-nine-year-old Staff Surgeon James McCutcheon was duly appointed to make the necessary preparations on *Vindictive*, and in time reported back that he had established

> 'Foremost dressing station, situated in the stokers' bag flat … After dressing station, situated in the warrant officers' flat, below the wardroom, [and] pre-landing dressing station, situated in the flat abaft the stokers' bag flat.'

In his report, McCutcheon also noted that in addition to these facilities, 'Eight cabins opened on to the after dressing station, each cabin now having been fitted with an extra bunk, [with] deck accommodation for three cases on mattresses.'

McCutcheon later admitted that these various efforts, while well intentioned, had proved hopelessly inadequate to meet the 'truly horrific conditions' that actually prevailed at Zeebrugge.

CHAPTER 4

The Suicide Club

Frank Brock, the Zeebrugge operation's pyrotechnics expert, was the latest in a long line of adventurous British eccentrics who seemed almost to exult in the joys and dangers of battle – a 'whiz-bang man and warrior-poet dedicated to the art of warfare as much as to the pursuit of intellectual study and reflection,' Alfred Carpenter fondly recalled. Another colleague wrote simply: 'Frank was a man who combined brains and brawn.' We've seen that Brock was an all-round athlete, a world traveller, a philatelist and a Bible-reading Christian. Although meticulously efficient in his way, he was also self-willed and, by the strict terms of the rulebook, a bit insubordinate. As Carpenter acknowledged, 'He would never have made a sound staff officer, but was a natural for special operations.'

Brock was also as demanding on himself as he was on others. Wanting to assess the waterproof qualities of a particular explosive compound one day, he promptly stripped off and swam two miles out into the straits of Dover with a waxed polythene bag filled with volatile chemicals tied to his waist. One of the team waiting anxiously for his return long remembered the sight of 'the skipper, semi-naked, body thickly oiled with workshop grease, and only the whites of his eyes visible through a mask of slime', calmly emerging to announce, 'Well, boys, I'm alive.' Certain of Brock's other experiments were 'less satisfactory,' his colleague was forced to admit, after an injudiciously mixed compound blend of TNT and ammonium nitrate took the roof off the men's hut one day. Brock himself wrote to a brother officer: 'I don't doubt that the [Zeebrugge] affair will cost lives. But how many of them will be ours?'

If Brock was worried about the dangers, however, it clearly wasn't from the perspective of his own safety. 'This very brave and ingenious officer worked with great energy to obtain materials, designing and organising the means and the plans, and eventually developing the resources with which we finally set out,' Admiral Keyes later wrote in his official report of Operation ZO. He tactfully failed to mention in the same document that Brock had had a price for his involvement in the Zeebrugge preparations, and that this was that he should personally accompany the raid. Not only that: he proposed to be at the head of the advance storming party when it attacked the Mole, which in his own measured phrase, 'might prove a lively affair'.

Keyes later explained his having agreed to this plan on the grounds that Brock was 'very keen to acquire knowledge of the enemy's range-finding apparatus mounted [on the] shore batteries, which might be of use to our country. His efforts to do this were made without any regard to his personal safety'. One Zeebrugge author has characterised this as an 'amazing and foolish' lapse of judgement on Keyes's part. 'To risk [Brock's] capture or death was short-sighted in the extreme,' she writes. 'It was akin to allowing Barnes Wallis to fly as a bomb-aimer on the Dams raid in the Second World War.'

Perhaps we can be more charitable towards Keyes's decision to include one of Britain's foremost technical brains in a so-called suicide mission in light of the many other 'compelling [and] often damnably conflicting' duties then jostling for his attention. The resumé of Keyes's daily routine in early 1918 discloses a regime that combined some of the qualities of a particularly hard-pressed businessman with those of a circus ringmaster. By the middle of February he was doing everything from coordinating the work of the assembled Royal Marine units rehearsing as far afield as the Orcadian moors, to personally overseeing the bow-to-stern refit of half a dozen warships, individually mustering and briefing the ships' officers, and constantly monitoring both the critical variables of wind, weather and cloud conditions, and of the possible changes to enemy coastal defences, unfolded before him on a nearly hourly basis.

Keyes also retained day-to-day responsibility for the vital work of the Dover Patrol, and, as we've seen, took decisive steps following the German hit-and-run raid in the area on the night of 14/15 February. It says something about the true nature of the man that he had at first demanded the harshest possible punishment for the negligent commanding officer of the screening destroyer *Amazon* and then quietly allowed the same individual to atone for his disgrace by joining the Zeebrugge task force. Keyes even had to intervene when one of the Liverpool newspapers began to ask questions about why the city's beloved ferryboats *Iris* and *Daffodil* had been mysteriously withdrawn from service, sending his chief naval censor, Sir Douglas Brownrigg, to intercede. 'Having fixed the press,' Brownrigg recalled,

> I then went and saw the Speaker of the House of Commons and told him what was going on, and begged him to stop any [parliamentary] questions. He agreed to see any MP who wished to put any question on the commandeering of these two vessels, and tell him the circumstances and ask him to refrain.

Often Keyes was called on to personally supervise units of the Zeebrugge raiding party, as in his rushing to the scene of yet another window-shattering explosion in Frank Brock's workshop, located uncomfortably close to his own office, from which 'the great rocket man emerged look[ing] a bit sheepish, with singed eyebrows, collar askew, but otherwise unharmed'. Although Keyes himself had 'only partly appreciated the full comedic aspect' of that particular flap, no one could ever question the tireless energy, unflagging enthusiasm and personal charm he brought to the task at hand. Even at his moment of supreme triumph, Keyes's biographer writes, 'his humility never forsook him; and he was far more anxious to obtain recognition for those – living and dead – who had served him so gallantly and well than to claim any credit for himself.'

This configuration of qualities had obvious appeal for Admiral Wemyss and the other Sea Lords, as well as their civilian masters. Keyes did not rise through the ranks as far and as fast as he did purely by means of the levers of bureaucratic manipulation. Clearly he had an enormous appetite for paperwork. Keyes's preparation for an October 1915 interview with the First Lord of the Admiralty (and former prime minister) Arthur Balfour to discuss the future course of the Dardanelles campaign had impressed even the career politician by its

> extreme assiduity … the Commodore spoke for two hours, and laid out a supremely rational argument for the most robust approach, fortified by a wealth of minutely researched statistics, down to the precise strengths of individual Turkish shore units, and the unique navigational hazards faced by a British destroyer as opposed to those confronting an Invincible-class battlecruiser.

But such assets would have been useless to Keyes if he had not also been able to lead by personal example when the need arose. Not only as an administrator but as a man of action – with a proven track record in just the sort of bold and maverick endeavour now planned for the Belgian coast – he seemed to fit the requirements of Operation ZO's command better than any other possible candidate.

By early March 1918, Keyes was personally briefing the near-daily reconnaissance parties sent by both sea and air to report back on German defensive deployments at Zeebrugge and Ostend. He was in overall command of the naval personnel and of the marine boat parties then yomping around the British Isles, many or most of them still under the impression that they would be attacking an enemy position somewhere in mainland France. And he continued to be intimately familiar with the daily existence of grease, noise and massed humanity of his own headquarters base at Dover.

'On the 2nd March,' Lieutenant-Commander Ronald Boddie wrote,

> Rear Admiral Keyes now gave the assembled officers a full explanation of the intended operation. The general scheme was for the *Vindictive* to go alongside the Mole, on the seaward side, and to land storming parties on it, and to create a noisy and flashy diversionary demonstration, to enable the blockships to sneak undetected into the harbour.
>
> If successful, this operation would put the U-boat base at Bruges out of action for some considerable time …

In some cases, the combined-services nature of the operation produced a healthy degree of intramural competition. After a few days on board HMS *Hindustan* at Chatham, Leading Stoker Norbert McCrory wrote:

Our jobs came along, the sailors to learn all about trench warfare, bomb throwing and special bayonet drill. Our seamen did their share and came out with most marks, after the Marines had a good try to beat them. The hours of drill were at intervals from 5.30 a.m. to 7.30 p.m.

On other occasions, however, the spirit of inter-service discipline proved less satisfactory. Someone in authority, if not Keyes himself, thought it wise to put the navy contingent among the Zeebrugge storming party into khaki uniform and have the men train alongside regular army personnel. A clash of military culture ensued. One hardened Jutland veteran named Henry Groothius remembered of a session spent on the drill square with the 5th Battalion, Middlesex Regiment:

> We had a row with the army instructor … He started bullying [a] sailor. We knew that a hell of a lot weren't going to come back and he found out to his cost that he was surrounded by 100 men with fixed bayonets. Our Lieutenant came up and asked what was the matter, and we told him that he was bullying the sailor.

Sometimes the altercations were less of a technical or procedural nature, and simply reflected the normal course of military life when hundreds of young men are thrown together for long periods of intensive training interspersed with occasional spells of shore leave. Policed only fitfully, the bars around Chatham high street were often lively places on a weekend, and one inter-denominational social affair held in the Lord Nelson pub on the Easter Saturday night of 30 March ended in a full-scale street brawl, in the course of which a marine and a sailor plunged through the plate-glass window of a nearby shop. In Dover, Admiral Keyes lamented the incident as 'rather unfortunate'. The mayor of Medway, on the other hand, was 'appalled … It was carnage on a royal scale … Men were running all over, singing and shouting. Traffic was stopped as a result, and the normal life of the town was suspended in the chaos'. Several men from the 4th Battalion, RMLI, would find themselves confined to barracks or in forfeit of a day's pay – about two shillings – as a result.

In the meantime, Keyes was sending a steady stream of nighttime motor-launch parties to reconnoitre the Belgian coast. Forty-one-year-old Captain Percy Douglas, a Gallipoli veteran now attached to the navy's hydrography department, would remember setting off on five or six such sorties early that spring: 'It was a rum sight,' recalled Douglas, who in recent years had grown used to spending much of his time sitting at an Admiralty desk studying beaches and sandbars on a map, a cup of tea at his elbow.

> The men all had blackened faces and carried torches stuffed with tissue paper, which were our only form of communication. We would shut down the motor and drift silently outside the great bulk of the [Zeebrugge] sea wall, and take readings, the Mole itself and even sometimes the enemy sentries walking on it quite plain to see. Two flashes of the torch meant 'Forward' – paddle slowly ahead. Three meant 'Stop!' Once we were close enough to shore to hear men talking together on the breakwater in German.

In time, Douglas drew up a detailed chart showing the entrance to the harbour, making special note of the channel where silt collected – even the scouts' motor-launch had once briefly run aground there until one of the men dropped into the water and wrenched it free – and giving an account of the various 'medium-calibre guns, searchlights, and other obstacles and impediments' the British task force could expect on the night.

At this stage, neither Keyes nor anyone else on the planning staff of Operation ZO knew that there was also at least one British PoW living in captivity close to the very spot where HMS *Vindictive* was due to land her raiding parties. This was Sub-Lieutenant Alec Seton, RN, whose torpedo boat *Bolero* had been intercepted by German patrols after becoming separated from her sister ships one night while on escort duty in the North Sea. Seton had since found himself confined in a disused heavy-gun emplacement about 80 yards from the head of the Zeebrugge Mole, quarters he later shared with a captured air-service pilot named Allerton Smith. The door of this keep was steel and furnished with three narrow slits designed for rifle fire. By peering upwards through the gaps, Seton could see that there were four observation balloons tethered above the harbour, which was constantly swept by powerful searchlights trained out to sea at night. There was also a 'wooden tower [actually a working lighthouse] on the extremity of the Mole, numerous signalmen, anti-aircraft gunners, [and] soldiers briskly marching to and fro, as well as barbed-wire liberally strung up in such a way as to repel any unauthorised entry.' Set among the various defences, a prewar sign in both Flemish and English rather incongruously read: 'No fishing from this pier.'

Captain Douglas's report – augmented by somewhat rudimentary aerial reconnaissance photographs – again made clear the challenges the men and ships of Operation ZO could expect to face. The lead vessels in the convoy would not only have to pass through a likely ferocious barrage from the German shore defences. Having done that, they could anticipate a further sustained pounding from the medium-calibre guns on the Mole, as well as small-arms fire from the enemy troops housed there. The three Zeebrugge blockships would then be exposed to what Douglas called a 'quite possibly uncomfortable few moments' as they swung into position in the main channel and left themselves 'in parallel line, athwart the canal gate, prior to the ships' destruction and abandonment'. According to the plan, it was all meant to happen in ten minutes.

Even under peacetime conditions, this phase of the operation would have provided a distinct navigational challenge, involving as it did steering three 110-yard-long, concrete-filled cruisers and beaching them at such an angle as to close off a minimum width of 340 feet of a narrow, imperfectly dredged canal mouth. Between running the gauntlet of the massed German guns and the precise technical demands of the blockships' approach to their target, Operation ZO presented some of the same general characteristics of the Charge of the Light Brigade before it combined with those of the dam-busting Operation Chastise that followed 25 years later. The success of the plan

> involved the intricate combination of various classes of naval units, and called for the concurrence of favourable physical conditions – and depended absolutely upon their nicest attention to a pre-arranged timetable: motor craft ahead to lay the fog screen; vessels carrying landing – and demolition – parties to clear the Mole; a submarine assault; destroyers in attendance; and the block-ships themselves all forming this elaborate machinery,

Keyes later wrote, the whole assembled into what he called the 'infernal dance' of the raid. Reviewing the same set of intricately moving pieces, Commander Carpenter of the *Vindictive* said: 'The operation, on the face of it, did not seem to be altogether simple.'

It would be hard to pinpoint the single most hazardous component of the Zeebrugge raid. Some of the challenges were technical, others were more issues of strategy and training. But it was widely accepted at the time that the crews of the blockships and their accompanying support craft faced perhaps the longest odds of survival.

'One cannot wage war without "breaking eggs",' Carpenter remarked bleakly of this phase of the operation.

> Bearing in mind the main object which had to be attained, it will be understood that all such questions as rescue work and retirement, however important from the point of view of humanity, must be relegated to a secondary consideration.

Even so, a small number of motor launches would be assigned to following the three blockships into Zeebrugge harbour, laying a few yards off while they explosively wrecked themselves, and then picking up any survivors. 'In spite of the almost incredible difficulties and tremendous risk involved, the number of applications for this dangerous job was almost embarrassing,' Carpenter later wrote. 'Eventually lots were drawn and the winners were greatly envied by their less fortunate confrères.' That was certainly true, but at the time Carpenter also 'sensed that British sailors are only human, and will always endeavour to explore the limits of acceptable naval discipline'. His intuition was correct. As Petty Officer O'Hara remembered: 'While at Chatham no leave was given, but trust us not to find a way out. The most simple [way] was to put up a leading badge and a change of cap ribbon, which was very easy to do as there were many ships in the yard.'

In fact, the peril of being in enemy waters 'didn't concern [O'Hara] half as much' as the boredom and claustrophobia he encountered during the training period. Living conditions below decks on *Hindustan* were 'cramped and miserable – as cheerless as in Nelson's day' – and not helped by the continuing secrecy about the men's final destination. 'There was great speculations as to what we were there for but no one could satisfy our curiosity,' O'Hara wrote. A few of the men were eventually billeted (or 'kenneled', as one of them put it) in more comfortable surroundings at Gads Hill Place,

Charles Dickens's old home just across the Medway in Higham, although even then they were 'bunked in twelve to a room, with food and drink reduced to the minimum'.

While the blockships and *Vindictive* were being fitted out in Chatham dockyard, a motley collection of other redundant or semi-retired navy surface vessels and submarines, joined by civilian pleasure boats, was being rapidly modified into what the Operation ZO plan called a 'single, fully cohesive marine strike force'. It has to be said that a certain degree of inspired amateurism again ran through this side of the arrangements. A skeleton crew sailed the Mersey ferries *Iris* and *Daffodil* the 600 nautical miles from Liverpool to Portsmouth, a journey that took the fat little boats nearly a week and caused some comment in the various towns where they put in along the way. Once in dry-dock they were each hurriedly painted grey and given protective armour consisting of half a dozen mattresses and a few assorted sandbags. Both vessels were just 159 feet long, but more importantly drew less than nine feet of water, allowing them to pass over any enemy minefield in relative safety. The ferries' peacetime crews have been described as 'mostly Liverpudlian Irish, hard men who kept the boats running in the foulest waters, never complained while out at sea and as a rule drank themselves insensible on shore'. In time, Frank Brock arrived from Dover to fit *Iris* and *Daffodil* with a somewhat haphazard array of flame ejectors and smoke canisters. No one appeared quite sure if any troops from *Vindictive* would need to clamber over the decks of the two ferries, or vice-versa, as they butted the larger ship against the Zeebrugge Mole, as it was agreed that conditions on the enemy quayside would likely 'call for a degree of extempore adjustment to events' and thus might best be left to individual judgement.

Some of the same spirit of improvisation applied equally in the case of the motor launches included in the Zeebrugge armada. Of *ML 4452*, based at Ramsgate, the author Percy Westerman wrote in 1919:

> Every man of the crew was an amateur yachtsman. In private life they were respectively barrister, mining engineer, Manchester merchant, two ex-public schoolboys, a stockbroker, and a bank clerk. The barrister, senior in point of age, was ship's cook. Altogether they were a jovial, hard-working band of comrades. The discipline on board would have turned the hair of a pukka R.N. officer grey.

In time Lieutenant Frank Farnborough, *ML 4452*'s 26-year-old skipper, received orders to patrol the waters off Zeebrugge while a squadron of Sopwith Camel triplanes – basically a series of rectangular boxes supported by bicycle wheels – softened up the German shore defences by hand-dropping 20-pound bombs on them. In Westerman's recreation of the scene on board *ML 4452*:

> 'All plain sailing?' asked Farnborough of his crew. 'Good! If you'll take her out, and call me at eight bells, I'll be eternally grateful to you. So, the old hooker's going to have her baptism of fire!'

Only later did Farnborough pause to wonder why a motor boat designated for patrol duty should have first received a supply of two dozen fast-acting ampoules of morphine before she set out for Zeebrugge.

On 4 March 1918, with the various air, land and sea preparations now well underway, and in some cases already nearing completion, the Admiralty board at last formally signed off on Operation ZO. Their lordships had been unhappy about some of the fine detail of the plan up to the end, and even now expressed certain reservations about it. There was the choice of the 'hitherto only reasonably belligerent' *Vindictive* – until recently, used as a training school, or on rather desultory home patrol – as the main assault vessel, for instance, and the question of how best to secure a nearly 6,000-ton warship against a concrete breakwater some 15 feet higher than her own deck while fully laden troops filed up a narrow wooden ramp under heavy fire. 'The essence of these storming parties being successful,' the Third Sea Lord noted presciently, 'is celerity in actually getting ashore.'

Doubts remained, too, about Keyes's preference for conducting the raid in the dead of night. The experience of Operation EC1 just five weeks earlier off the Isle of May had painfully highlighted the potential for disaster when a large number of navy vessels found themselves operating at close quarters in the dark. Keyes overrode all these arguments, in part by stressing that the landing on the Mole 'clearly require[d] an element of bluff in its execution' and that this one-time diversionary tactic was in fact now 'a, or the, principal land component' of the operation. The storming parties, therefore, found themselves moving from a limited liability at Zeebrugge to taking the major burden in directly engaging the enemy. In due course, the orders were passed down the chain of command until they reached Sergeant Harry Wright and the men of No. 10 Platoon, still busily square-bashing on the parade ground at Deal: '[We] were issued with a Lewis gun and flame-thrower,' he later wrote.

> There was also a special platoon of machine gunners, a signal platoon with telephones and a demolition party for blowing up the concrete shelters and sheds. Each man carried Mills hand-grenades, and every NCO had a stunning-mallet for close fighting. The officers were armed with revolvers and canes weighted at the handle-end with lead … Each man had an India-rubber under his tunic in case he fell into the sea during the landing.

Strange as it seems in the context of a 20th-century military engagement, the task of announcing the various phases of the battle was entrusted to a troop of Royal Marines buglers and, these men requesting weapons, each was issued with an 1880s-vintage cutlass that one diary account characterised as an 'agricultural implement [more] suited to clearing vines than advancing on a machine-gun nest'.

At 4.40 a.m. on Thursday 21 March 1918, a German artillery bombardment opened up over a 150-square-mile area of the Western Front, the signal for the start of the *Kaiserschlacht*, or spring offensive, that produced the most significant territorial gains since 1914. By the end of the first day, the British had suffered some 47,000 casualties, of whom as many as half were captured, and the Germans had broken through at several key points around the Somme. Although the advance faltered as it became increasingly difficult to move artillery and supplies forward to support it, the situation was grave enough for Field Marshal Haig's Order of the Day of 11 April to read:

> Many amongst us now are tired … With our backs to the wall and believing in the justice of our cause, each one of us must fight on to the end. The safety of our homes and the freedom of mankind alike depend on the conduct of each one of us at this critical moment.

The first 30 days of the spring offensive resulted in 270,000 British and French casualties, with 320,000 German losses, or some 20,000 soldiers killed, wounded or captured on each day of the action. In Dover, this was what Admiral Keyes called the 'ghastly spur' that lent new urgency to 'make the most prodigious efforts to actively contain the enemy in the days and weeks immediately ahead'. Neither Keyes, nor anyone else on the Allied side, had realised that the final victory might yet come before Christmas. Operation ZO was undertaken not so much to hasten the end of the war per se, but to help ensure Britain's continued survival until 1919.

Germany's commitment to the concept of the 'knockout blow' in March 1918 was not restricted to the land campaign. Even before the heavy guns had opened up on the Western Front that Thursday morning, a raiding party of nine destroyers, six large torpedo boats and four small A-class motor launches of the Flanders Flotilla left port to carry out a bombardment of the Allied lines between Dunkirk and Nieuport. In the cold pre-dawn mist a few miles out in the Dover straits, a squadron of British and French ships met them and returned fire. The resulting action again demonstrated the hazards of a large-scale naval operation undertaken in imperfect light without radar or other modern navigational aids. The British destroyers *Botha* and *Morris*, and the French ships *Capitaine Mehl*, *Bouclier* and *Magon* sortied from Dunkirk, and in short order (something of a theme of Allied–German naval encounters of the years 1914–18) the attackers thought it best to break off their raid and turn back for home port. In the confused mist-shrouded action that followed, *Botha* rammed and sank the enemy torpedo boat *A19*, but was then mistaken for a hostile ship and torpedoed by the *Capitaine Mehl*. That effectively concluded the engagement. In the words of one naval historian: '*Botha* was towed back to Dunkirk by the *Morris*, with the French destroyers forming a protective screen, bringing up the rear like the mourners in a funeral cortège.'

Although Keyes apparently omitted any direct mention of the *Botha* incident in his situation report for the week of 18 March, he would have known very well about the continued enemy presence in the straits. He could hardly have avoided it, since the monthly totals of merchant shipping losses (the vast majority of them to U-boat attack) remained 'quite disquieting' both in terms of matériel forfeited and ships sunk. The Allies lost 231 fully laden supply vessels to enemy action in March 1918. British-registered ships were relieved of 215,045 tons of food in the same period, less than half the near-ruinous figure of 566,000 tons of March 1917 but still enough to ensure long queues in British shops and the phased introduction of compulsory rationing over the winter of 1917–18.

It was at this time that Keyes, already making his final plans to choke off the enemy's bases on the Belgian coast, first learned of the full severity of Britain's supply crisis. 'We had barely a month's worth of wheat,' he later confided. Lord Lee, the government's director of production, added that there had in fact been only two weeks' stock of most basic foods in the country: 'This was the deadliest secret of the war, [and] to the very few of us who were in the know it was as ceaseless and nerve-racking an anxiety as the powers of hell could devise.' Ration books were soon introduced for butter, margarine, cheese, lard, meat and sugar. It's true that mortality rates among some Britons gradually fell, as the new provisions guaranteed at least a minimum weekly quota of fruit and vegetables. It's also true that this was an era in many British households, at all levels of society, of icy nights spent in gaslit rooms, of dried soup powder and whale fat – the comically vile ingredients of a serious sacrifice that Keyes made clear in his final briefing to his officers it was now their duty to help 'directly redress'.

Keyes himself, we've seen, would personally accompany the strike force. Apparently expecting to be rebuffed, he had first suggested this at a War Office conference early in March. 'Why not?' Admiral Wemyss had replied. To Commander Carpenter's consternation, among others, however, 'the most important Naval figure in securing British home defences' had then gone on to seriously propose that he take up position on the bridge of *Vindictive* as she lay under what was confidently expected to be sustained close-range fire on the Zeebrugge Mole. It was only with some difficulty that Keyes was persuaded he might better direct proceedings from the outlying HMS *Warwick*, which was probably tactically sound but itself problematic with regard to command structure.

As Keyes's biographer writes:

> Carpenter was still a comparatively junior commander; and though there could have been no objection to his holding the post under the Admiral's flag, the position would now be different, because Captain Halahan, in command of the naval landing-parties to be carried in *Vindictive*, was senior to him … The problem was solved by Halahan generously offering to waive his seniority – and Keyes then arranged that Carpenter should remain in control of *Vindictive* with the acting rank of captain. He emphasised, however, that the storming-parties must at no time be regarded as under Carpenter, and that his responsibilities would be confined to acting as Fleet Guide, laying his ship alongside the Mole, keeping her there, and then bringing her back to Dover.

It seemed to some that it was all a somewhat tortuous and peculiarly British jumble of a control stricture, with a supreme commander on one capital ship, two subordinate commanders in charge of separate but overlapping operational matters on a second leading ship, and as many as 140 lesser officers responsible for the performance of the individual assault or support craft that would constitute the bulk of Keyes's 'infernal dance'.

In the event, strict adherence to service rules and etiquette – an almost comic situation, were so many lives not at stake – soon broke down under battle conditions, and something of an enforced social experiment ensued 'with men shouting orders at one another without distinction, and more than one private soldier forced to take action in the absence of any higher authority'. It would be a stretch to say that this particular instance of enlisted men operating in extremis on level terms with their superior officers set a long-term precedent, but it demonstrates how the intensity of war can forge a spirit of mutual comradeship not always available in peacetime.

Alfred Ewing (who now spent what he called the 'more irenic' part of his life as rector of Edinburgh University) and his team in Room 40 meanwhile continued to supply the Admiralty with accurate and important details about German defences. One disturbing possibility was that the various garrisons at Zeebrugge and Ostend might not be taken entirely by surprise. Ewing reported that the battery personnel stationed between Wuerttemberg on the western side of the Bruges canal and Goeben on the east had recently held a series of *Alarmbereitschafts*, or armed drills, apparently designed to sharpen their response to any enemy attack. When he learned about these, Keyes sought another meeting with the Sea Lords. He later told Edward Renouf that the essence of what he had said was: 'The enemy may be waking up. If we're going, we're going soon.'

The Germans may not have been expecting Operation ZO in every detail, but it now seems clear that they were alive to the possibility of at least some sort of massed attack on their submarine bases. Apart from the obvious strategic logic involved, there was the fact that early in April they would capture the British motor launch *CMB 33* when she grounded herself near Ostend harbour in the course of the first abortive attempt to raid the area.

'In this boat,' wrote Kapitan Eric Schülze, the senior intelligence officer attached to the German coastal garrison,

> we found a map giving us first hand information concerning the plan of the expedition. It was the English naval chart Nr. 125 'Ostend Roads': written in black ink was the inscription 'No. 33 Boat Chart April 9th 1918'. This map indicated the course to be steered, with full explanations such as 'Line of Blockships approach'. It was not difficult for us to draw the necessary conclusion for Zeebrugge.

But despite any qualms he may have had about the strict secrecy of Operation ZO being compromised, Keyes wisely adopted a pragmatic attitude. This was plainly a mission in which old-fashioned British grit and buccaneering spirit had a role to play, whatever the shortcomings of some of its finer detail. Keyes was 'not only confident, but excited,' Edward Renouf said. 'He was always very much someone who combined the dignity of office with the general air of a boy on a holiday.' Keyes and his planners clearly saw at least the Mole-storming part of the raid in semi-piratical terms. A directive to the Royal Marine units at Deal read: 'Officers [are] to imbue their commands with the idea of carrying the operation through with the bayonet; rifle fire, machine-gun fire and bomb throwing are only to be resorted to when necessary to break down enemy resistance.' Conscious of both the need for stealth and perhaps also the example of his own swashbuckling role in the Boxer uprising, Keyes and his executives stressed the commando-like approach, with the Hun 'suddenly encounter[ing] silent dark figures breaching his citadel, blades outthrust'.

Again, a strong sense of both the plucky and the makeshift runs through even the final phases of the preparations for Operation ZO, of which Richard Sandford said, 'No one seemed to be focused on the true goal.' Harry Adams added,

> Our training consisted chiefly of Trench Warfare – long point – short point – jab and butt stroke stuff. Revolver practice – and night exercises against the Regiment … We did quite a lot of jujitsu, armed and un-armed; it's astounding how easy it is (after practice of course) to disarm a man armed with a rifle and bayonet, and yourself with nothing – no matter how big he is.

In late March, a rare Marines exercise using live ammunition ended badly when a Stokes mortar crew miscalculated their range and a high-explosive shell landed close to the reviewing stand where the Admiralty lord commissioners had assembled to watch, injuring two enlisted men who were standing nearby.

A more serious training incident came on 1 April, on the hillside above Deal, when a Stokes shell exploded prematurely, killing four Royal Marine gunners and injuring five others. Apart from the central part of the tragedy, the speed of subsequent events is what most strikes the modern observer. Lieutenant-Colonel Bertram Elliot convened a court of inquiry on the same afternoon the incident occurred. He reported:

> We can offer no other explanation than that the burst was due to a premature explosion due to faulty ammunition. An inquest was held at the R.M. Infirmary, Deal, at 2.15 p.m., 2 April, on the bodies of the deceased, when a verdict of Accidental Death was returned.

Later that same evening, the families of the four victims would each see a young man on either a motorbike or a bicycle pull up at their door and silently hand them a telegram beginning: 'The Secretary of State regrets to inform you …' Even this mild courtesy was marred a day or two later, when one of the dead men's parents received a letter from him deposited in a field post box at Walmer on 31 March with the word '*Killed*' scratched across the envelope. All four Royal Marines, the first British victims of the Zeebrugge raid, were buried at Deal cemetery on 4 April.

No one doubts the brilliance and audacity of the overall plan of attack at Zeebrugge, nor the indomitable spirit of the men who carried it out. But it seems fair to say that at least some of the preparations for the event fell short of the ideal even as that was defined in the exigent military climate of spring 1918. Captain Carpenter (as he now was) of the *Vindictive* would remember attending briefings in which

> reconnaissance men [had] sometimes not had adequate photographs [of Zeebrugge], and had suggested that we instead study colour tourist post-cards of the area to provide the necessary detail on everything we needed to know on matters such as anchorages and the exact location of shore batteries. They were hoping for pies in the sky.

Carpenter later wrote of the moment his ship emerged out of the night fog at Zeebrugge:

> Though none of us had ever actually seen the Mole itself we felt pretty sure of being able to recognise any portion of it immediately. In that we were over-confident ... The smoke, the intermittent glare and flashes, the alternating darkness and the unceasing rain, added to the disturbance of one's attention caused by the noise and the explosion of shells, rendered observation somewhat difficult,

he added, with a touch of understatement.

Of course, criticisms of any part of the advance programme for Zeebrugge should be applied with caution. Admiral Keyes and his subordinates operated in a world without mobile phones, jet engines, proximity fuses, lasers, nuclear submarines, guided missiles or computers, among many other staples of modern warfare. As we've seen, Keyes's force also lacked the sort of detailed aerial intelligence of their target any self-respecting special-ops team would take for granted today. It was equally deficient when it came to precise information about the strength and deployment of the defensive garrison awaiting it, and only partially briefed on basic matters of local navigation. Shortage of time and resources forced it to improvise in ways that might seem to us either ludicrously inadequate or endearingly British, according to taste. When the demolition parties on board *Vindictive* found that they would need some means of running their detonators and fuses off the deck of the ship and up a ramp onto the Zeebrugge Mole, they asked the local Chatham post office to lend them some straw-sided parcel carriers on wheels. There was a degree of the ad hoc and makeshift to the arrangements as a whole that may well have been forced on Keyes and his staff, but which in at least some cases proved detrimental, if not worse than that, to the final outcome. As the Zeebrugge author Deborah Lake writes, '[Even] the choice of [the codeword] Operation ZO underlines the essentially amateur approach that runs like a thread through the planning.'

Among other arrangements that might seem to us to have a touch of the slapdash to them, there was the critical matter of the task force's medical provisions. We've seen that Staff Surgeon James McCutcheon, whose 14 years' naval service contained little front-line experience, was briefed to make the necessary plans to treat casualties on board *Vindictive*. Lieutenant-Commander Rosoman, the officer in charge of refitting the ship, remembered his first meeting with McCutcheon:

> He joined with no idea of what we were playing at, and asked me if I could tell him how many dead or injured he was to be prepared for. I asked him if he knew anything about the show. He did not, except that he understood he had joined a Suicide Club.

When the Royal Marine detachments began their own training, this was devoted as much to matters such as cross-country runs, route marches and martial-arts fighting as it was to preparing them for the reality of encountering organised German artillery and machine-gun fire. There was initially some question of whether the landing parties would be issued with plimsolls to help them clamber up the slick gangways onto the Mole parapet, but in the end most of the men wore their regulation boots with the metal heels filed off for added stealth – another slightly haphazard detail in the overall plan. We've seen that many of the exercises involving the actual point of contact at Zeebrugge used a roped-off patch of the grassy Kent countryside to represent the concrete bulk of the Mole, rather than attempting a more lifelike model. There was at no time any dress rehearsal using a real ship or involving a steep harbour breakwater.

Once on dry land, the plan called for the naval and marine storming parties to then 'establish an ammunition and bomb dump on the Mole, abreast of [*Vindictive*]. Demands for ammunition and bombs should be sent to Battalion Headquarters or to this dump ... Reports should be sent to this position which will be indicated by a white flag' – all of which, again, was badly to underestimate the sheer pressure of events on the German redoubt.

These same shore parties also set off with insufficient ladders or even functional gangways with which to attain their objective, creating a sometimes lethal bottleneck on arrival. The various signalling arrangements in place once debarked on the Mole were antiquated even by the standards of 1918, and arguably more suited for use on a marine parade ground than in the heat of battle. On the day no one thought to provision *Vindictive* with adequate supplies of food or fresh water, although luckily for at least some of the ship's company there was no shortage of dynamite-strength rum. When the time came, the plan for laying calcium buoys in order to light the entrance to Zeebrugge harbour broke down almost immediately when the motor launch carrying the markers was hit by enemy fire, killing her captain and leading deckhand, and forcing the remaining crew members to scuttle their boat by chopping holes in her with an axe. As Deborah Lake writes, 'It is a legitimate criticism that nobody considered specialist navigators necessary on [the] venture. That neglect cost dearly.' Even without the benefit of hindsight, it's clear there were other lapses and shortcuts within the overall plan of attack that qualified it more as one of those inspired British-seafaring adventure tales of the Nelson era than as a feat of 20th-century mechanised warfare.

This is not necessarily to cast any aspersions on Admiral Keyes, however, nor on any lesser military or civilian planner of the Zeebrugge raid. They had few of the technological assets or other resources available to their modern counterparts, and like much of society as a whole they were generally more phlegmatic about the prospect of early death than we are today. In at least some senses, Keyes was a supremely able administrator. From early March onwards he held a daily conference at which his senior officers were expected not only to appear but to clearly articulate any concerns or misgivings they might have about their individual duties. He consistently impressed on officers and ratings alike that they were part of a team, that their work was crucial to the greater war effort, and that any man could honourably withdraw at any time up to the actual point of embarkation. None did.

Keyes himself would not only escort the raid, but had an unblemished personal history of the utmost valour and enterprise in broadly the same sort of operation. His crews knew that and he was popular for it. Richard Sandford said that 'men were always pleased to know that they were attached to his command'. Private 'Beau' Tracey of the Royal Marine Light Infantry later remembered peering out from the deck of the converted ferry *Iris* onto Keyes's flagship *Warwick* as the Zeebrugge task force left port to engage the enemy. Even for an enlisted man serving in a separate branch of the armed forces, it was a stirring sight. 'It gave one a certain degree of pride to be able to look in that direction and see that massive Admiral's flag,' Tracey recalled.

Keyes's other outstanding quality as a commander was the latitude he allowed his subordinates, and the respect, loyalty and – without ever prejudicing the frontiers of discipline – the genuine affection he inspired as a result. It seems fair to say that his whole intent was to establish the overall framework of the plan and then to encourage the spirit of individual enterprise within it. The partially sighted Francis Sandford and his professionally chastised younger brother Richard were perhaps the most obvious beneficiaries of this policy. Keyes trusted them and their fellow officers to prepare the submarine detail of the raid. They seem to have done this by equal parts diligent rehearsal and more recreational activity on a series of requisitioned high-speed boats in the waters off Portsmouth. One day Francis Sandford, in shorts and singlet, found himself standing on the deck of a particularly palatial cabin cruiser on which 'civilian personnel in various costume, or no costume at all, could be seen reclining' as she sailed past the fully manned HMS *Warwick* on her way into port. The unabashed young officer had come to attention, saluted his supreme commander and the ship's company massed on the quarterdeck, and continued on his way to his berth. Soon afterwards Sandford accepted the command of the converted picket boat that would follow the two C-class submarines into the thick of the fray at Zeebrugge. The ink on his papers was barely dry when the combined task force set off to meet the enemy.

Keyes the leader was multifaceted. He was a micromanager who spent long nights poring over detailed weather reports and the exact disposition of sandbars and silt deposits off the Belgian coast. He nonetheless allowed for a marked degree of personal initiative, if not wholesale improvisation within the context of a given plan. He was a team player who sometimes thought and acted like an old commando. Practised in the arts of departmental compromise, he later attacked the 'brass hats of Whitehall' for 'frustrating every worthwhile offensive action I have ever tried to take'. He was a fatalist not given to excessive self-doubt. Depending on circumstances, Keyes displayed all these traits at once or accentuated some while concealing others. Lieutenant Sandford once said of him, 'He left you impressed, inspired and sometimes also a little dazed ... You were never quite sure which side of his personality he might reveal.'

On 4 April 1918, Keyes seemed to show a combination of mild apprehension and pronounced optimism when he wrote to Admiral Beatty:

> I only hope we can get light northerly weather – otherwise we will have to do it in moonlight, can't afford to wait until May. The hour is 'written' and I feel sure when it comes it will be the best possible for the operation – anyhow I am happy and confident.

Later that same night, the assorted ships of the Zeebrugge flotilla left their home bases and assembled in the Swin, at the mouth of the Thames Estuary, just out of sight of land. 'It was a curious looking squadron that steamed down the Medway,' Captain Carpenter wrote, 'the blockships with their funnels looming extra-large in the absence of masts, and the *Vindictive* with her gangways protruding into the mid-air like almonds in the side of a tipsy cake.' Such a widespread movement of a naval force equivalent to the total of all three fleets involved at the Battle of Trafalgar was hardly the best way to ensure secrecy, but Keyes had a schedule to keep.

Two days later, Keyes himself visited the anchorage and spoke to all the ships' companies in turn. It was only now that men like Harry Adams, one of the sailors who had volunteered for special service back in early February, finally learned of their objective. Adams's reaction to the various briefings that followed was one that might strike us as fully human. 'All of us in turn were marshalled on a certain mess deck; different officers gave us lectures, we were shown maps, and enlarged photographs of the Mole and the German defences – Ugh!' Adams wrote.

Keyes's formal battle order, dated 7 April 1918, read:

> The object of the enterprise we are about to undertake is the blocking of the entrances of Zeebrugge and Ostend. These ports are the bases of a number of Torpedo craft and Submarines, which are a constant menace [to our] country ... I am very confident that the great traditions of our forefathers will be worthily maintained, and that all ranks will strive to emulate the heroic deeds of our brothers in the Sister Service in France and Flanders.

Later that mild early-spring evening, Captain Carpenter added his own open-air address to the officers and men of *Vindictive* in which he remarked, 'Many of you may not return. Others may see out the war in a German prison camp.' Conditions on the Zeebrugge Mole would likely be 'somewhat hectic,' he added, and should the men at any time hear a 'thunderous report' nearby, this was just as likely to be one of the other constituent parts of the mission in play as it was a reaction on the part of the German gunners. Carpenter concluded his remarks by reiterating that any man wishing to withdraw from the raid, now that they had heard the full story, had his unconditional permission to do so. Although none did, both he and his fellow commanding officers of Operation ZO would receive a number of urgent requests in the days ahead.

'In the *Vindictive* there were several men, of non-combatant rating, who, in the ordinary course of events, were destined to be left behind when the expedition started,' Carpenter noted. 'They comprised cooks, stewards, canteen-servers and the like. They naturally knew the secret and they openly expressed their desire to remain in the ship so as not to miss the fun.' Carpenter accommodated as many of these surplus personnel as he could, using some to act as mortuary or sick-bay attendants.

Meanwhile, some of the ship's company of HMS *Intrepid*, similarly discovering that they were slated not to go all the way to their objective, came perilously close to mutiny. The men's spokesman put it this way to their commanding officer Lieutenant Stuart Bonham Carter, as recorded by Carpenter: 'Well, sir, me and my mates understands as how some of us have got to jump the ship on the way across to Zeebruggy. The jaunty [master-at-arms] says it is us lot and we ain't a-goin' to leave.' Bonham Carter remembered that he had listened to these remarks and decided that perhaps he could use the men's services in action after all. He later explained that most of the sailors had wanted to fight because they had only one idea in their heads: 'The Huns must be stopped.' After the fleet had set sail and it was too late to turn back, a number of other individuals began to emerge from the remote parts of their own ships where they had hidden themselves – a court-martial offence today, but widely accepted at the time as showing a British serviceman's proper sense of duty, and one of the reasons for his country's status as a great power.

Of course, there was also a healthy degree of apprehension among the assembled sailors and marines that they were to attack a heavily defended enemy position from the sea at night, and this same natural sense of disquiet adds to their humanising contradictions. Captain Carpenter and the other commanding officers imposed postal censorship on their crews following their final full briefing of 7 April. The men were 'not ... to communicate the details of their commission to any other individual either before or after the event, until expressly permitted by written directive to do so'. But there again seems to have been a certain degree of leeway to the arrangements. '[It was] a most peculiar feeling deep down,' Harry Adams remembered of this period.

> You realised this 'arsenal' would greet you – hard and heavy. One even began to think of those at home quite a bit more sincerely – I know lots of men, myself included, who addressed wee

parcels – keepsakes maybe – to be forwarded if there was no return for them. This was kindly undertaken by the Chaplain of the *Hindustan*.

During this same period, the submarines *C1* and *C3*, each with a crew of six, had left Portsmouth and now sat at anchor at Dover. Richard Sandford spent the night of 8 April in his cramped forward compartment aboard *C3*, later recalling that he had read a few pages of Thomas à Kempis's biblical treatise *Of the Imitation of Christ* before turning in to the 'not disagreeable noise of a light swell slapping steadily against the side of the boat', the bows of which had been packed with five tons of high explosive. The plan called for the two submarines to be taken in tow to a rendezvous point with the rest of Swin Force, as it was now called, and then to proceed under their own steam to Zeebrugge.

While Lieutenant Sandford slept, others were busy. Clerks in the Admiralty's Room 40 hurriedly typed up the latest situation report on the state of German armoured defences on the Belgian coast. These included the familiar concentration of 'huts, hangars, barracks and other dens and coverts' situated at intervals on the Zeebrugge Mole, but showed no apparent reinforcement of the number of enemy personnel based there. On board *Warwick*, Admiral Keyes was also examining the latest high-altitude (and by our standards, crudely basic) aerial reconnaissance photographs of the area. Keyes later wrote in his official report,

> In order to guard against [German detection], which would have meant the certain failure of the expedition, it was necessary for the sea patrols and air forces to show the utmost vigilance and energy. There is every reason for believing that, as a result of their efforts, the enemy remained up to the last entirely unaware of our intentions.

This begs the question of whether Kapitan Schülze and his colleagues on the coastal batteries yet had any specific information that a British battle fleet was preparing to sail towards them, or if the German garrisons – at Zeebrugge, if not Ostend – merely continued to expect that there might at some time be such an attack, quite possibly by long-range artillery, on their positions. In fact, both British field guns and a squadron of RAF Handley Page bombers operating from Dunkirk would target the Zeebrugge–Ostend area at regular nighttime intervals during early April – the main idea was to probe the German shore batteries and pinpoint the number and range of their searchlights. As a result of this, the boffins in Room 40, if not Keyes himself, may have been dangerously overconfident about the prospects awaiting the men of Operation ZO.

There are two other curious incidents that touch on the matter of whether or not the raid achieved total secrecy. The first came on the Saturday morning of 6 April, when the 4th Battalion, RMLI, left its barracks in Deal and marched smartly through the town centre towards the main rail station, where the marines would board four reserved compartments of a normal passenger train to take them to join their ships waiting at the Swin. Sergeant Harry Wright remembered this progress as being less of a clandestine troop movement and more of a municipal street fair. 'At 06:00 hours the battalion was paraded, and after being inspected by our Colonel we marched through the town to the station, preceded by the band,' he recalled. 'The people of Deal turned out en masse to give us a hearty send-off, and no one ever saw a happier crowd of men.' Other contemporary published reports have the marines 'fil[ing] off to the jaunty strains of *The Girl I Left Behind* and *Rule, Britannia*, accompanied by the lingering cheers of the throng' – if so, an apparent lapse from the official movement order calling for the 'orderly, silent and swift transfer' of the units involved.

The second and more serious incident came when a civilian deckhand on a Thames Estuary lightship, seeing the Swin Force assemble on 5 April, wrote an excited but incautious letter to his family, in which he said:

> If you hear the newsboys shouting about five British cruisers being sunk you can laugh at it. We have five of them close to us taking in a lot of cement. They are going to Zeebrugge, and our people are going to sink them in the mouth of the harbour and trap the Germans so they can't get out.

This particular account seems to reveal a double breach of security: that the writer should have known quite as much detail of Operation ZO as he did, and that he should have communicated this quite as freely as he did. He was subsequently tried and sentenced by Southend magistrates to two months' hard labour, 'so as to impress upon him his duty in the future and as a warning to other people'.

At four o'clock on the wet afternoon of 9 April 1918, naval and marine personnel began to leave HMS *Hindustan* in small boats and transfer to their own designated ships for the attacks on the Belgian ports. Admiral Keyes sent a movement order to the waiting fleet, and shortly before five the urbane, monocled figure of the First Sea Lord, Admiral 'Rosy' Wemyss, who turned 54 that week, addressed the assembled men standing in the drizzle on the deck of HMS *Vindictive* – 'His lordship's voice sound[ing] like a record being played at half speed,' according to one of those present. Keyes had determined that the tidal and lunar conditions were suitable for the attack to be launched that night. The entire flotilla actually put to sea, flags flying, the ferryboats *Iris* and *Daffodil* taken in tow by *Vindictive*, but then turned around again some 90 minutes later. Below decks on *Daffodil*, Harry Adams remembered:

> Night had fallen by this time, and alas … the Admiral realised that owing to weather conditions and the wind changing, it would simply court disaster and failure if we went on that night; so we shared his disappointment – but return we did – and by next morning we were all back aboard the *Hindustan*.

The wind and rain continued for the next two days.

On the night of 11 April, all 85 vessels again set off. The two ferries under tow reeled drunkenly in the heavy seas, the submarines appeared on cue at a point five miles off Ramsgate, and on board the blockship HMS *Thetis* Commander Ralph

Sneyd treated his officers to a caviar-and-stilton supper from a Fortnum & Mason 'Epicure' hamper he had thoughtfully brought with him. This time the armada was within 15 miles of its target, and able to see the flashes of the RAF's bombs and the return artillery fire bursting over Zeebrugge, when Keyes, on the bridge of HMS *Warwick*, again ordered it to turn around. The wind had suddenly dropped, and without it Frank Brock's all-important artificial fog would have been 'quite useless – it would mean us going naked into the spotlight,' Captain Carpenter said. As *Warwick* herself came about, a burst of German 15-inch shells fell out of the night sky and landed in the water just behind her. There was a noise like 'a violently rude clap of thunder.' The men momentarily froze at their posts, waiting for something more to happen. Nothing did, but the sound 'rolled and echoed,' Carpenter said, 'a salutary warning of what lay ahead.'

A few minutes later, one of the Handley Page bombers circling overhead lost power and crashed into the sea near the village of De Haan, midway between Ostend and Zeebrugge, killing its 22-year-old pilot, Canadian-born Captain John Allan. He was one of two Allied troops initially known to have perished in this second miscarried attempt to launch the raid. The other was Leading Seaman Reuben Pearce, 43, who accidentally shot himself through the thigh while on his way home on *Vindictive*, causing his death through loss of blood. 'This was rotten luck as he had gone through the siege of Ladysmith and the Boer War,' a shipmate noted. It was later established that in addition to these two fatalities a six-man naval motor boat had run aground on shoals near Ostend, and in the stark words of the official report: 'All crew believed died of exposure, washed ashore.'

The return journey was not without further incident. Another of the British naval motor launches had become detached from the main fleet and as a result missed the 'break off' signal when it was flashed from the deck of *Warwick*. The young commanding officer of this boat had instead made full speed for Zeebrugge, overshot it in the dark by about three miles, and turned about only at the unusual cry by one of his crew of 'Houses ahead!' Having narrowly avoided running ashore at the small town of Blankenberge, the boat made smartly back for Dover as German shells screamed out of the dark behind it.

Yet another of the British coastal motor boats (CMBs) ripped a gash in her bow in the sudden turn for home, and would almost certainly have sunk but for the resourcefulness of her young commander. According to Captain Carpenter on the *Vindictive*, 'this officer ordered one of [his] men to sit on the hole. This reduced the inflow of water, but can hardly have been a comfortable proceeding for the individual concerned.'

By increasing speed to 27 knots, the CMB's commanding officer managed to raise the fore part of his boat into the air at a sufficiently steep angle so that the hole in the bow no longer made direct contact with the sea. 'The man who had found a new use for his anatomy then withdrew himself,' Carpenter noted, with justifiable pride at this

> outstanding example of British naval ingenuity … *Vindictive* was steaming at a modest 10 knots or so … The CMB could not afford to proceed at less than 27 knots, so it steamed round and round the remaining vessels until daylight, when it was detached to its base.

Two nights later, on 13 April, the entire fleet set out once again. The first vessels away, the twin monitors HMS *Erebus* and *Terror*, were to take up position off the Dutch town of Middelburg, some 20 nautical miles from Zeebrugge, and then use their heavy guns to soften up the enemy shore batteries. The main attack force would follow about an hour behind, until it reached a marker buoy 16 miles off the Belgian coast. At that stage, a flotilla of a dozen combined blockships, motor boats and fast launches would break off from the convoy, rendezvous with a detachment of British and French destroyers from Dunkirk under the command of 43-year-old Commodore Hubert Lynes, a world-class ornithologist in civilian life who also proved to be a supremely brave naval officer, if, in the event, one only modestly gifted as a navigator, and make for Ostend. The bulk of the attack group would then proceed southeast to Zeebrugge.

Soon after the task force had cleared the Swin anchorage, a destroyer hove in view and flashed a signal that she had a letter for the commanding officer of *Vindictive*. The two ships stopped, and in time Frank Brock himself appeared in a small boat bearing the message. According to Captain Carpenter, 'the tenor of it was "We must push on to-night." This was passed round the ship and semaphored down the line of blockships. It reflected our own feelings – "We must push on to-night".'

Again, it was not to be. Within minutes, the wind had freshened to gale force, and for the third time Keyes made the decision to abort the mission in mid-passage. Once more, everyone returned to The Swin. Added to the natural frustration of the men, the planners of Operation ZO now had serious doubts about the wisdom of their proceeding at all.

Captain Arthur Chater, adjutant of the Royal Marine battalion billeted for the crossing on the ferry *Daffodil*, wrote:

> The Admiralty now became apprehensive that some news of all our comings and goings must have reached the enemy … Their lordships wished to call off the whole operation on the preparation of which so much time and material had been expended. The Admiral [Keyes] came to ascertain the feeling amongst officers and men. The First Sea Lord also came to visit the ships. All those who spoke said they were keen to go on, and one more try was agreed.

This again begs the question of whether three separate sailings of a full-dress British battle fleet had alerted the Germans that an attack on their positions might be imminent. 'Such an eventuality was by no means outside the pale of probability,' Carpenter admitted, 'and we had to reckon with the chances of having been seen, and almost certainly reported, by a large number of neutral vessels, [as well] as by enemy aircraft and submarines.' There was also the troubling matter of the captured set of maps found aboard the launch *CMB 33* when she foundered off Ostend. It's hard to believe that the Germans failed to go on high alert as a result, although with so many last-minute postponements and revisions of the British plan they can hardly have known the exact date of the final strike.

When the moment eventually arrived, legend insists that at least some of the German marines stationed at Zeebrugge were attending a party in a nearby hotel to celebrate the apparent success of the spring offensive in rolling the British up against the Channel ports, and had to hurriedly rejoin their units. With a Teutophobia it might be difficult to carry off in public today, Carpenter wrote: 'The Germans were past-masters at chicanery. The first inclination of such individuals is to disbelieve others; a prevaricator always labours under that disadvantage.' The enemy were so devious, in other words, they simply assumed that the British were playing some vast, inscrutable trick on them by repeatedly seeming to signal their intentions to storm their harbour. Part of the charm of the eventual raid was that it was so illogical.

Perhaps just as great a challenge as maintaining the security of the mission was the strain of keeping some 1,600 armed men in a state of battle readiness. Admiral Keyes himself returned to his office in Dover. 'The week that followed,' he was to say with some restraint, 'was one of the more trying I have ever spent.' Keyes and his staff used some of the time to make eleventh-hour navigational changes in the fleet's course to the Belgian ports. There would be further use made of Aga buoys, equipped with acetylene flashers, to mark the gap between the minefields. Once past the last of these buoys, a dozen miles off the enemy coast, the group would be committed to the attack – or 'There would be no possible return without the spilling of blood,' as Carpenter put it.

After four days of staff work, Keyes appeared on the deck of *Hindustan* on the afternoon of 18 April, told the assembled crews that the raid was still on, and soaring into Nelsonian mode, added that men who had already been through the dark days of Gallipoli and Jutland and the rest would surely rise to the occasion now that the final victory was in sight, that their names would be famous down the ages, and that in the words of Second Chronicles, they were 'not to be afraid nor dismayed by reason of a great multitude; for the battle is not yours, but God's'. Listeners were grateful for confirmation that all their hard work in training had not been in vain. At least one of the young ratings who heard Keyes's words was so moved that he broke down in tears.

The next possible date when wind and tidal conditions were likely to be conducive for the mission was the night of Monday, 22 April, which meant an enforced eight-day wait between sailings. Some of the men passed the downtime in spiritual contemplation under the guidance of Reverend Charles Peshall, RN, a rugby-playing Church of England padre who seems to have personally embodied the term 'muscular

Christianity': volunteering to accompany the raid itself, his subsequent citation for the DSO notes that he 'showed great physical strength and did almost superhuman work in carrying wounded from the Mole over the brows into *Vindictive*'.

Other individual members of Swin Force waiting at anchor in the Thames estuary found more secular release for their energies. Although all shore leave was denied, there seems to have been at least one illicit visit made to the newly opened Kursaal amusement park at Southend-on-Sea, as well as in savouring what one man quite seriously described as the 'raw fun, juicy nightlife and gay times' of nearby Canvey Island. Other, more officially sanctioned activities included a lively tournament below decks on *Hindustan* of the dice game Crown and Anchor, as well as what Harry Adams called 'General quarters, general evolutions, boat-pulling, boat racing, a dance or two – in fact anything to keep your mind occupied.'

Altogether no fewer than 22 vacancies opened up during that long week of nervous anticipation. Several men went sick, and a junior officer from HMS *Sirius* was temporarily blinded when one of Frank Brock's smoke cylinders exploded in his face. There was no shortage of volunteers to fill the newly available places created among the ships' companies as a result. Perhaps the most significant change in personnel came when Lieutenant Ivan Franks, the commanding officer of the blockship *Iphigenia*, collapsed with appendicitis. Before being taken to Chatham hospital, Franks dashed off a note to Admiral Keyes asking him to appoint 22-year-old, Tasmanian-born Lieutenant Edward Billyard-Leake in his place. Despite his youth, Leake, as he was known, crew-cut and muscular, with a jaw that seemed to have been built in a foundry, was already a decorated Jutland veteran who later told an interviewer of his experience there:

> I was watching the prospects of the battle when, suddenly, the deck and top hamper of one of our great battleships lifted and flew skywards, and in a few moments the sea showed little trace of her. My superior officer turned to me and said evenly: 'Are you ready, Leake? We're next.'

Keyes seems to have made up his mind on the matter of *Iphigenia*'s command when in short order he received a second written request, this one signed by the entire ship's company, supporting Lieutenant Franks's choice of replacement. Leake told Keyes that he was 'very pleased indeed to be sent for [to] lead a cement ship' at Zeebrugge.

While Keyes made these enforced last-minute adjustments, the German high command continued to insist that their enemy was destined for oblivion. Although it was they themselves who were thus destined, the overall war situation in the middle of April 1918 was anything but a foregone conclusion. Apart from the advancing spring offensive – where the Germans now overran the British and Portuguese positions around Estaires and continued to both threaten Ypres and push on Paris – the High Seas Fleet still promised to deliver the victory that would solve their country's growing domestic problems. Speaking on the 19th of the month, Admiral Eduard von Capelle, head of the German navy, told the Reichstag: 'Even the greatest pessimist must say that the position of our opponents is deteriorating rapidly, and that any doubt regarding the total success of the U-boat war is unjustified.'

Later that same night there was a desperate scene in the waters off Zeebrugge when a German UB 111-class submarine lost contact with its convoy, hit a mine possibly laid by one of its own boats, and began to sink rapidly by the stern. According to the writer Henry Newbolt, in an account that may owe something to his poet's imagination:

> Some of the crew lost control and behaved like madmen. They crammed cotton waste into their ears and nostrils, and plunged beneath the water, which was now knee-deep. One man turned his revolver upon himself; it missed fire; he hurled it from him and plunged after his comrades. One, who still kept his head, with a final effort forced open one of the torpedo tubes and let in the water … Perhaps twenty in all thus made their way out of the ship; but it was only passing from one death to another. Human lungs are not adapted for the sudden change from a deep-sea pressure to surface conditions. The shrieks of those unfortunate men were heard by a trawler which happened to be passing near. Only two lived.

Apart from the obvious human tragedy, the point of the story is that the Germans were still freely making use of the Belgian ports for U-boat raiding purposes in April 1918, and that the Allies lost some 171 merchant ships, carrying 320,000 tons of urgently needed food and matériel, that month. On the very night of the Zeebrugge raid, German and Austrian submarines attacked the British ships on patrol duty 1,300 miles away in the Otranto straits of the Adriatic, killing eight men and allowing Admiral Capelle to again deliver a glowing report to the Reichstag on the 'ever improving economic and maritime conditions' that would lead to his nation's victory.

On Friday evening, 19 April, Admiral Keyes issued 'Memorandum 001/18 – Orders for the passage of forces for Operation ZO, [with] Accompanying Memoranda 001/19 – Orders for the operations at Zeebrugge, with recognition and letter signals and orders for embarkation.' Barring another sudden change in wind or sea conditions, the mission – preceded by the codeword 'Nascent' – would go ahead the following Monday night. Keyes later remarked that the entire force had felt 'immense relief' at finally being about to attack, and that few if any of them would have now walked away voluntarily.

Two separate British saboteur teams landed after dark on the coast near Zeebrugge during the intervening weekend and attempted to cut German communications cables, although it's not thought they did significant damage. A Saturday-night volley from British artillery units in Flanders was more effective, hitting a radio mast erected on the beachfront at Ostend and sending it tumbling into the sea. In final briefing sessions held after church parade on Sunday, 21 April, Keyes made clear to his senior officers what was expected of them. The gist of it was summed up by Lieutenant Bonham Carter when he wrote: 'The goal that the Admiral had in mind was an immediate and radical end to the enemy's ability to cause hell to British shipping – and shorten the war as a result.'

The component parts of the raiding fleet had all been fitted with the requisite amounts of rubble and cement, supplies of chlorosulphuric acid for the smokescreens, assorted flamethrowers, medium- and short-range Stokes mortars, pom-poms, Lewis guns, folding gangways, false decks, howitzers, and, in the case of the submarines *C1* and *C3*, enough high-grade amatol to blow a significant part of the Zeebrugge Mole into the next Belgian municipality.

There was one final touch added to the superstructure of HMS *Vindictive* when on the morning of 22 April Keyes's wife Eva presented the crew with a good-luck horseshoe, which they nailed to the middle funnel of the ship. A number of the men posed for a group photograph in front of this talisman, which survived the subsequent action. In addition to this, there were several ad-hoc adjustments to personnel right up to the actual moment of sailing. Coming aboard *Vindictive* on the sunny late morning of the 22nd, Keyes found a young officer lurking below decks who he knew full well had no business to be there. Asked to explain himself, the man replied that he seemed to have misplaced some of his personal equipment and had come aboard to retrieve it. 'Not buying this tale for an instant,' as he later remarked, Keyes returned the man's salute and allowed him to stay.

At 1.10 p.m., *Vindictive* and the blockships left their moorings and proceeded in formation to a rendezvous point off the coast of Margate. The wind at that stage was northerly, blowing about 5–7 mph, and the sea was calm. While the ferries *Iris* and *Daffodil* in turn took their places in line, Wing Commander Brock transferred to *Vindictive* from the motor launch *Whirlwind*. It was noticed that he was dressed for the occasion in khaki, and that he carried two holstered pistols and a short sword with a blade curved like a scimitar. Brock also brought with him a box which Captain Chater of the RMLI, watching from the deck above, recalled

> bore the label *Explosives – Handle with Care*. This was hoisted on board very gingerly. It was taken down to the Wardroom, and in time found to contain several bottles of excellent vintage port, which were consumed with relish. Brock landed on the Mole, and was never seen again.

Keyes himself had meanwhile returned to Dover, where shortly before five on a now overcast early-spring afternoon he was piped on board his flagship *Warwick*. The entire surface assault force, from the most modern W-class destroyer down to the virtual floating fortress of *Vindictive* and the utilitarian ugly ducklings of the Mersey ferries, every larger vessel towing a smaller one, with two squadrons of outlying motor launches fussily threading their way to and fro to shepherd the whole ungainly convoy into place, turned east from the Goodwins just after six that evening. Captain Carpenter noted that morale was high. 'Our confidence in the face of the many obstacles, when considered in cold blood months afterwards, may have seemed to be almost an impertinence,' he wrote in his memoirs. 'Everybody knew exactly what was expected of them. There was no actual excitement, except that inseparable from intense enthusiasm.'

Vindictive's rear ensign was ceremonially struck at sunset, after which there was an issue of hot soup and cocoa, along with a generous rum allocation for anyone wishing to take it. Many did. Just before he boarded *Warwick*, Keyes's wife had reminded him that by the time they reached Zeebrugge it would be 23 April, or St. George's Day. The date perhaps had more resonance a century ago than it does for us now. As dusk fell on the evening of the 22nd, *Warwick* flashed out a signal to the nearby *Vindictive*: 'St. George for England.' Carpenter promptly flashed back, 'May we give the dragon's tail a damned good twist!' which his superior officer would later note was 'very apt and to the point, but did not fit in with my mood at that moment'.

※

At long last, under seemingly favourable, if not idyllic, conditions, the British task force now made for its appointment with the enemy. It sailed in three columns, *Warwick*, with its distinctive admiral's ensign, slicing through the water, *Vindictive* on her immediate port bow, the assorted destroyers, blockships, minesweepers, ferries and CMBs bringing up the sides and rear. According to Lieutenant Billyard-Leake on the bridge of *Iphigenia*, 'Darkness arrived with the suddenness of a thrown switch.' A light rain soon began to fall, with banks of mist seeping in the surface of the water. The clammy, damp conditions came as a relief to Lieutenant-Commander Rosoman on *Vindictive*, who was 'somewhat afraid of fire, owing to the large amount of wood in the ship – assembling platforms, ramps, brows, etc, which I had drenched in some anti-fire mixture supplied by Brock, but of the value of which I knew nothing.' In time a rising moon broke through the clouds, throwing a silvery light on the whole ghostly procession. There might be no sight on earth like that of a massed naval convoy moving at night. The wind was also freshening, churning the dark, rolling sea white and sending the smaller boats dodging back and forth, keeping under the sheltering protection of the destroyers. 'There's one thing about it,' Captain Wilfred Tomkinson, appraising the conditions, remarked cheerfully to Keyes on the bridge of *Warwick*. 'Even if the enemy does expect us, they'll never think we could be such fools as to try and pull it off on a night like this.'

'The main thing at this stage was just to keep everyone going,' Keyes himself later noted. It was not to be. At around eight o'clock, roughly 15 miles out of port, the motor boat *35A* fouled her propellers and dropped out of her place in line. According to one naval historian writing in the 1950s, 'From their respective decks the crews of her sister-ships watched her drop behind, commenting between them with sympathy or jibes according to nature.' Such observers underestimated the obstinacy and resilience of the boat's commanding officer, 23-year-old Lieutenant Edward Hill. Hailing a nearby drifter, he

> bullied or cajoled her captain into towing him straightaway back to Dover, and within half an hour of arrival his craft was hoisted out of the water and half the available dockyard staff were working like blacks to free his jammed propellers and repair secondary damage ... At 9.40 p.m., *CMB 35A* again cleared Dover harbour, and with a fine disregard of such dangers as excessive fuel consumption or minefields, sped like an arrow across to Zeebrugge.

This was not quite to be the only technical mishap of the outward journey to the Belgian coast. The submarines *C1* and *C3* had both left port under tow shortly before 2 p.m. and rendezvoused successfully with the main surface fleet at the somewhat unimaginatively styled 'Point A' off the Goodwin Sands. As Richard Sandford later wrote in his report: 'C3 proceeded out of harbour and, being taken in tow by HMS Trident, proceeded to Pt. A. On arrival of Swin force, [I] proceeded in company for Pt. G.' With commendable precision, Sandford continued:

> Fifty-six minutes after passing G, slipped tow as arranged [and] proceeded on a course of S.O.E. at 8 ½ knots, seven minutes later. After 18 minutes smoke was encountered, but this cleared three minutes later and after 21 minutes on this course, course was altered to S. 48 E. according to instructions, and C3 proceeded direct for Zeebrugge viaduct.

Somewhat before this point was reached, Lieutenant Sandford had become uneasily aware that *C3*'s sister ship *C1* had vanished into the night. It later transpired that this latter vessel had snapped her tow rope, lost her place in the line, been fired upon by the destroyer HMS *Mansfield* which mistook her for a marauding U-boat, and eventually limped back to Dover. Sandford knew none of this at the time. For now he and his men were alone on the dark sea, about to be confronted by the uncompromising bulk of the Zeebrugge Mole and the iron-clad viaduct they were meant to destroy. Two months earlier, Sandford had admitted to his brother that the whole mission seemed to him 'quite hairy' even under the best of circumstances, but that he believed he and his crew would deliver the result expected of them on the night.

He would soon learn if he was right.

CHAPTER 5

Into the Cauldron

When the men of Operation ZO left home waters in the early evening of 22 April, they faced almost seven hours of nervous anticipation before their arrival on the Belgian coast. They filled the time according to collective assignment or personal taste. Some of the landing crews on *Vindictive* started up another high-stakes round of the game Crown and Anchor, while just a few feet away Staff Surgeon McCutcheon and his team of sick-bay attendants were busy at work laying out rows of scalpels and field dressings as part of their last-minute preparations for receiving casualties. Most of the marine contingent remained below, while out in the air naval personnel, some of the officers muffled in scarves and greatcoats, squinted through binoculars or pored over charts to plot their positions and express the hope that each successive dark shape bobbing up in the water in front of them was a marker buoy and not a mine. Before he went down to his own billet on *Vindictive*, Private James Feeney of the 4th Battalion, RMLI, remembered standing on deck with some of his comrades watching the setting sun, their unsaid thought being whether or not they would see it rise again in the morning.

Quoting from his diary, Feeney later told the *Globe & Laurel* newspaper:

> At 7 p.m. I can count 57 vessels all going the same way. We got tea at 8 p.m. and our usual rum ration at 10 o'clock. If the wind is right at half past ten we are to see it through tonight, no matter what happens. Going down now for a short sleep before the landing starts. I hope it won't be my last short one on this planet.

Captain Carpenter, who was also concerned with the men's wellbeing while en route to Zeebrugge, restlessly paced in and out of *Vindictive*'s wheelhouse to study the voluminous Admiralty instructions – 'as always, punctilious in the extreme' – on the subject. '*Excessive Fatigue, Seaborne Precautions Against*' one impressively detailed paper read. 'Arrangements were made to provide each [ship] with a variety of men, over and above the minimum required at the climax of the operation,' Carpenter later wrote. 'These could handle the vessel and its engines during the passage overseas, whilst those men required for the "final run" would be resting.' One man actually was ordered to bring his bass banjo along for 'mass entertainment' purposes, even though it was nearly as big as he was.

This flexibility in quotas among the ships' companies continued even when the moment came to transfer surplus crew members to the waiting minesweeper HMS *Lingfield* and from there return them to Dover. According to Captain Ralph Collins, speaking for the record in his report:

> I regret to note that the excess personnel were not taken off HMS *Intrepid* when the fleet stopped. *ML 555* was detailed for this duty, but when proceeding alongside *Intrepid* fouled both screws with lines that had been used for towing the CMBs, was totally disabled, and eventually was towed back to port.

Lieutenant Bonham Carter, commanding *Intrepid*, was not the only one to subsequently wonder whether *ML 555* had in fact broken down as described. As a result of this mishap he now carried a crew of 87 instead of 54, 'many of whom bore an air of distinct self-satisfaction' that they would continue with him into the thick of the fray at Zeebrugge. The naval writer Barrie Pitt adds the detail that 'even from the blockships *Thetis* and *Iphigenia*, the numbers removed were not as high as they should have been, for when the time came for the Masters-at-Arms to parade the excess steaming-crews and see them over the side, the decks became unaccountably deserted.'

On *Iphigenia*, the entire 12-man engine-room crew somehow failed to muster on deck when the launch came alongside to remove them. In time they, too, reappeared from the depths of the ship and jauntily went on their way to Zeebrugge. Another 'extra' emerged from out of his asylum in the hold of HMS *Thetis*. 'At 9 o'clock we were 25 miles out, and the weather was turning,' he wrote. 'I came [on deck], and as I watched the mist closed in front of us like a curtain at the theatre.' Mugs of tea, in some cases liberally spiced by rum, went round again. On board *Vindictive*, Frank Brock and his entourage finished the last of their 'particularly fine' vintage port. Captain Carpenter makes no reference in his report to any particular tippling on board his ship, but later recalled the sense of isolation throughout *Vindictive* as a whole as she drew nearer the enemy. By ten o'clock, several units began silently taking up action stations, crouching in turret gun rooms, magazines or bunkers, while the men of the storming parties assembled in makeshift shelters amid the deteriorating weather on the ship's upper deck. 'The visibility at this time can hardly have amounted to a yard – the forecastle was invisible from the bridge,' Carpenter said.

At 10.30 p.m., 17 miles out from Zeebrugge, Admiral Keyes flashed the signal, '*No alteration of zero time*'. The operation would go ahead. A fine, sizzling rain was then falling. The attack force sailed on from there in total radio silence, its commanders well aware of the potential for a collision – 'if not with an enemy mine, then by way of one of our own ships slicing through you,' Lieutenant Bonham Carter mused. As the fleet approached the coast, the motor-boat squadrons forged ahead to prepare to open the valves that would release Frank Brock's smoke. The whine of the small boats' engines as they sped past seemed unnaturally loud to the men gathering on the upper deck of *Vindictive*.

One of the assembled marines was silently loading his weapon when he suddenly saw the man standing next to him shudder, as if he were about to let out a scream. The first marine turned his head sharply. He saw that a pair of seagulls had flown out of the dark and startled his comrade. The birds were now perched together on the narrow rim running around the ship's forward funnel and staring down at them. The marines tried to remain silent and not break out laughing.

'The wind had dropped again,' Carpenter remembered, 'but it was one of those fickle spring nights with moments when the moon suddenly flashed through the clouds, and others when visibility again shrank to near-zero.' These were ominously similar conditions to the ones that had wrought such havoc on the men and ships of Operation EC1 just 81 days earlier. Although there were no fatal crashes this time around, the blackout conditions meant that the outlying monitors *Erebus* and *Terror* were late in opening their scheduled bombardment of the Flanders coast, an event German gun crews and Belgian civilians alike had come to wearily regard as a near-nightly ritual, and thus not one that seemed to herald the arrival of a mixed-force enemy armada in their midst.

While the fleet closed in on its target, other British assets also worked to enhance the raid's chances of success. On the morning of 22 April, 'Blinker' Hall, director of Admiralty intelligence, called in six of his senior colleagues in the cryptographic department and briefed them on the coming night's activities. They and their staffs were not only to pay close attention to that day's German military and diplomatic cables, but to immediately begin transmitting a series of faked battle signals intended to draw the enemy's defensive fire on the Belgian coast. 'This is the most important assignment you have ever received,' Hall announced, fixing his audience with his rapidly flashing eye for emphasis. It was a dramatic brief, but that was the way he wanted it. From his years as a gunnery officer, Hall believed that it was 'no bloody good just asking a naval man to do his best – what he wants is precision'.

In practice, this meant that while the Admiralty sent out bogus movement orders 'to induce the Hun to make faulty dispositions of his shore batteries' and 'create confused thinking on his side', the German garrison at Zeebrugge would also be forced to deal with a simultaneous bombardment from the air, the heavy siege guns of the Royal Artillery in Flanders, and the outlying navy monitors. 'Enough fireworks for anyone,' Hall believed, although in the event a combination of British inter-service communication problems (or apparent reluctance to help other arms) and adverse weather conditions limited the ploy's effectiveness. Meanwhile, at half past seven on the evening of 22 April a fleet of 23 vessels under the command of Commodore Reginald Tyrwhitt left Harwich to patrol the approaches to the Flanders Bight. Other battle cruisers steaming down from the north would rendezvous at midnight with Tyrwhitt's group and form an outer guard screening Keyes's force from any U-boat attack in their rear.

At 10.52 p.m., on *Warwick*, Keyes himself reached the calcium buoy a dozen miles northwest of Zeebrugge denoting 'Position Z' – the final point of no return. The ropes used to tow *Iris* and *Daffodil* were slipped, and a detachment of six ships broke off from the main strike force and turned south for their attack on Ostend. We will return to their exploits later. There was one further issue of cocoa, rum, or both combined, to the crews on their final approach to Zeebrugge. At 11.15 p.m., seven miles out, all the ships' lights were turned off. They would proceed from there to their destination by dead reckoning, plotting their course by chart and ruler rather than any more advanced navigational aids. Harry Adams, on *Daffodil*, remembered the dark and the silence, and the moment in the still of the night when the motor launches went forward to release their artificial-fog canisters:

> The CMBs set up [this] screen, and we began to run into it or through it. Just like the white smoke that emerges from a long train tunnel as the engine rushes out. The 'drone' from the CMBs became more and more distinct – seemed to be rushing all over the place … The wind was playing its part splendidly – if it would only do its job as well to the end, we thought. We [were] within half an hour run of the Mole – At last.

Somewhere in the dark to the west of the main strike force, Lieutenant Sandford and his five colleagues on board the submarine *C3* had reconciled themselves to the fact that they were now alone in their mission to ram the Zeebrugge Mole viaduct, which they continued to approach from the seaward side at a brisk 9–10 knots. Shortly before midnight, *C3* altered course to S. 45. E, lining up for a headlong collision, and switched on her own artificial fog canisters. These proved counter-productive when the smoke promptly blew back into the crew's faces, and Lieutenant Sandford ordered them shut down again. At 11.45 p.m., Stoker First Class Henry Bindall came topside from the submarine's engine room.

> With [every]thing running smoothly the boat glided into the shoal waters of Zeebrugge, the whole crew being on deck … The Mole bulking up black in the darkness and the Viaduct joining it to the shore were clearly seen. It was a silent and nervy business … I do not think anybody said a word except 'We're here all right.'

Elsewhere in the British flotilla there seems to have been a mood of quiet determination during the last few minutes before the attack. This mutual resolve should not be confused with any sense of active pleasure among the men at what awaited them. Aboard *Iris*, the young Air Mechanic George Warrington, who would lead one of the parties storming the Mole, remembered the moment when 'Lieutenant Henderson said to me, "Get your men together and cover the top deck with sand." I asked him why, and he gave me a look of pity, and said, "Lad – to soak up the blood."' Warrington had been brought up on a pig farm, 'where nothing among the slaughter one saw prepared you for what followed.'

On *Vindictive*, Captain Arthur Chater recalled, 'Earlier in the passage across, very careful precautions were taken to see that no man got more than his own ration of rum … In spite of this, one old soldier must have borrowed someone else's tot, for when I went round the mess decks with the Sergeant Major as the men were closing-up, he shouted at us, "We are going over the top! We are all equal now!"' Chater recalled a very different atmosphere aboard *Vindictive* as she made her final approach to her target. 'I remember catching sight of the same soldier some three hours later, and thinking what a changed and sober man he now looked.'

✳

'We took up our action stations,' Captain Carpenter noted evenly.

> The guns in the fighting-top on our foremast were in readiness to engage. Rocket men had been stationed to fire illuminating flares for the purposes of locating the Mole. Crews were standing by the bomb-mortars and flame-throwers … It was a decidedly tense period, but there were others to follow.
>
> At a given moment by watch-time *Vindictive* altered course towards the Mole – or rather towards the position where it was hoped to find the Mole. Almost immediately we ran into the smoke screen. *The wind had now changed to an off-shore direction*, diametrically opposite to that on which the screening plans had been based.

A moment later, the troops mustered on *Vindictive* could suddenly see the frothy rim of surf breaking against the sea wall in front of them, and the figures of men, running, walking, literally dead ahead. It was a mutually stunning moment.

To the night crews manning the German gun batteries stationed on the Mole, the fully armed British cruiser now looming up at them out of the sea mist must have seemed both a disconcerting and an irresistible sight. For what seemed like a very long time, no one on shore reacted. Then a German star shell burst overhead, instantly turning the scene from night to day.

'Although there was plenty of light about,' recalled Lieutenant Edward Hilton Young on *Vindictive*,

> a few hundred yards from the ship everything was blotted out in wreaths, eddies and whirls of glowing vapour. The German gunners, I imagine, were peering into the smoke, unable to perceive any definite object in the shifting, dazzling glow … So we steamed on until we were some four hundred yards away.

At this point the scales had fallen from the Germans' eyes and the shore batteries opened up at point-blank range, some of the British storming crews mown down as they stood waiting on deck, falling side by side, their uniforms cut to shreds. *Vindictive* completed the last agonising quarter-mile of her journey amidst a hail of shells and machine-gun fire, finally grinding up against the Mole, where to one marine lined up on board with his colleagues from No. 12 Platoon, 'It seemed as if hell had been let loose, as the ship closed in against the wall and was struck by heavy fire around the forecastle, the control top and the foremost funnel, flame-throwers on the port side and burning pieces of metal flying everywhere …'

In the midst of this inferno, on the control tower of *Vindictive* Captain Carpenter glanced at his watch. It was a few seconds after midnight on 23 April, St. George's Day.

'We were one minute late on scheduled time, having steamed alongside at 16 knots,' Carpenter later noted, before describing his attempts to berth his ship in an operation that combined some of the challenges of parallel-parking an overloaded lorry while supplying the sitting target in a shooting gallery.

> The engines were immediately reversed at full speed … The conning position in the flame-thrower hut [where] we now stood was well chosen, our heads being five feet above the top of the Mole wall. As far as we could see we were to the westward of our desired position. The engines were, therefore, kept at full speed astern and the ship, aided by the three-knot tide running to the eastward, rapidly drifted in that direction. When sufficient sternway had been gathered the engines were put to full speed to check her. The order was given to let go the starboard anchor. A voice tube, for this purpose, led from the flame-thrower hut to the cable deck. The order was certainly not given *sotto voce*, but no answer was heard in reply. Anyway, the anchor was not let go.

These are the orderly facts of the matter, the navigation officer's dry account of what happened. The reality was considerably more chaotic and bloody. Though the German gunners were both wide awake and fully alert to the general prospect of a British attack, the stealth and swiftness of *Vindictive*'s arrival in their midst temporarily paralysed them. Kapitanleutnant Robert Schütte, the battery commander on the Mole, was interviewed by a British journalist after the war and told him,

> I looked through the fog and saw an enemy battleship approaching our position at high speed. The distance was deceptive, but he appeared to me to be terrifyingly close – when a star shell burst suddenly overhead the whole scene was bathed in a ghastly bright red. You could see the faces of the individual enemy troops standing on deck staring back at you.

An unnamed colleague of Schütte's added expressively: 'It was as if we had closed our eyes for an instant in a dark room and opened them again to see the devil himself standing before you.'

But if the Germans were momentarily stunned by events, they recovered with commendable speed. Waiting to disembark on the deck of *Vindictive*, Sergeant Harry Wright recalled of the next few moments:

> Then the silence was broken by a terrific report, followed by a crash as the fragments of shell fell among us, killing and maiming the brave fellows as they stood to their arms, crowded together as thick as bees … A very powerful searchlight was also turned on us from the sand dunes at Zeebrugge, and the heavy batteries there began to fire. The slaughter was terrible.

Kapitan Schütte – known by his men, half admiringly, as 'The Pope' – later reported that he had waited only an instant or two more before picking up the phone in his hut located just a few yards further south down the Mole from where *Vindictive* surged up towards him into her makeshift berth. 'Gun teams to shore defence. Infantry to positions,' Schütte ordered. As an afterthought, he added: 'Enemy troops are about to land.'

Right: Roger Keyes, reforming naval officer, saboteur, politician, and the principal organiser of Operation ZO.

Left: Reginald 'Blinker' Hall of the Admiralty's Room 40. The American ambassador wrote of him to President Wilson: 'He is the one genius the war has developed. Neither in fiction nor in fact can you find any such man to match him.'

Left: Admiral John Jellicoe, who as First Sea Lord frequently warned of the threat the Flanders-based U-boats posed to Allied shipping. 'The First Lord made his usual statement about losses', the cabinet secretary took to writing.

Right: Admiral David Beatty, Jellicoe's successor as commander-in-chief of the Grand Fleet, who in December 1917 signed off on the plan to attack the enemy submarine bases.

Above: Zeebrugge harbour, showing the 'Mole', or breakwater, jutting out into the North Sea to screen the port like a vast concrete claw, seen in peacetime.

Below: The Mersey passenger ferry *Iris ll,* requisitioned with her sister *Daffodil* to take part in the Zeebrugge Raid, where both boats took heavy losses. (*Wirral Archives Service*)

Left: Lieutenant Rowland Bourke, RNVR, who won the Distinguished Service Order for his part in the first raid on the Flanders coast. Just seventeen days later, he would repeatedly steer his small boat back into the firing line in order to rescue survivors of the follow-up attack. Bourke was awarded the Victoria Cross for this latter action.

Below: Sgt. Norman Finch, who won the VC for his action in remaining at his battered and exposed position on the foretop of HMS *Vindictive*, exchanging fire with the enemy troops standing just a few yards away on the Zeebrugge Mole.

Right: Stuart Bonham Carter, the cricket-playing commander of the blockship HMS *Intrepid* at Zeebrugge.

Right: Frank Brock, the fireworks man and all-round technical genius who insisted on joining the landing parties on the Zeebrugge Mole. 'He would have attained to the highest power and eminence in his field,' *The Times* wrote of him after he fell in action.

Below: The Venerable Ernest Sandford, archdeacon of Exeter, seen at home with his large family. Francis Sandford and his brother Richard, each later to play a major role in the Zeebrugge Raid, sit cross-legged to the extreme left and extreme right respectively. (*Daniel Sandford*)

Above: A demonstration of Frank Brock's 'artificial fog' on the deck of the ferry *Iris ll* before setting out for Zeebrugge.

Left: Lieutenant Richard Sandford at the conning tower of HM Submarine *C3*.

Below: A 1964 depiction in the comic *Victor* which captures some of the spirit, if not the factual detail, of the Zeebrugge Raid.

Above: Charles John de Lacy's painting of HMS *Vindictive* alongside the Mole, showing the storming parties going ashore.

Below: Charles Dixon's representation of the same event, with *Vindictive* and the two ferries bumping up against the Mole.

HMS *Vindictive*, showing the scars of the Zeebrugge Raid, shortly before she returned to action at Ostend.

Above: The deck of HMS *Thetis,* left wrecked just out of position at the entrance to Zeebrugge harbour.

Below: Some of the damage at Zeebrugge, with both German and British ships abandoned in the narrow canal mouth, at the time of the Armistice.

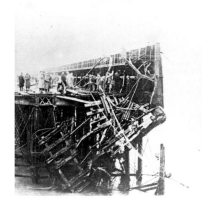

Left and below: The wrecked Zeebrugge viaduct after being blown apart by submarine *C3*. Standing nearly a mile further up the Mole, one of the British troops described the moment of explosion as 'a terrible thud that shook Heaven and Earth – the nearest approach to an earthquake one could imagine.' (*Charles Keyes*)

IWM

Zeebrugge

Brèche de 66 mètres de long sur 20 m. de large, provoquée par l'explosion d'un sous-marin anglais chargé de 6,000 kilos de dynamite.
The breach, 66 metres long and 20 m. wide, made by the explosion of an English submarine laden with 6,000 kilos dynamite.
Bres van 66 meters lengte op 20 m. breedte, geopend door het ontploffen van een engelschen onderzeeër geladen met 6,000 kilos dynamiet.

Above: The German kaiser visits his U-boat commanders at Bruges shortly after the British raids, assuring them that their war effort had 'in no way been impeded by the enemy's foolishness.'

Below: A panorama of Zeebrugge harbour soon after the St. George's Day raid. HMS *Thetis* lies about half a mile out of position in the background, with HMS *Iphigenia* and HMS *Intrepid* parallel to each other in the canal mouth itself.

Above: Captain Carpenter of the *Vindictive* accompanies President Wilson on a tour of the Zeebrugge Mole at the time of the Paris peace conference in June 1919.

Above: Some of the crew of *Vindictive* pose on deck after returning to England. Note the mattresses used for the ship's protection at upper right.

Below: Captain Carpenter, VC, with his injured arm in a sling, seen with other survivors of the *Vindictive*. (*Imperial War Museum*)

No 9   Zeebrugge   Ustende   Le Vindictive coulé devant le port.
The "Vindictive" sunk in front of the harbour.
De Vindictive gezonken vóór de haven.
Tombes des héros du Vindictive.
Graves of the heroes of the " Vindictive ".
De graven der helden van den Vindictive.

Above: The hulk of *Vindictive* after being wrecked at Ostend. Most of the ship was broken up for scrap in 1920.

Below: Vindictive's bow section preserved today as a war memorial.

Right: Richard Sandford, VC, recovering in hospital after the Zeebrugge Raid. Returned to duty in September 1918, he died just two months later at the age of 27.

LIEUT. R.D. SANDFORD,
ROYAL NAVY.

22-23.
APR.
1918.

Left: Sandford's medal. (*Britannia Royal Naval College*)

Above: Nineteen-year-old Able Seaman Albert McKenzie, seen with his mother Eliza after collecting his VC and barely three months before his death from influenza. *(Colin McKenzie)*

Below: The memorial and graves of some of the Zeebrugge victims at St. James's Cemetery, Dover.

'We got pretty near shore before they saw us, and then the fun began,' Carpenter wrote in his report. 'Up went the star shells, the guns began blazing, and we went pell-mell for the old Mole.' This *Boy's Own* attitude, as it might seem to us, continued even as *Vindictive* came under steadily heavier fire. Able Seaman Cyril Ablett was one of the members of a gun crew stationed behind a flimsy mattress barrier on the ship's upper deck. 'The boys were falling right and left,' he told his daily newspaper shortly after the event.

> But still we kept on and eventually reached our objective, but minus most of our landing gangways. Those that were left we immediately lowered, and with a cheer 'over the top' went our storming parties and then Fritz got a surprise as the bayonets got to work and ran in all directions.

Again, this account was perhaps to minimise or condense the actual ordeal of the men on board HMS *Vindictive* as she steamed ever closer to the German wall. Most observers agree that *Vindictive* emerged abruptly out of the night at 11.57 p.m., at which point she was roughly a third of a mile from her final destination. Up until then it had been literally a case of the fog of war, as an advance group of half a dozen coastal launches and motor boats had flitted protectively around her, plumes of thick grey smoke belching from the steel containers welded to their masts or strapped close to their hot exhausts. From the moment the wind changed direction, *Vindictive*, now in the full glare of enemy searchlights and star shells, had some three minutes' steaming time before reaching the relative shelter of the Mole parapet. As Carpenter later remarked: 'A journey of even 500 yards can seem quite a long one when heavy guns are firing at you continuously from point-blank range.'

During that last desperate run, *Vindictive*, devoid of any cover, had to pass through both a maelstrom of artillery shells and volleys of machine-gun and rifle fire raining down on her from the German shore units immediately ahead, as well as a sustained barrage from the enemy entrenchments on the Belgian mainland only a mile or so to the south. Despite his ordering as much speed as was feasible without ramming his ship headlong into the Mole, Captain Carpenter wrote,

> *Vindictive* [was] a sitting duck … Everything was in favour of the defence as soon as we had been sighted … From that moment, [the] battery guns had a clear target, illuminated by star shell, of a size equal to half the length of the Mole's own outstretched causeway and lighthouse extension.

Carpenter later speculated that the very nearness of the German guns had worked in *Vindictive*'s favour. 'To my mind,' he reasoned,

> a longer range would have entailed more deliberate firing, and this in turn would have given time for more deliberate choice of aim. A few projectiles penetrating the engine or boiler rooms, or holing us at the waterline would have settled the matter … the range being so short, we can conjecture that the German gunners, realising they literally could not miss, pumped ammunition into us at the utmost speed of which they were capable without regard to the particular damage they were likely to cause.

This 'loss of serenity', as Carpenter put it, seemed to him to demonstrate that while the enemy training manuals presumably stipulated how to fire at just such a target as now presented itself in the form of an approaching 6,000-ton British warship, 'all the slick, smooth drills on the artillery range counted for nothing when the adrenalin began to flow'.

What ensued was something more akin to a close-quarters Nelsonian carnage than more impersonal modern warfare. Carpenter later asked one of *Vindictive*'s own gunners what ranges he had fired at. The man replied that he had opened up at 200 yards and continued until he was 'quite near' the Mole. Questioned further about how close he had come to the German positions, he said, 'Reckoning from the gun muzzle, I should say it was about three feet.'

In their initial shock, the Germans may have fired at *Vindictive* in a reckless and almost frenzied manner. But at that range it could hardly be an entirely ineffective one. During the first minute of the engagement, the Mole batteries each got off five to six rounds per gun, meaning that roughly 30 high-explosive shells tore into *Vindictive*'s upper works, quite apart from the attentions of the enemy machine gunners and individual riflemen. A similar barrage followed over the next 60 seconds. 'Almost every moment there was the sight of a flashing muzzle and the sound of a thundering crash,' Carpenter remembered.

> In the course of the first two minutes, Lieutenant-Colonel Elliot [the officer who just three weeks earlier had conducted the inquiry into the deaths of the four Marines lost in training at Deal] and his deputy Major Cordner were both killed instantly when a shell landed within a few feet of where they stood on *Vindictive*'s upper deck ready to lead the storming parties onto the Mole.

Lieutenant Hilton Young was stationed nearby, ready to open fire,

> and saw one blinding flash of blue light in my eyes. It was at this moment that [the marines] were killed, but at the time my attention was wholly fixed in listening impatiently for the first shot from the top, in order that my 6-inch guns might begin.
> It was afterwards that I remembered the eruption of sparks where the shells struck, the crash of splintering steel, the cries, and that smell which must haunt the memory of anyone who has been in a sea-fight – the smell of blood and burning.

At this point, Captain Carpenter decided to alter course and make for the Mole by the shortest route possible. *Vindictive* accordingly swung to port, smoke and sparks shooting up from her ruptured funnels. Carpenter himself was stationed in a crudely fashioned flamethrower hut-cum-conning tower built on a platform above the main deck. His first lieutenant, Robert Rosoman, stood on the bridge below him, periodically picking up his brass speaking tube, blowing into it, and then inquiring if his captain was all right. If Carpenter ever failed to reply, Rosoman was to assume command. The flamethrowers themselves – meant to have liberally sprayed the German defenders as *Vindictive* came alongside – proved only partly effective. 'The aft *flammenwerfer*, in charge of Wing Commander Brock, was used, but the oil failed to ignite owing to its apparatus being shot away,' Carpenter reported.

Brock's weapons were not entirely ineffectual, however. One German soldier stationed in a hut towards the north end of the Mole later remembered the 'monstrous scene' that had ensued when a jet of liquid fire from *Vindictive*'s upper deck ignited a flash grenade held in his friend's ammunition belt. 'This accursed individual [had] become a screaming human beacon,' he reported. Some of the crew standing on *Vindictive*'s port side could clearly hear the man's anguished cries, and had watched as he staggered towards the parapet's edge, apparently meaning to put an end to his blazing hell by throwing himself into the sea. The soldier crumpled before he could get there, 'the flames still licking his now mercifully lifeless body'.

Those last few moments of *Vindictive*'s own agony must have seemed like an eternity for the men waiting on board. At least two German shells struck the ship's main engine room, which rapidly began to fill with choking ammonia fumes as a result. Lieutenant Arthur Lougher, the officer in charge below decks, ordered his men to don goggles and respirators, further adding to the unworldly atmosphere aboard. 'The noise was deafening, and the ship rocked like a cradle,' Lougher recalled. Another German salvo killed *Vindictive*'s forward howitzer crew. A relief team then rushed up to take their place and were themselves killed. A young marine stationed in the flamethrower hut beside Captain Carpenter later wrote of these minutes: 'My, what a din, it was shattering! Although [Carpenter] put the ship full speed ahead to run her alongside, I think we suffered more casualties running the gauntlet of the Mole battery than in the rest of the action.'

The planners of Operation ZO had made wildly optimistic claims about *Vindictive*'s ability to tie up alongside the enemy wall without attracting undue attention. In reality it was a 'hellish vista,' Carpenter wrote. Air Mechanic William Gough, whose age was given as either 19 or 20, added: 'Our casualties during this bombardment were fearful. Out of the platoon to which I was attached – over forty men – not more than eight to ten got up to land when the signal was given. The remainder were either dead or wounded.' An unnamed member of No. 11 Platoon, waiting with his comrades at the ship's rail, later told an interviewer that he had been knocked unconscious by a German shell and woke up at the bottom of a gangway with the bodies of his friends piled up on top of him.

In his official account of this part of Operation ZO, Admiral Keyes wrote in February 1919:

> According to the time-table, the hour at which the *Vindictive* should have been laid alongside the Zeebrugge Mole was midnight. She reached her station one minute after midnight, closely followed by the *Daffodil* and *Iris*. A few minutes later the landing of the storming and demolition parties began.

Again, this sense of an orderly, regulation arrival and disembarkation at Zeebrugge perhaps understates the true chaos of events. The plan called for *Vindictive* to come alongside the outer northeastern extremity of the Mole, at the point where a narrow stone causeway extended out some 300 yards to the lighthouse. This was the most heavily fortified part of the enemy garrison, and the first marine storming parties were meant to have rapidly attacked and subdued the gun batteries there, while others crossed the roof of an adjacent barracks hut, dropped down onto the Mole itself, neutralising the nearby machine-gun emplacements, and then proceeded down the wall as far as they reasonably could, sabotaging any further armaments or equipment they found on their way, and in general diverting the Germans' attention from the imminent arrival in their harbour of the three British blockships.

In the event, this was not quite what happened. *Vindictive*, if punctual, found herself badly out of position, some 400 yards further down the Mole than the plan called for. The storming parties would have to make good the difference on foot, fighting their way through machine-gun posts mined and protected with barbed wire they had hoped to attack from the rear. The ship was also rolling badly, and her landing brows – those not already shot away by German fire – were found to be too short to reach the Mole parapet. 'This was a trying period,' Carpenter was later forced to admit, as heavy shells, mortars and machine-gun fire continued to rain down on his ship from close range. It's true that there was a 'great deal of smoke and noise about', and that at least some of the German garrison had been understandably shaken by the sudden sight of *Vindictive* bearing down on them – so much so that one of the marines on board later insisted that he had 'heard the cries of a Hun praying desperately out loud' as the ship closed in – but none of this diminishes the still-formidable defences the raiders were forced to face.

The Mole itself acted as a shield for *Vindictive*'s lower decks as the ship bumped up alongside, but above the level of the parapet top the ship continued to offer an unmissable target to both the German gun crews and enemy ships, including at least one fully armed U-boat out of its stall and steaming nearby. Lance-Corporal Calverley later wrote:

> The *Vindictive* took the brunt of the fire from the guns on the Mole as she went alongside … All hell seemed to be let loose, her troops were [attempting to] climb the wooden scaling ladders onto the Mole and flame-throwers were shooting flames across the Mole. It was like Dante's Inferno must have been.

'We were rather badly gassed down below,' Lieutenant-Commander Bury recalled of his experience during the next few minutes in *Vindictive*'s engine room.

> In fact, a perfect bedlam broke out all around, and the old ship shook all over. It was impossible to say which were Hun hits and which were our own explosions. Our pom-poms barked away merrily for a while, and then stopped, all the crews being wiped out … Our brows were nearly all shot away, the crowded marines falling down on their faces all around me, so that I was

much too frightened to look for a ladder, but directed my attention to business on the upper deck … The ship was enfiladed for a while by a destroyer, which came round the point of the Mole astern of us, and she did a good deal of damage, but was sunk by a CMB, and our crews claimed some shots into her, too. It did not matter what position of the Mole we went alongside, for the whole place bristled with guns.

Landing the men required good luck, lest either a sudden swell or equipment failure drove *Vindictive* off the Mole; audacity, since the first arrivals on the parapet would be staggering upwards under the weight of their packs into the teeth of the enemy; and extraordinary effort, in the form of pinning a fully laden cruiser against a heavily defended sheer wall in the dark. This was perhaps the moment in the whole exercise when the disparity between the training regimen on the Kent downs and the conditions encountered on the night was most painfully obvious. While Carpenter tried vainly to secure his ship, whose port bow repeatedly banged against the stone breakwater like an ineptly parked car, the casualty lists continued to grow. Surgeon McCutcheon would later remark that there had been the 'most sanguinary and awful scenes' as the landing parties had stood to on *Vindictive*'s upper decks, 'cruelly exposed as machine-gun fire, bombs and shrapnel' raked the men's muster stations.

Speaking to the press just two days later, a young gunner's mate named Seaman Dowell remembered:

> With all that firing, with dazzling light one minute and darkness the next, and with the decks covered with dead and wounded, it wasn't easy to get our chaps together … Five of our seven crew went down at once. I don't know if it was shrapnel bursting overhead or whether we got splinters from a shell that had struck the superstructure. Anyway, only two of us were left standing. But the five who went down were not dead, and some had begun to drag themselves off the forecastle. We half lifted, half carried the others, one by one, into shelter, and then beckoned to some stretcher bearers to come and take charge of them. There were a lot of bearers passing here and there all the time, and very busy.

Having come under the full force of the Germans' guns in the last excruciating minutes before she reached the Mole, *Vindictive* now faced a second merciless ordeal. The marines' Captain Arthur Chater, a Gallipoli veteran, recalled of the furious efforts to put the ship alongside:

> Although only 22 years old, I probably had a more intimate experience of shell fire than either [my] CO or the second in command … We were still some distance from the Mole and now instinct told me to keep my head down. I suggested that my two seniors should do the same, but they either did not hear me or they did not agree with me. Anyhow they took no notice. A moment later, a shell appeared to hit the front part of the lower bridge beneath us. My two seniors dropped to the deck on either side of me. I grasped hold of them and spoke to them in turn, but neither of them answered me.
>
> 'B' Company, stationed in the port waist, had to some extent been protected from shell fire whilst the ship was approaching the Mole – by the built-up deck. 'C' Company, in the starboard waist, had little protection and suffered considerable casualties before the ship was placed alongside. The plan was for No. 10 and 11 Platoons of 'C' company to land first, but

when the moment for this arrived, both platoon officers and most of the men were already casualties. The platoons as such appeared no longer to exist.

The Germans may or may not have immediately realised that *Vindictive* meant to put troops ashore, but whatever their initial grasp of the situation they lost no further time in obstructing the ship's progress towards them. The surviving British gunners returned fire, and a thunderous artillery battle raged. Close-range bursts from maxim guns and the steady clap of star shells overhead both added to the air of what Captain Carpenter called 'an infernal and deafening lightning storm' all around. During this exchange, the two sides were close enough together for the men standing on *Vindictive's* deck to be able to clearly hear the German soldiers talking to each other in between salvoes. According to Carpenter, their tone was one of 'apparent resolve, mingled with some bewilderment' at finding the weirdly remodelled enemy warship staring down at them.

Most Britons of that era were expected to be nonchalant about death, and many of the contemporary accounts of Zeebrugge quote the mortally wounded as meeting their end with lines such as: 'By Jove! That was a bit of a ripper' or 'Quite all right, thanks. A little embrocation will soon set matters right.' There was a widely reported incident among the ranks of Sergeant Harry Wright's 10 Platoon of the marine troop mustered in the dark waiting to transfer from *Vindictive* onto the Mole. Wright recalled:

> We were packed tight in five ranks. The two rear ranks were standing directly underneath one of the ship's cutters.
>
> It is usual, of course, when boats are hoisted inboard for the plug to be removed for the water to drain. This had not been done and the cutter was half full of rain water.
>
> The first shell inboard, fired from the battery at the sea end of the Mole, exploded directly overhead and some 30 members of my platoon were killed. Those of us standing under the cutter escaped unhurt, the water breaking the force of the fragments of the shell.
>
> Lying mortally wounded on the deck of the *Vindictive* was my young officer, Lieutenant Stanton. As I knelt beside him he had just enough time to whisper, 'Carry on, Wright' before he died.

While there is no reason to doubt the truth of Harry Wright's account of the impressively calm manner in which Lieutenant Stanton met his fate, other British casualties reacted in more robust fashion. One officer on *Vindictive* reported that

> Many of the men who were hurt used the most awful language, some of them laughing hysterically even after being knocked over. I longed to be able to say that I wasn't frightened, after all we had heard about being under fire … I pretended to myself that I was cool enough for a bit, but it was no good.

Private Jack Finney of No. 9 Platoon, RMLI, later had the painful duty of writing to the family of his friend Arthur Burnell, who had been crouching next to him on the port side of *Vindictive* as she first made contact with the Mole:

> We were all layed down at that time, and when Lieutenant Bloxham shouted 'come along' orders, of course I said to Arthur, come on, he's shouting at us and Arthur never spoke. So I says, 'Arthur you are not hit are you', and then he said quietly, 'yes'. 'Where are you hit' I said, he then said, 'in the head.' So I said come on down to the sick bay … So I got hold of him to lift him and then he said, '*leave me alone.*' That was the last thing he said to me.

The often quietly heroic words of young men as they lay bleeding and dying on the decks of *Vindictive* haunt the pages of many of the eyewitness accounts of the survivors.

Once having reached the Mole, it took *Vindictive* a further 15 minutes to successfully berth herself, an interval during which every enemy gun within a radius of two miles steadily turned the cruiser's funnels and upper works into a giant sieve. Lieutenant Hilton Young was the officer in charge of securing a grapnel to hook the ship in place as she continued to bang up and down in the heavy swell. After several failed attempts, many of his fellow crew members lay dead or dying, and Young himself was temporarily *hors de combat* with a smashed shoulder. At that stage, *Vindictive*'s starboard anchor was lowered. It failed to grip. Lines were then thrown in the faint hope that they might attach to something solid. They also failed. It might almost have been comic had it not been so tragic. One of the ratings engaged in desperately trying to secure *Vindictive* to shore recalled of this phase of the operation:

> We were fitted with special grapnels to drop over the two-feet ridge on the upper part of the Mole. Under the guidance of Lieutenant Young, who, although wounded in the arm, carried on as usual, we strove under a heavy and raking machine gun fire to place our hook … I shall never forget the coolness and bravery of the aforesaid officer. With one hand and quietly smoking a cigar (and the everlasting monocle in his eye), he tried to drop our grapnel.

During this protracted ordeal, Lieutenant-Commander Rosoman, situated in the relative safety of the lower bridge, continued to inquire politely through the speaking tube connected to Captain Carpenter's room located several feet above the eye line of the German gunners, 'Are you all right, sir?' The question was no mere formality, as three men were shot down at Carpenter's side while he struggled to hold *Vindictive* against the sea wall. Later in the proceedings a shell burst just outside the ship's conning tower as she was preparing to turn for home. Rosoman fell with shrapnel through both ankles, a young petty officer named Edwin Youlton had his arm all but severed, and Carpenter himself suffered a deep wound to his left shoulder. All three men survived. It was found that Carpenter's soft cap had also been pierced by a bullet during the raid. He later told an interviewer that he had either not noticed or only half-noticed the event, and that he had simply been too busy to care about it. 'There was no time for philosophising,' he added.

As the assault parties were waiting anxiously on deck for *Vindictive* to lash herself to the Mole, the ship was being continuously pounded by both land and sea. In addition to the sustained artillery barrage, several German surface ships opened fire on the intruder in their midst from only a few hundred yards away across the harbour. Lieutenant Hilton Young remembered of this 'quite testing' time:

> I was sitting down for a minute on a mushroom head in the battery, to look after my arm, [as] shells struck our upper works and the funnels and cowls which stuck up above the sheltering Mole … when a round struck [us], a spray of splinters from the thin steel structure dashed down into the battery and caused many casualties there. But the fire directed on them at point-blank range did not affect the resolution of [Lieutenant Charles] Rigby and his crew of six Marine artillerymen in the top.

As we've seen, at least one fully armed U-boat had been in the vicinity when *Vindictive* arrived at the Mole, and a brief but lively sea skirmish ensued – the steep angle at which the submarine then submerged suggesting that her departure was neither 'completely voluntary, nor totally unhurried', according to one observer.

The fighting on both sides was merciless, but at least the Germans had solid ground under their feet. Throughout these torturous few minutes, *Vindictive* continued to lurch up against the smooth stone surface of the Mole before repeatedly bouncing off again into the open sea. Manning the ship's forward guns, Seaman Dowell remembered of this farcical and dangerous time:

> A derrick had been rigged out to let down a specially made anchor by means of a 3 ½ in. cable. The idea was to make the anchor fast against something or other on the Mole. But the derrick, though it held the anchor some 18 or 20 feet off the ship, didn't quite go far enough.
>   You see, there is a part of the Mole which projects under water, so it was impossible for the *Vindictive* to come closer than she did. The anchor hung just short. Some men on the Mole eventually tried to draw it in, but when we lowered away the anchor proved too heavy for them, and there it hung alongside the Mole instead of on it.

The whole grim pantomime might have ended there, with *Vindictive* ignominiously forced to slink home, but for the arrival out of the mist five minutes later of the ferries *Iris* and *Daffodil*. There are surely few sights and sounds more British than a flawed master plan being rescued by the spirit of improvisation and personal fortitude of its individual participants. Lieutenant Harold Campbell, commanding *Daffodil*, bleeding profusely from wounds received when a German shell exploded on his bridge, now expertly put his ship's nose against *Vindictive*'s starboard flank, and, calling for every ounce of pressure his stokers could raise in the engine room, bodily shoved the cruiser's port side in place against the wall.

'Really, [Campbell] might have been an old stager at tug-master's work, pursuing his vocation in one of our own harbours, judging by the cool manner in which he [acted],' Carpenter wrote. Due to the relative positions of the two vessels – and the fact that the men queuing up on both their decks were being strafed by German soldiers standing directly above them on the Mole – only a fraction of the naval storming parties arriving on *Daffodil* were able to pass safely to the deck of *Vindictive* and from there struggle onto shore. One of the officers who did so remembered: 'I and four men were able to land, but the remainder were unable to follow, as the *Daffodil* was being shelled all the time, and the captain ordered my men who were left to throw the Stokes bombs overboard' – Lieutenant Campbell's concern being that a stray German shell might ignite these arms and send both *Daffodil* and *Vindictive* to the bottom.

As *Daffodil* strained at the seams to keep *Vindictive* in place, her sister ship *Iris* loomed into view behind them, bobbing drunkenly in the heavy swell, and eventually came to a stop some 200 yards further down the outer Mole. She, too, encountered some difficulty in holding fast. Lieutenant-Commander George Bradford, who had turned 31 on the day before the raid, clambered up the derrick which held a large grapnel in place on *Iris*'s port bow. In the words of his subsequent citation for the Victoria Cross (VC):

> During the climb the ship was surging up and down and the derrick crashing on the Mole. Awaiting his opportunity, [Bradford] jumped with the parapet-anchor on to the Mole and placed it in position. Immediately after hooking on the parapet-anchor, he was riddled with bullets from machine-guns and fell into the sea between the Mole and the ship. Attempts to recover his body failed.

Lieutenant-Commander Bradford was not the only casualty during the extended struggle to lock *Iris* in place alongside the Mole. The ship's navigating officer, Lieutenant Claude Hawkings, did not look very martial with his pink, cherubic face and somewhat floppy ears, but was remembered as a 'pragmatic, unflappable personality who would get the job done'. Hawkings now made a further attempt to secure *Iris*, climbing up a scaling ladder and trying to hook this on to the Mole parapet. He was last seen firing his service revolver at the half-dozen German soldiers armed with machine guns advancing towards him. Meanwhile, Petty Officer Michael Hallihan, seeing Bradford fall, either jumped off a ladder or dived headlong into the water over the shouted warnings of his comrades in order to rescue him. He was crushed to death when the heavy swell drove the 480-ton *Iris* against the sea wall. At that point Captain Valentine Gibbs, the ship's commanding officer, reversed course and in time placed his vessel alongside *Vindictive*'s starboard quarter. At least some of *Iris*'s waiting troops would thus be able to scramble across the bodies of the dead and wounded on the cruiser's deck to go ashore.

As *Vindictive* came at least precariously into position at 12.16 that morning, Captain Carpenter was now able to attach two gangways to land and to pass down the general order: 'Storm the Mole.'

The first Royal Navy party ashore consisted of 203 men and eight officers arranged in four groups, and their primary mission was to engage the nearest German infantry troops, spike their gun batteries, lay explosive charges, and in general harry the enemy forces while the three cement-laden ships entered the harbour behind them. There was a touch of the piratical about both the landing itself and the issue to the raiders of daggers, grappling hooks, chopping axes and bayonets. One marine who followed in the first wave onto the Mole recalled the moment with soldierly satisfaction. 'It would be difficult to conceive a finer spectacle,' he wrote. 'The sky was brilliantly lit by the different conflagrations, star shells bursting aloft, guns roaring, and a sheer white light flashed out of the muzzles of cannon and machine-gun alike, sufficient to permit each man to view distinctly his enemy's face.'

The element of surprise no longer applying, many of the men of *Vindictive*'s storming crews took the opportunity to hurriedly smoke a last pre-landing cigarette. Several also fortified themselves with a generous tot of rum in addition to the fixed allowance. The men would have to step over the fallen bodies of their friends and then climb one of only two working gangways, the ends of which heaved up and down on the Mole parapet in the heavy seas. They could hear the shouted orders and cries that marked the animation of the German troops waiting to receive them above. 'It was an infernal cauldron,' a British officer noted. An Australian sailor named Dalmorton Rudd added the detail: 'Fellows were literally shitting themselves. I was shitting myself so much there was nothing left.'

There is some discrepancy as to the exact order of arrival of the first British boots on the ground at Zeebrugge. Captain Carpenter, who was looking down on the proceedings from his conning tower, wrote: 'The two foremost brows reached the wall, and the seaman storming parties, led in the most gallant manner by Lieut-Commander [Arthur] Harrison ran out along them.' Other eyewitness reports suggest that the honour properly belonged to Lieutenant-Commander Bryan Adams, who rushed ashore at the head of four or five men and promptly dropped a stick grenade through the slit of an adjacent concrete shed before engaging individual enemy troops in close-range combat. An account written not long after the event by the American author-adventurer Lowell Thomas gives something of the overall flavour of the action when it quotes an unnamed German officer on the Mole:

> I have never seen such horrible hand-to-hand fighting as took place … The sailors from the Vindictive swarmed down, and many of the defenders were unarmed [*sic*] … I saw an Englishman bayonet a German through the body, and then the dying man sank his teeth in the throat of his adversary.

Lieutenant-Commander Harrison's claim to glory as the first man to go ashore at Zeebrugge was also advanced by his colleague William Bury, watching from the deck of *Vindictive*, who wrote shortly afterwards:

> The bluejackets were first over the top, led by Harrison, who was shot through the face, but, however, kept on, until again shot through the neck. They suffered badly from the machine-guns' cross-fire from Huns under cover … Chamberlain walked down to the after-flat unaided, with one of his lungs blown out through his back, but died almost at the foot of the ladder. Walker had his left arm blown off, and much shrapnel in his head and neck, but sat up and shouted encouragement to his men.

If the Germans were truly caught unawares at Zeebrugge, some of their garrison attending a celebration party at a seafront hotel, they roused themselves with notable speed. From the moment the sea fog parted like a curtain to reveal *Vindictive* steaming full pelt towards them, the Mole batteries were in constant action. 'Every man was serving the guns,' an *Artillerie-Maat* petty officer named Richard Policke later told the German press, 'dripping with sweat, covered in powder marks, everybody from the Battery commander to the youngest sailor work[ing] to keep every gun firing as rapidly as possible. It was a wonderful thing.' Policke's only cause for complaint was to see a number of shells from the German coastal batteries miss their mark and hit some of their own side's infantrymen on the Mole by mistake.

Adding to the general mêlée, many of Zeebrugge's 4,000 civilian population, awakened by the sounds of an artillery battle in their town, began running from their homes in a panic. By 12.15 a.m. there was a bottleneck of pedestrians and bicyclists making their way across the old wooden Zwankendamme bridge to the immediate south of the Mole, and a Belgian nun named Godelieve Deprez hurriedly scribbled in her diary by candlelight: 'Guns roaring on all sides, shells shuffle [*sic*] above our heads, nothing but death and destruction. What is going on?' Even in a country that had already suffered so much in the war, it was a fearful night. Deprez later added that a shell presumably fired by one of the British monitors lying offshore had 'fallen from over the sea on to a small farm, inhabited by poor people, [and] the youngest child was pulled from its crib which was covered in glass and plaster'. One graffitist marked the sooty wall of Zeebrugge's seafront Palace Hotel with a damning comparison: 'Huns wreck this town after 2 months campaign. British do it after 1-hour raid.'

Thanks to a combination of shellfire before *Vindictive* reached her berth and the ferocious small-arms attack following her arrival, some of the first storming parties mustered aboard had to be hurriedly rearranged. B Company of the Royal Navy, for instance, went ashore without officers, all of whom had been killed before setting foot on dry land. As a result, a young rating named William Childs found himself at the head of a 'highly excited and also very jittery' group of a dozen men as they clambered up what was effectively a seesawing wooden plank into the face of the enemy. Childs himself was about to jump from the head of the gangway onto shore 'when I was knocked silly by a 303 bullet, which struck my tin hat and cutting its way through the rim, parted one of my putties. A lucky escape. I soon came to my senses again, through hearing someone shout "Over the top, boys …!"'

This was clearly among the most hazardous moments of the whole exercise – not only dangerous in itself but 'excessively crowded,' Carpenter noted, many of the men being so tightly wedged as they groped their way up the gangways that 'few if any can have seen much over the heads in front of them and the dark outline of the wall ahead'. Another naval officer compared the disembarkation process to 'something out of Hieronymus Bosch'. As each newly wounded seaman collapsed at the top of the landing ramp he fell backwards into the man immediately behind him, often creating an horrific domino effect. Of a group of 56 officers and ratings crossing over from the deck of *Iris* to *Vindictive*, and from there to the Mole, only seven survived, most of them wounded, to reach land. A direct hit from a mid-range

German gun killed 29 more men below decks in *Iris*'s sick bay. For those who yet lived, there was the constant threat of machine-gun and other small-arms fire directed at them from the Mole.

'Our demolition charges had been moved from the conning tower to a safer position,' Carpenter wrote of the critical period when he had struggled to keep *Vindictive* alongside.

> This change of arrangement was indeed fortunate, for the deck on both sides became a regular shambles. Yeoman of signals, John Buckley, who had volunteered to take up a position outside the tower in readiness to fire illuminating rockets had remained at his post until killed. We found him there at the foot of his rocket tube in the morning. All the signalmen except one were either killed or completely disabled: and almost every soul on the conning tower platform made the supreme sacrifice.

Elsewhere on the Mole, the advance orders calling for the British forces to 'establish an ammunition and bomb depot on arrival' and to submit requests for supplies from this 'through Battalion channels' soon broke down amidst the blood and detritus of war. One of the first marines to reach the Mole was Lieutenant Theodore Cooke, who was almost immediately wounded but carried on to lead his platoon down the wall to confront a nest of German snipers. Following this decisive engagement, Cooke endeavoured to help one of his stricken men back to the *Vindictive*, but as he did so he was shot a second time and rendered temporarily unconscious. He was then in turn picked up by his soldier-servant Private John Press, who was himself wounded but carried his officer back through the gauntlet of machine-gun fire on the Mole to the comparative safety of *Vindictive*. Another marine was blinded by a shell burst just as he was about to embark on the gangway to shore, but was 'very heartened' to then hear the voice of Captain Edward Bamford shout: 'Come on lads, let's get at them!' Alfred Carpenter remembered of these moments, during which he left his conning tower to monitor developments on deck:

> At the top of the foremost ladder the men, in their eagerness to get at the enemy, were stumbling over a body. I had bent down to drag it clear when one of the men shouted: 'That's Mr. Walker, sir, he's had his arm shot off.' Immediately Walker, who was still conscious, heard this he waved his remaining hand to me and wished me the best of luck. This officer survived.

Meanwhile, what Carpenter called 'the very tip of the spear' of Operation ZO – the squadron of three blockships – was about to enter the sustained and confused fighting around the harbour basin. The ships' passage to Zeebrugge had not been free of incident. All three vessels carried excess personnel owing to these individuals' reluctance to leave them when asked to do so, and all three subsequently had to endure the heavy and prolonged rain of German shellfire. Lieutenant Bonham Carter, commanding officer of *Intrepid*, later wrote of the group's final approach to its destination:

When Thetis came within sight of the Mole *only about 50 yards away*, they found themselves some way out [of position], due no doubt to the set of the tide. They had therefore to turn to port and go along the Mole on which there were mounted at that part six 3 ½ inch guns. They then had to turn to starboard again after passing the lighthouse.

Thetis, leading, fouled the barge which supported the net-defence on the port-side, jammed her propeller and went aground. She widened the entrance in so doing and burst a light to show the Intrepid, which came next, on which side to pass her. The Germans seemed to have concentrated their guns on the Thetis and when Intrepid passed her, she was apparently being blown to pieces. As Intrepid cleared the boom, the wind shifted and blew all our smoke back and over us and, as the Huns were also throwing up star shells, the whole place was lit up as light as day.

For a minute or two more after encountering the harbour defences, HMS *Thetis* steamed on, taking the heavy underwater nets with her, proceeding with what Kapitan Schütte called 'great impetuosity' towards the mouth of the canal half a mile to her south. Apparently the ferocity of the German response from shore was more than the commanding officers of the blockships had counted on. While the heavy artillery batteries kept up a steady barrage from their seafront positions at Zeebrugge, other units stationed on the Mole peppered the new arrivals in their midst with a variety of shells, bombs and machine-gun fire, one explosion killing the two-man gun crew on the forecastle aboard *Thetis*. An Australian stoker named Norbert McCrory later remarked of the damage inflicted on the leading blockship:

Our forward gun was blown overboard, taking the crew with it. We also had a shell go right through from starboard to port side. It blew a hole immediately above our heads in the engine room. I remember the crater quite distinctly. It was big enough for three men to walk through.

CHAPTER 6

'The Firing was a Bit Severe …'

The phrase 'Going over the top' is often associated with the obliterative violence of the Somme or Passchendaele, and with all the other horrific convulsions of the Western Front. It might also be said to apply all too literally to events on the seaward side of the Zeebrugge harbour Mole in the early minutes of 23 April 1918. We've seen how Lieutenant-Commander George Bradford, less than an hour after sharing a convivial drink to celebrate his birthday, lost his life while attempting to secure *Iris* alongside in order for his men to then follow him ashore. Within minutes of his arrival, Bradford had shinned up the ferry's forward davit and leapt from there to the lower part of the sea wall, taking the ship's anchor with him. In the same split-second that his feet touched the ground he was shot by German machine gunners and, frozen in silhouette, swayed in place for a moment before toppling backwards into the sea. Watching from on board *Iris*, Petty Officer O'Hara saw Bradford's dying struggle: 'We managed to get a line to him, which he grasped,' O'Hara said.

> But as he was badly wounded he did not have the strength to hold on and be pulled up. A ladder was procured and placed over the side, but unfortunately just as a volunteer was descending to his aid a rather heavy swell dashed Iris against the Mole and he was crushed between.

George Bradford's act of valour was only one of several desperate attempts to establish a means of landing the British troops on the Mole. After reversing course to bring his vessel alongside *Vindictive*, *Iris*'s commanding officer Valentine Gibbs was at least able to put a token force ashore. No greater deployment was possible than that, as *Iris* lost fully 77 men killed and 105 men wounded out of her four onboard platoons, a nearly 50 per cent casualty rate. Later in the action, Gibbs himself was mortally wounded when a shell crashed through the side of his bridge. A Marine private watched with a mixture of horror and admiration as 'Commander Gibbs … lost both his legs, and while tourniquets were being applied he died with devotion to duty on his lips with the words – "Leave me alone, leave me alone, I want to get these men back"'. Marine Lieutenant 'Willie' Sillitoe and Private John Bostock were in all probability killed in the same explosion, and were later laid to rest side by side in a Kent cemetery.

On *Vindictive*, Captain Carpenter recalled of the final landing process:

> It was an extremely perilous task, in view of the fact that the ends of the brows at one moment were from 8 to 10 feet above the wall, and the next moment were crashing on it as the ship rolled. The way in which the men got over those brows was almost superhuman. I expected every moment to see them falling off between the Mole and the ship – at least a 30-foot drop – and be crushed against the wall.

It's worth remembering that these individuals were each carrying the equivalent of two fully laden suitcases as they ascended a narrow, juddering plank, without handrails, and that they did so headlong into a hail of German bullets. 'The crackle of musketry and machine guns grew into a considerable din as we found shore,' one young rating remarked in a subsequent letter home to his parents. Some of the men queuing up on deck were spattered with the blood of their comrades falling backwards above them in the dark. The upper half of one navy officer, his tin helmet still on his head, fell in the middle of one of the waiting groups.

Captain Arthur Chater, the marine adjutant in *Vindictive*, later confirmed that there had been the 'gravest difficulty' in getting men to and from the ship and the sea wall.

> I found that there were no steps near to where the vessel had been berthed, and that the height was too great to jump down. Returning on board, I gave instructions for hook ropes to be taken ashore for men to get down on to the parapet-top, and I made Sgt-Major Thatcher personally responsible that, after the men had landed, scaling ladders were taken ashore and placed and maintained in position ... Having given these orders, I returned to the sea wall, slid down a hook rope and crossed over to the enemy's No. 3 shed on the far side of the Mole.

Captain Chater assessed the frightful carnage of the scene in front of him in dispassionate terms: 'The defenders were shelling the Mole and their shells were striking the sea wall and their own sheds,' he wrote, later remarking that he had seen 'one young soldier, moaning, impossible to tell if he was British or German, with his intestines out under his battle-dress. He soon died.' This was not the end of the various challenges facing the landing parties. *Vindictive*'s being out of position meant that the British troops would have to fight their way through an additional quarter of a mile of pillbox and barbed-wire defences in order to reach and hopefully destroy the main gun battery at the lighthouse end of the Mole. For the most part the men advanced on their target in complete darkness, although at intervals they were bathed in the flash and glow of a star shell overhead, or by a burst of automatic gunfire directly ahead. One marine remembered seeing the funnels and foretop of *Vindictive* suddenly becoming visible to his left as he prowled up the Mole, and that the ship was then illuminated by a spray of sparks and an eerie electric-blue light flickering on and off somewhere near the bridge. Many of the British forces going ashore wore white arm-bands to identify themselves to each other.

Impatient at the lengthy wait to debouch onto the Mole by one of the two working gangways eventually secured to *Vindictive*, Able Seaman Charles Pooley, carrying a cutlass, a revolver and some 25 pounds of high-explosive detonators, leapt down 12 feet in the dark onto dry land. He twisted his ankle on landing. A rugby-playing Welshman, like others Pooley struggled to cope with the sheer physical ordeal facing him. 'It was hell while it lasted,' he later told a reporter, 'but the boys were splendid. They were in the best of spirits, and never faltered, the uniforms giving them an excellent lead.' Elsewhere, Pooley remembered the ghastly sight of officers and men alike, themselves often grotesquely wounded, staggering to and fro with their fallen comrades on their backs. 'This is no simple task,' said Pooley, who was celebrating his 21st birthday on 23 April 1918. Close-arms fire soon reduced to six the original demolition team of 22 naval personnel set on silencing the main Mole-extension guns before the arrival in their sights of the three British blockships. Another challenge presented itself in the form of a fully manned German warship, probably either a 1,700-ton G101-class destroyer or a similarly sized large torpedo-boat, moored just to the south of *Vindictive*'s position on the inner side of the Mole. In time this led to the strange spectacle of what one British sailor called 'a periodic big flash, clouds of smoke and deafening noise' as the two ships engaged one another from a range of just 80 yards away across a concrete breakwater.

According to the commanding officer of the naval demolition party, Lieutenant Cecil Dickinson,

> We did not advance … on account of fire from the German destroyer alongside, and the question of demolition was therefore rendered impractical. One or two of my men endeavoured to approach this ship to place a charge, but this too was rendered out of the question owing to the fire from her. I believe some bombs were thrown by [us] on board.

Coming up on the deck of *Vindictive*, Lieutenant-Commander Bury was torn between his feelings of revulsion at some of the horrific injuries he witnessed and his concern with the practical difficulties of conveying the victims to the ship's sick bay. 'It was a most difficult job,' Bury later wrote. 'The small hatches, steep ladders and darkness made it so. Never again shall I believe yarns about people rushing about [with] the wounded on their backs. I could hardly move some of them, and my chief stoker, a huge strong chap, couldn't help.'

By the time the marine storming parties came to join their naval counterparts on the Mole, the scene was approaching one of Gothic carnage. The young Air Mechanic Francis Donovan was meant to run up *Vindictive*'s forward gangway onto land with a portable flamethrower strapped to his back with which to accost the enemy. A bullet cut through this device before he could use it, so Donovan, improvising,

> dropped it and ran onto the Mole … the only weapon I had was a rather blunt cutlass. All I could see through the drizzling rain and under the glare of the star shells was blazing gun-fire and barbed wire entanglements, and the parties of our men and Germans firing at each other.

Another marine crew accomplished what an eyewitness described as 'a splendid charge' on a fortified German shed located on the Mole immediately opposite *Vindictive*. 'The men raced across the parapet-top, skipping over the dead as they went, their upturned cutlasses flashing with intent in the shellfire light.' Fighting in these conditions quickly brought home to even the youngest recruit the harsh reality of close-quarter combat. Able Seaman Wilfred Wainwright, who was just 19, wrote:

> Once on the top of the Mole one was assailed by the overwhelming feeling of nakedness and maddening desire to go forward at all costs and stop the hail of death that swept the upper Mole. Your sense of reason was replaced by insane fury and the events that followed cannot be remembered coherently. It was a horrible nightmare of sweating and cursing men thirsty for blood, the sickening 'sog' of bayonets and of shots at close quarters.

Although the marines came into their own as a fighting force at Zeebrugge, some individual troops reacted poorly to battle. Private Jim Clist of No. 12 Platoon remembered meeting two of his comrades on the Mole parapet. 'I told them where to go, but they were in such a state of shock that they would not move. They were in the most dangerous part ... I shouted and told them to lie down, but they took no notice.' These individuals were not seen alive again.

Despite isolated cases such as the one Clist described, the marine storming parties as a whole revealed considerable courage and dedication. They could also lay an undisputed claim to have been the first unit ashore to seize German guns. Speaking to the British press just two days later, an unnamed officer remembered:

> We formed up and forced our way on land at the point of the bayonet. We charged the [artillery] crews which had been giving us so much trouble, and after killing a number dispersed the rest and captured the guns ... All around us we could hear the noise of the conflict, the cries and shrieks of the dying and wounded. It was horrible, but our men behaved magnificently.

As the attack continued, the scene on the Mole increasingly broke down into one that resembled a series of hand-to-hand skirmishes rather than a fully integrated assault. In some places individual German units pushed the British raiders back over the same ground so dearly gained just a few minutes earlier. Men were shouting incoherently and flailing at each other with clubs and swords in the eerie, strobe-like flash of the bursting star shells. Normal command structures broke down almost completely. After the fighting, Captain Carpenter asked one of the seamen from *Vindictive* who had run ashore where the rest of his raiding party was. The man replied, 'Dead on the field.' Both of his group's officers and 18 out of 20 of the men were gone.

We've seen how Lieutenant-Commander Arthur Harrison, in charge of the naval storming parties embarked on *Vindictive*, was knocked cold by a shell splinter as the ship came alongside the Mole. His jaw smashed, he rallied sufficiently to lead a group of men onto the parapet top, waving his cutlass in the direction of a murderously active enemy machine-gun post. Harrison, a former England rugby union forward, had covered roughly half the distance to his objective before he was cut down, his fallen sword clattering across the blood-soaked cobblestones in front of him. A later German press account said: 'He remained there for a moment in the same upright position, still staring, and it was only when the blade fell from his hand that one realised he must be dead.'

The build-up of forces in that area, described as a 'mass of wreckage, of men and materials, and bodies spouting blood', continued. A sailor named Harold Eaves managed to reach Harrison's corpse, but was himself repeatedly shot from close range as he tried to lift it onto his back. Able Seaman William Lodwick, a merchant navy veteran, watched Eaves 'stagger and fall heavily to the ground. We could not get to him on account of heavy fire from machine guns … He was left on the Mole'. Initially reported dead, Eaves was taken prisoner by the Germans, treated in hospital and repatriated after the war. Arthur Harrison's body was never recovered. He was posthumously awarded the VC, having, in the citation's words: 'Displayed indomitable resolution and courage of the highest order in pressing the attack, knowing as he did that any delay in silencing the guns might jeopardise the main object of the expedition, i.e., the blocking of the Zeebrugge–Bruges canal.'

Nineteen-year-old east Londoner Albert McKenzie was another of the naval ratings who joined Arthur Harrison's headlong rush down the Mole. With a dry cockney wit and an essentially pragmatic approach to life, McKenzie, already a three-year veteran of the service, was not one to be easily deterred. When his Lewis light machine gun was shot from his hands, he paused only to draw his service revolver before continuing his advance. It was impossible to see any concerted plan of attack by this stage, and in the confusion individual British troops were doing stop-gap jobs where the need seemed greatest. Casualties were heavy on both sides. After disposing of several Germans as he ran pell-mell in the general direction of the Mole lighthouse, and being repeatedly hit in the arms and legs, McKenzie began to improvise:

> I found a rifle and bayonet … All I remember was pushing, kicking and kneeing every German who got in the way. When I was finished I couldn't climb the ladder [back to *Vindictive*], so a mate of mine lifted me up and carried me back up and then I crawled on my hands and knees inboard.

Three months later, Able Seaman McKenzie was able to limp forward with the aid of two crutches to receive the VC at an investiture held on a hot summer's day at Buckingham Palace. Immediately after the ceremony, which his family attended, he returned to the naval hospital at Chatham to continue his convalescence. McKenzie died there of pneumonia on 3 November 1918, barely two weeks after his 20th birthday and just eight days short of the Armistice. One newspaper reported: 'Shortly before the end he asked his sisters to read him the war news. Then with the utterance "P-e-a-c-e", followed by a feeble "hurrah" he passed away.'

The men who coursed onto the Zeebrugge Mole faced an unenviable prospect. Apart from the challenges of actually making landfall, the Germans, recovering from their initial shock at the intrusion, soon laid down a heavy defensive fire with artillery and small arms. The raiders charged full bore, some leaping into the dark; many were scythed down by the shore batteries, and others by the guns of the enemy destroyer trained on them immediately across the Mole. For the survivors, the fight that followed was desperate, a hand-to-hand duel between men who fought like savage animals. Soldiers used their bayonets as knives, their guns as clubs. Some favoured weapons of an older generation, swinging axes and fighting with their fists and feet. It was brutal. Able Seaman Bernard Devlin, who clambered ashore from *Daffodil*, said of the experience:

> The place was an inferno. Machine gun bullets whizzed above and past us, shells burst over our heads, gas choked those men who in their excitement had allowed their respirators to slip from their faces ... With cutlass drawn in one hand and a bomb in the other, each one of us rushed along the Mole towards the concrete gun stations. Those Germans who tried to get away were blown to atoms by our bombs which we pelted at them. Those who showed fight were slain by cutlass. It was a case of teeth, feet, hands or anything. No quarter was given.

But grim as the struggle was on the Mole, at least it was relatively fluid and mobile. For the men who remained on *Vindictive* as she lay tied alongside, the next hour more closely resembled a siege, 'a relentless pounding from artillery close and far, with enemy infantry also helping themselves to a sitting target the length of a full sports field,' Captain Carpenter wrote. The carnage was fearful. Henry Halahan, the married naval captain who had politely asked if he could accompany the raid, had been killed even as *Vindictive* nosed forward the last agonising few yards to her berth on the Mole, cut down when the first shell-and-machine-gun salvo slammed into the ship's hull. The two marine battalion commanders were both lost in the same incident as they stood waiting to lead their men ashore. Lieutenant Hilton Young's right arm had been shattered, and eventually had to be amputated, although, as we've seen, dismissing this setback he continued to help supervise *Vindictive*'s landing while nonchalantly smoking a cigar. Lieutenant Arthur Chamberlain, the officer in charge of leading the navy's B Company ashore, also lay dead. Forty-two-year-old Commander Patrick Edwards, the man who had been unable to sleep from excitement on first being asked to join the storming party on *Vindictive*, now lay paralysed on the ship's foredeck, shot through both legs. When Edwards ordered two of his men to carry him up the gangway on to the Mole they instead hurriedly took him below, where the surgeons managed to save his life. All these casualties, and many more besides, took place even before *Vindictive* successfully came alongside. That represented the relatively free-flowing part of the ship's role in the mission. The young Sub-Lieutenant Felix Chevallier, having managed to get ashore, looked around in the midst of the fight to see 'The Vindictive being shelled all the time ... A pom-pom was going in the foretop of the ship, [and] I heard afterwards there was only one man left alive there, and he carried on all the time.'

Captain Carpenter recalled of the same scene:

> Every available space on the mess deck was occupied by casualties. Those who could do so were sitting on the mess stools awaiting their turn for medical attention. Many were stretched at full length on the deck, the majority being severely wounded. Some had already collapsed and were in a state of coma. It was a sad spectacle indeed. Somehow, amidst all the crashing and smashing on deck, one had not realised the sacrifice that was taking place.

Meanwhile, fortified by his onboard reserves of vintage port and dressed in a khaki outfit equipped with two equally antique pistols and a cutlass, Frank Brock had found his way across the shambles of *Vindictive*'s deck and up the seesawing gangway onto dry land. One account has him impatiently remarking before leaving his berth that he was damned if he would stay behind listening to the terrible cries of 'I'm hit! I'm hit!' coming from all directions. 'It's awful to feel ineffectual,' he added. At that Brock had dropped down onto the parapet top, noting in the same level tone that he meant to get a closer look at the enemy's range-finding equipment and other points of interest. Beside him a small group of men similarly filed from the darkness into the open night. One of them, a fresh-faced airman named Roland Entwisle, cleared the way ahead with the aid of a Lewis gun and a tray of grenades. He later remembered the reek of cordite, the drizzly rain, the hunched bodies, the irregular flashes of shellfire momentarily turning the night into day. Albert McKenzie witnessed the Brock party's arrival, and watched as they broke into a crouching run in the general direction of a nearby enemy observation post:

> I turned to my left and advanced about 50 yards then lay down. There was a spiral staircase which led down to the [inside of] the Mole and Commander Brock fired his revolver down and threw a Mills bomb. You ought to have seen them nip out and try to get across to the destroyer tied up against the Mole, but this little chicken met them half way with his box of tricks, and I ticked about a dozen off.

After that Brock's further progress up the Zeebrugge Mole passes into the realm of legend. Speaking to his hometown Coventry newspaper just a week later, an unidentified marine sergeant recalled:

> Without any arms, Frank Brock rushed among the German gun crew, fighting out with his naked fists and knocking over the enemy who tried to bar his path. Behind the brave officer came our men in increasingly large numbers.
> The Germans put up a hard fight, but they were driven back step by step and all through one of the finest fights I have ever seen there was Brock letting Jerry have it with his fists. Every time he got his fist a fritz went home or at least went down. Very soon they gave him a wide berth, contenting themselves with firing at him. I can't say what happened. He disappeared from sight soon after that.

Other accounts differ in the matter of Brock's choice of weapons, but agree that he was both progressing rapidly up the Mole and full of fight. One of the men in his immediate party remembered the Commander advanc[ing] steadily up the extension towards the lighthouse. He was signalling vigorously, summoning us to follow. After a few moments there was a loud report and a cloud of smoke, and when this cleared Brock seemed to be rising slowly from his knees and for a second or two stumbling on. Then there was another roar, and this time when the fog lifted he was gone.

A voice that might have been heard in the highest councils of British science and technology, and certainly as an expert adviser on future special-forces operations, was stilled forever somewhere in the fog and chaos of a Belgian harbour wall. Frank Brock's body was never recovered. His mysterious fate is one of the most heroic and enigmatic episodes of the raid, and the only further clue as to what happened lies in the account of a German torpedo-boat officer named Ernst Baer. Baer had hurriedly left his craft on hearing the heavy guns open up above him and soon found himself, equipped with a ceremonial sword 'of Franco-Prussian vintage', engaged in a series of close-quarter duels with similarly armed British invaders rushing headlong towards the lighthouse some 200 yards behind him. 'It was a truly hellish scene,' he said, long remembering the moment when he had come across 'a dead Englishman with a gaping hole in his upper head, a burning pipe still clutched between his teeth'.

Extraordinary confusion prevailed. Whatever the state of advance intelligence on the subject at headquarters level, the sudden arrival of enemy troops in their harbour had evidently come as a total surprise to the German boat crews spending the night in the Zeebrugge basin. To Baer, however, the British raiders seemed only barely better prepared for their task. 'So far as I could see, none of the men had torches, none knew the terrain, and there was evidently uncertainty about objectives – their bewilderment was as obvious as our own.' In the raggedly broken fighting that ensued, Baer saw a fellow Torpedoboot *S-53* crewman named Hermann Künne locked in mortal combat with a khaki-clad British officer. 'It was an orchestration of violence, and before I could intervene both men had repeatedly stabbed each other about the throat and chest. They fell together virtually in each other's arms.'

It's impossible to know with total certainty whether the British officer whom Künne killed was Frank Brock, and Admiral Keyes's official report on the subject says only: 'I cannot leave ... without recording my indebtedness to [Brock] for the indispensable share he had in the operation ... When on the Mole he was very keen to acquire knowledge of the range-finding apparatus which might be of use to his country, and his efforts to do this were made without any regard to his personal safety ... I greatly deplore the loss of a man so well qualified to carry experiments in this matter further,' Keyes added, which was undoubtedly true even if it left unsaid the whole question of Brock's presence at Zeebrugge in the first place. Keyes's own obsessive desire to be close to the centre of action led him to take up position on the bridge of HMS *Warwick*, which for much of the night lay well within the range of German artillery just off the north end of the Mole.

The Times similarly believed that Brock had 'rushed ashore, [with] the smoke of battle swirling', and that but for this he 'would have attained to the highest power and eminence in his field' had he lived. A friend wrote to the same newspaper to say that 'Frank would never have yielded to the enemy', and it can only be assumed that his body was either pulverised by shellfire or fell into the sea. He is remembered today by a worn stone in Zeebrugge churchyard dedicated to three British officers and a Royal Navy mechanic 'who fell on St. George's Day 1918 and have no known grave'. Frank Brock was just 29 at the time of his death.

*

Lieutenant Richard Sandford and his five colleagues on board the surfaced *C3*, finally coming in sight of the Zeebrugge viaduct at close to midnight, were completely ignorant of the fierce land battle raging just a few hundred yards in front of them. After altering course to S. 45. E. – bringing them up for a head-on collision – they had proceeded in total radio silence and, thanks to both the patchy night rain and their own artificial fog, only limited visibility. A few minutes earlier, Sandford had flashed a signal back to one of the outlying motor launches, but the mate there 'couldn't read a flipping word of it, it came out so fast,' as he later recalled in his diary. Shortly after this, *C3* came under attack from a German shore battery which seems only to have aided the submarine's progress by shooting a flare into the sky above it. 'The viaduct was duly [silhouetted], about two points on the port bow,' Sandford reported. 'Two searchlights were also switched on and picked us up but were then switched off. By this time the viaduct was clearly visible.'

Standing at the conning tower of *C3*, a trim figure in navy-blue sweater and corduroy trousers with a short white scarf knotted at his neck, Sandford stared intently at the looming iron bridge now just a quarter of a mile, or about two minutes' sailing time, in front of him. Situated some 300 yards up the Mole from the Zeebrugge coastline, the viaduct was raised up on a trellis of wooden pilings designed to allow a tidal flow to wash through the gaps into the harbour proper, and thus prevent it from silting up into a giant sandbar. The structure also served as both a pedestrian overpass and a railway line bringing men and supplies from the mainland to the far extremity of the Mole. As such it was a vital communications link, and severing it would significantly delay any enemy reinforcements trying to make their way up to the heavy gun emplacements at the lighthouse end. If the Mole itself could be seen as a giant arm crooked protectively around Zeebrugge harbour, the idea was to now snap this at the elbow. 'The German supply line will be destroyed, and they will get nothing up from their reserves,' Keyes had written in the original plan.

Although the viaduct was in some ways the weakest link in the enemy stronghold at Zeebrugge, it was still closely guarded from both north and south. Nearby defensive units included a row of powerful searchlights, a concrete shed or pillbox for machine guns protected by strands of coiled barbed wire, and a battery of four-inch artillery pieces trained out to sea. Critically, though, these were all primarily means of dealing with an enemy intruder lying somewhere off the Zeebrugge Mole, rather than one whose mission plan was to physically ram it.

Standing at the open hatch, Lieutenant Sandford was facing the most critical decision of his life: exactly how and where to strike the enemy position, and to carry off what he at least half-seriously called the 'death-wish' element of Operation ZO. It was still less than three months since his disgrace in the disastrous fleet exercise off May Island, and we can speculate about issues such as guilt and atonement. On a more practical level, Sandford had to decide whether to use the automatic gyro mechanism that would have allowed his crew to abandon ship at a comparatively safe distance from their target, or to take the riskier but navigationally more reliable course of manually steering the 300-ton submarine to the point of impact. He chose the latter option. There were also technical questions of speed and angle of attack to be considered – Sandford had been briefed by his brother Francis on the relatively untried technique of deliberately inserting a moving vessel between two vertical rows of wooden piers – and for that matter of the crew's subsequent evacuation into the freezing waters of the North Sea. After setting their fuses, the men would have less than three minutes to make good their escape before five tons of amatol exploded into the night sky, and even in this brief lull they risked being used for target practice by the German troops lined up on the wall directly above them, or else being dragged under by their heavy clothes and drowned.

All these calculations passed through and were resolved in Sandford's mind in 60 seconds. He altered course at 12.03 a.m., and a minute later came about to N. 85. E to ensure a right-angle collision, at the same time bringing up his speed to a brisk ten knots. 'The firing from the shore was a bit severe at 200 yards,' Sandford noted dispassionately in his official account of events, 'and only the fact that the sea was a bit rough and we were up and down a good deal saved us.' For several minutes the submarine had been bucking with the waves, and cutting through the night air the crew became conscious of what Sandford called 'fizzing' noises nearby. 'When a couple of these then clanged loudly off the superstructure, it became clear that we were within the enemy's sights.'

Curiously, the Germans then ceased firing altogether as *C3* completed the last critical minute of its passage to the viaduct. Peering up at the enemy soldiers standing in a row above him, Sandford thought that 'surely they would hit us with every weapon they had', but in the event there was 'nothing but shouting and a distinct peal of laughter to be heard' in the final seconds before impact. The German reaction seems to have been one of perplexity mingled with mild amusement that a British submarine had apparently lost its way while on a mission to violate their harbour, and would now be trapped in the viaduct cross-spars as a result of this navigational blunder. 'The men took the position,' Georg von Müller, head of the German naval cabinet, wrote in his diary, 'that the English boat had gone astray in the night, and that it was momentarily to be ensnared like a fat man who had incautiously poked his head between the iron railings of a park fence – a defenceless spoil of war to be seized at our leisure.'

This was not quite what happened. As a single German spotlight played on the approaching submarine, Lieutenant Sandford first gave orders to increase speed to a rivet-shaking 12 knots, and then invited his five crewmates to join him post-haste on deck. Clambering up the ladder from the engine room, Stoker Henry Bindall watched as the huge bulk of the Mole 'now seemed to blot out the very stars in the sky … We were going full tilt when we hit [it]. It was a very good jolt,' he added, 'but you can stand a lot when you hang on tight. We ran right into the middle of the viaduct and stuck there as intended.' It was only then that one of the crew, possibly Bindall himself, remarked: 'Well, we're here all right.'

This certainly conveys the proper note of British composure under fire, although other sources suggest that on first striking the viaduct Lieutenant Sandford uttered an oath that his father the archdeacon might have disowned. It was 12.07 a.m., and roughly three-quarters of a mile away to the northeast *Vindictive* was then desperately struggling to make herself fast to the Mole. *C3* hit her mark with a hideous rending of steel and then surged upwards, her bows lifted by the force of the collision into the mesh of girders and stanchions above – 'tilted towards the sky like the great snout of a beached whale,' one witness recalled. The vessel came to a complete stop only when her conning tower crashed emphatically against one of the iron piers above her. At that point Sandford disappeared below to light his three-minute fuses and simultaneously gave the order to abandon ship.

'Our skiff was then lowered and manned by the crew,' he wrote precisely, 'who had mustered on deck prior to the collision taking place.' Leading Seaman William Cleaver remembered of this part of the exercise:

> We all waited with bated breath. The shouting on the Mole above increased. There was the clatter of rifles. At last we saw the figure of our commander. He was hurrying along the deck towards us bending low. 'Come on, sir!' we yelled in chorus.
>
> There was a fusillade of rifle bullets from the Mole that whizzed menacingly past our heads. 'Everything OK,' said Lieutenant Sandford as breathlessly he jumped aboard the skiff. He told us afterwards that his delay was due to difficulty in lighting the fuses. He had also seen that the lights were out.

The 'skiff' in question was a 12-x-6 foot, flat-bottomed wooden boat with a small outboard motor and no pretension to comfort. On coming aboard, Sandford gave the order to 'set course to the westward, heading against the current' and more pertinently to make with all due speed out into the open sea, putting as much distance between themselves and the ticking bomb of *C3* as possible. Things did not go entirely smoothly. 'Immediately on the skiff leaving the submarine, two searchlights were switched on and fire was opened with machine guns, rifles and pom-poms,' Sandford wrote. 'The boat was penetrated many times, [but] kept afloat with a pump which had been fortunately fitted. I was myself wounded, and then two of the crew.'

For the men of *C3*, the next two minutes proved to be the most collectively nerve-wracking and personally dangerous phase of the entire mission. Lieutenant Sandford was shot through the arm, but continued to issue orders as he lay half-conscious in the skiff's bows. Stoker Bindall and Coxswain Walter Harner were also wounded in the first desperate moments of the boat's flight. The German infantry standing overhead appear to have again reacted with a mixture of mild bewilderment and distinct hilarity as they watched the raiders hurriedly abandon their wrecked submarine before taking to the open sea in an unarmed wooden boat. None of the enemy soldiers seems to have suspected that the eccentric British behaviour might all have been part of some larger plan. There is no evidence that the Germans ever took the trouble to begin to evacuate the viaduct, and their steady but unhurried small-arms fire directed on the receding skiff was of the leisurely sort normally only associated with a fairground shooting booth.

Speaking to the press just a day later, Stoker Bindall remarked that he and his comrades had had 'rather a bit of bad luck' in their initial retirement in the skiff. 'The propeller fouled the exhaust pipe and left us with only a couple of oars and two minutes to get away,' he noted. 'The lights were now on us and the machine guns were going from the shore.' 'They couldn't hit a pussy cat,' the stricken Lieutenant Sandford is said to have commented to his men. At that same moment Sandford and Bindall were each shot for a second time, in both cases through the right leg. The three uninjured crewmen continued to paddle furiously to the west, taking the small boat away from the viaduct at what must have seemed to them an agonisingly slow two or three knots, meaning that they would have had time to put some 200 yards between themselves and their abandoned submarine while being systematically picked off by the enemy troops standing on the wall behind them.

At 12.12 a.m. the noise of German machine-gun and rifle fire from the viaduct top was abruptly lost in what was called the 'heaven-shaking roar' of *C3*'s detonation. To Richard Policke, manning a battery nearly a mile away on the Mole's northeastern extremity, it offered a curiously striking display that 'momentarily enthralled' the German petty officer in its 'sheer dazzling spectacle' even as he sensed that 'many of my friends-in-arms [were] dying in the inferno.'

'It was as if a rocket burst,' Policke recalled.

> There was a red-and-white spout of smoke high up above us somewhere in the direction of the land. This hung in the sky like a firework, and as I watched, another rocket seemed to burst behind it, trickling stars in the bright night sky. I saw the flash as it burst and another great plume of flame and smoke appeared and flashed across the horizon like lightning. It was incomprehensible. Some of my men were pointing, others were praying.

To Leading Seaman William Cleaver, rowing with all his might away from the immediate scene, it was an altogether more tangible and urgent experience: 'It was as though Heaven came to meet Earth in one momentary upheaval,' Cleaver recalled some 17 years later.

> *C3* and the viaduct were no more. Above the din of the raging battle the fearful fulmination rose. Great chunks of masonry fell in the water all around us. The boat rocked and swayed as though possessed. Flames shot up to a tremendous height. In their glare was visible a great break in the Mole. Out of the sea rose great twisted masses of ironwork bent into grotesque shapes.

Reliving these events in his official report, Lieutenant Sandford spoke in measured tones that still conveyed something of the sheer bedlam of the occasion:

> The charge exploded when the skiff was only 200–300 yards from the viaduct, as little progress could be made against the current.
> The effect of the explosion appeared to be great, much debris falling into the water around ... Both shore searchlights immediately went out and firing became sporadic.

Pausing for a moment in his bitterly contested attempts to land *Vindictive* on the Mole, Captain Carpenter witnessed 'a terrific explosion seen away to the westward, and we guessed that the submarine party had decisively attacked the viaduct. A seaman standing near me at the time [asked], "Was that it, sir?" The explosion presented a wonderful spectacle. The flames shot up to a great height – one mentally considered it at least a mile. Curiously enough the noise of the explosion was not heard.'

Standing just a few yards away from *Vindictive* on the deck of *Daffodil*, Harry Adams agreed with Carpenter about the visual aspects of the blast, but not its aural ones:

> There [was] a terrible deafening explosion, a thud that shook Heaven and Earth – The ships shivered and trembled – the nearest approach to an earthquake one could imagine. We had been warned to expect it, but amongst all this it had passed from one's mind – the convulsion threw you to the deck.

A six-man patrol sent by Kapitan Schütte, the battery commander on the Mole, was making its way through the fighting around a shed erected for servicing the nearby seaplane base, peering downwards at the strange sight of an enemy submarine hoisted up from the bows between the jaws of the viaduct pilings, its propeller still thrashing, when there was a sudden flash of light from within the boat's conning tower. Then *C3* exploded. From roughly 50 yards away, it seemed that there was 'a pillar of flame and an eruption that blew up the railway track and all the supports beneath, sending men and guns into the air, and setting fire to the debris which rained down into the sea'.

In the smoke and confusion, a Leading Seaman Potter, standing nearly a mile away on the flying bridge of HMS *Iphigenia* as she swept past the Mole lighthouse on her way into harbour, allegedly saw other 'vaguely unbelievable' shapes silhouetted in the explosion. According to one account,

Narrow-rimmed wheels spun out across the water, familiarly bent metal tubes and frames showed momentarily against the white screen: then, perfect and unmistakable, a complete bicycle, its rider still gripping the handlebars in a catalepsy of fright and astonishment, rode high into the air, somersaulted complete, and crashed down into the sea.

We'll return to the matter of the German bicyclist, or bicyclists, supposedly pedalling furiously into the molten core of *C3*'s eruption. For now it's enough to say that Sandford and his men achieved everything that they set out to do in their original mission. The blast tore a hole roughly 80 feet long in the viaduct. As a result, it would now be impossible for the enemy to bring up reinforcements onto the Mole from the mainland. As power and electrical lines were also destroyed in the blast, the various German gun batteries situated on either side of the viaduct could no longer communicate with each other. An unknown number of defending troops were also lost, and as the smoke cleared the men in the skiff saw 'German marines rushing up to the edge of the mangled [railway] sleepers, and injured soldiers, some lying broken on the steel below, crying for help'. One individual staggered out of the debris 'covered in dust ... His hair was scorched and his uniform singed, and as he reeled away we saw that his hand was blown off, the blood gushing from his upturned sleeve'. Grotesque as it might be to use the word 'successful' to describe an event that maimed or killed dozens of ordinary soldiers, it might with justice be applied here. The self-destruction of *C3* and the severing of the link between the Mole and the mainland was the one part of the whole intricate apparatus of Operation ZO to go entirely, and spectacularly, to plan.

The legend of the German cyclists who had failed to notice the plume of billowing flame and smoke directly in front of them as they rushed to reinforce the Mole, and instead rode to their doom like so many Merrie Melody cartoon characters still frantically pumping their legs after running headlong over the side of a cliff, seems to have been one of those cases, not uncommon in military history, where rumour and fact become difficult to disentangle. The story probably originated in Howard Keeble's book *The Glory of Zeebrugge* that first appeared, sponsored by the British government, just weeks after the raid. It's certainly a vivid touch, but it remains doubtful whether anyone standing on the bridge of *Iphigenia* could have seen that far away in the dark, and no men on bicycles were among the German troops whose bodies were later recovered from the silt under the demolished railway line. For all that, Alfred Carpenter seemed to endorse the story when he wrote in his 1921 memoir: 'We heard afterwards that a Hun cyclist corps was hurriedly sent to reinforce the Mole garrison, and, not knowing that the viaduct had been destroyed, they were precipitated into the sea and thus infringed the Gadarene copyright.'

Again, this version of events would seem to rely on hearsay rather than eyewitness testimony. Carpenter was asked further about it while on a promotional visit to New York, and said only: 'That was the story the men told themselves, though I don't believe there was ever a named declarant to swear to it.' Like the legend of the

Angel of Mons, or that of the vodka-swilling Cossack troops who had mysteriously appeared on the streets of Glasgow in 1914, it seems to be a mixture of rumour, speculation and deliberate disinformation of the sort that often flourishes in wartime. Captain Arthur Chater, who personally fought on the bloodied ground between *Vindictive*'s berth and the viaduct, later remarked: 'It belongs more in fairyland than the history books.'

Meanwhile, speaking to the *Daily Mail* from his hospital bed just 24 hours after the raid, Lieutenant Sandford made light of the whole ordeal:

> I set the fuse myself and I think the thing was done all right. We were lucky in being picked up afterwards. The crew did their duty, every man. They were all volunteers and picked men. We got in without difficulty and were not found by the searchlights until we were getting away.

What Sandford failed to mention was that after the explosion he and his five shipmates had flailed around in their leaking skiff for several more minutes in the burning sea before help arrived in the form of a crudely motorised wooden jolly boat rather gingerly making its way down the length of the outer Mole. This latter craft had initially been towed in by the destroyer *Moorsom*, and had twice keeled over in the heavy swell before slipping her line altogether. 'It is by no means clear how or why she righted herself,' her commanding officer reported. The man now steering her through the flaming debris of the viaduct to retrieve the survivors of *C3* was Richard Sandford's one-eyed elder brother Francis. One published account of the subsequent rescue concludes:

> Ten minutes after the explosion, the picket-boat [arrived] and a very worried and anxious Francis Sandford saw his brother and the crew of *C3* brought inboard. [They] could not have been in more considerate hands – but it is noteworthy that, with the limited medical attention on board a picket-boat, Richard Sandford insisted that Bindall and Harner were given aid and made comfortable before he would allow his brother to attend to his own wounds.

Lieutenant Sandford and his shipmates were then transferred to the destroyer HMS *Phoebe*, which circled the area for the next two hours looking for other survivors of the raid while coming under repeated attack from the German shore batteries before finally returning to Dover at around eight in the morning. The shed where the injured men were processed on landing lacked food and water, as well as medical assistance. 'The end to a perfect day,' Richard Sandford commented.

❋

Although *C3*'s role in Operation ZO was a uniquely bold and critical one, it wasn't the only instance of a small boat causing significant trouble for the German garrison at Zeebrugge. There was the motor launch *CMB 22B*, for example, which continued to surge tirelessly around the Mole lighthouse in order to lay smoke for the blockships and exchange somewhat unequal fire with the heavy-calibre shore batteries. Two days later, a young midshipman named David Morris wrote home of his experience on this vessel:

> We had a terrible fight, but quite enjoyed it, and of course we won. I got two Lewis Gun bullets in my left arm, just as we got to Zeebrugge Mole, but managed to keep on firing until all was over. When we arrived 15-inch shells were flying about and we got it pretty hot ... Our officers were wounded – one of them having 14 bullets through his chest – and I helped to bring the boat back. We had been 35 hours without sleep, and had hardly any food, so you can guess we were pretty exhausted.

Some of the other smaller boats displayed the same unfortunate tendency seen during Operation EC1 to crash into one another. Captain Ralph Collins was in overall command of a flotilla of four motor launches. He later reported to the Admiralty: 'ML 262 (Lieutenant R. Allen, RNVR) was in collision with ML 513 (Unit 1), and, temporarily disabled, the boat was towed seaward.' Another supporting launch, *ML 110*, was hit by three German shells in rapid succession as she approached the Zeebrugge lighthouse. Her commanding officer, 40-year-old Lieutenant-Commander James Dawbarn Young, stoically gave the order for the crew to scuttle the ship by smashing a hole in her hull with an axe, and then to take to her small life raft, before collapsing with a mortal wound to his chest. Young's body was brought back to Dover the following day, and on 28 April he was laid to rest near his family home at Saunderton in the Chilterns. A report said: 'There was a good turnout, and two Royal Navy riflemen pranged off a volley over the coffin.' A lawyer, author and chartered surveyor, Young was unmarried at the time of his death. In his will he left £1,262 6s (roughly £26,000 today) to his elderly parents. A magazine article published in June 1918 quoted an *ML 110* shipmate as saying: 'When he was caught by the enemy fire and put out of action, the skipper said: "Never mind me, lads, carry on."'

A similar fate awaited *ML 424*, which was caught by the German shore batteries as she emerged from the artificial fog at the lighthouse end of the Mole. Her captain, 28-year-old Lieutenant Oswald Robinson, a skilled mimic who had been the star turn at the previous year's dockyard Christmas party, was killed instantly, and two of her deckhands were seriously injured, one of them dying a few minutes later. The boat's second-in-command, Lieutenant John Robinson, then announced that he was blasted if he would allow his boat to be captured intact by the enemy, and at that stage the crew set fire to the engine room before taking to their dinghy. They were eventually rescued and returned to Dover.

Some of *ML 424*'s sister ships were meanwhile able to slip past the outer Zeebrugge guns and launch torpedo attacks inside the harbour basin. *ML 32A* successfully engaged an enemy steamship lying at anchor about halfway down the sheltered side of the Mole, although according to the official report: 'An explosion was heard, but Commanding Officer states that he could not see the effect owing to thick smoke screen. After firing he returned to Dunkirk.'

Much the same confused situation applied in the case of *CMB 5* when she too came in view of Zeebrugge a few minutes before midnight on 22 April: 'A large German destroyer was proceeding at 12 knots on E.N.E. course,' the boat's commanding officer, Sub-Lieutenant Cedric Outhwaite, noted placidly. Outhwaite's orders were to engage only those enemy vessels actually lying at anchor inside the harbour, but the prospect of attacking a 320-foot-long hostile warship equipped with at least four heavy guns and an equal number of pom-poms and torpedo tubes seems to have appealed to his sporting instincts. He immediately turned *CMB 5* around, and – to quote his official report – 'increased speed to 20 knots, setting course for collision with the enemy ship'.

Again in Outhwaite's words:

> The destroyer apparently observed CMB 5 in light of star shell, switched on foremost searchlight, lighting up CMB 5, and opened fire. At 00.05 CMB 5 fired her torpedo at a range of 650 yards, turning off to starboard as soon as torpedo was clear. Torpedo was observed to hit enemy beneath her forward searchlight, but damage could not be ascertained owing to heavy gunfire evidently concentrated from end of Mole and enemy vessel still continued, but in a lesser degree.

Shortly after this, it was found that *CMB 5* had developed a badly overheated main piston, and dense clouds of steam were seen to be pouring through her deck as a result. 'Our engine was not running satisfactorily,' Outhwaite was forced to admit as the wooden planks began to glow and warp under his feet. 'At 01.50, course was set as requisite for Dunkirk,' he continued. 'At 08.40, engines were stopped alongside CMB base.' Some weeks later, Sub-Lieutenant Outhwaite was awarded the DSC for his heroically insubordinate actions at Zeebrugge, although it's said that Admiral Keyes took the opportunity to quietly take him aside following the investiture and suggest that he might consider a return to civilian life as soon as practical after the war.

✳

Throughout this period of relatively fluid small-boat activity, *Vindictive* continued to lie immobile in her berth on the upper side of the Zeebrugge Mole, an increasingly misshapen hulk of twisted steel, dense smoke and appalling human carnage thanks to the persistent close-range attentions of the German guns, but remarkably still afloat. Combatants on both sides thought it one of the most curious sights they witnessed at any stage of the war. Of all the descriptions of the chaotic events surrounding *Vindictive*'s landing, perhaps that of the unnamed marine quoted in the next day's British press best captured the scene:

> It was raining hard and our storming party was forming up when a big burly German loomed out and made a dive for the nearest men, but before he could do anything our captain knocked him on the head with his truncheon. He was killed outright. We then received the order to charge and we rushed along the Mole to the shore. We bayoneted and shot all the men we came across.

The noise of the firing mingled with the shouts and cries of the men was terrible. It was fair slaughter, and all around us was hubbub, but we kept our heads and put the wind up the Boche completely. The Germans [who] scrambled up the hatchway to meet us, many of them only partially dressed and half-awake, were knocked on the head and tumbled back again.

Watching proceedings from *Vindictive*'s forward flamethrower hut, Captain Carpenter could only look on in horror as the commandeered ferry *Iris*, easing away from the relative shelter of the Mole, so low down and close in under the wall that the German heavy guns had been unable to depress sufficiently to fire on her, was now struck by a screaming salvo of artillery fire from shore. At least one shell scored a direct hit on the ferry's bridge. Carpenter later wrote:

Valentine Gibbs, Iris's captain, was mortally wounded. I had known Val since he was a boy of 13. Even at that age he had shown himself to be absolutely fearless. In peace days he had won the great race on the Cresta Run at St. Moritz; in war he had volunteered for every dangerous operation for which he had the remotest chance of selection. At last his opportunity had come and he lived for nought else than to put Iris alongside Zeebrugge Mole. I was told afterwards that in his short periods of consciousness after being wounded he asked and repeated but one question, 'How are things going?' and he continued to ask how things were going until he died.

When Gibbs succumbed, *Iris*'s command passed to the ship's navigating officer, 30-year-old Lieutenant George Spencer. Despite suffering a serious leg injury when another shell smashed into *Iris*'s bridge, Spencer remained at his post, gasping out orders and eventually finding the strength to jot down a return course to Dover on a bloodstained scrap of paper which is still preserved today. He died the following morning in a Kent hospital, one of at least 110 men to fall during the roughly 55 minutes *Iris* was at Zeebrugge. Below decks, the carnage was just as fearful as above. Lance-Corporal George Calverley could still remember his experience there sixty years later:

I said to one of my section, 'Well Cornforth, the worst is over – where are the others?' He opened his lips to answer, gave a sigh and fell forward at my feet. I bent down towards him and woke up about five yards from where we had been standing … I was on my side and was scared, then happy as I gradually moved my limbs and stood up, and as my hearing came back I could hear moaning and cries of pain and someone yell 'Put that light out' – We were in darkness except for an occasional electric-blue bulb which gave just a glimmer of light.

There was similar havoc on board *Vindictive* during her 60-minute vigil alongside the Mole. 'An hour can be a very long time indeed,' Captain Carpenter later noted. Two heavy rounds of shellfire had dispatched eight of the ship's nine-man forward marine gun crew early on in her tenure. The sole survivor was Norman Finch, the hearty young sergeant from Birmingham, who in the words of his citation for the VC:

… Severely wounded, nevertheless showed consummate bravery, remaining in his battered and exposed position. He once more got a Lewis-gun into action, and kept up a continuous fire, harassing the enemy on the Mole, until the foretop received another direct hit, the remainder of the armament being then completely put out of action. Before the top was destroyed Sgt. Finch had done valuable work, and by his bravery undoubtedly saved many lives.

During that hour of *Vindictive*'s agony she presented a shambles of buckled equipment and broken men that in time seemed so grotesque as to be part of some cosmic jest of almost unfathomable cruelty. There were figures suddenly illuminated by shellfire, their faces burned away, or blood running from an empty sleeve or trouser leg; others who continued to mechanically pace the deck, chattering busily away to themselves before collapsing from their wounds; and those who gasped pitifully for breath as fuel-oil tanks ruptured or gas shells invaded the mess decks. 'The first batch of wounded began to arrive, and from then on until *Vindictive* left the stream of casualties was almost continuous,' Staff Surgeon McCutcheon wrote with some restraint. 'It was soon found necessary to utilise the ward room, aft deck, sick bay, all cabins, and, in fact, all available space of the ship between the decks for the disposal of the wounded.'

Above McCutcheon's head, Captain Carpenter, seeking to boost morale during this critical hour, shouted over the noise of the explosions 'about everything going splendidly ... The cheer that went up will live long in my memory,' he wrote. 'The crowd almost barred my way in their excitement, and the question which caught my ear more than any other was, "Have we won, sir, have we won?" It was just as if the whole affair was a football match.'

The German artillery fire, which was disconcerting enough for *Vindictive* as she lay partially screened by the sheer bulk of the Mole, was a far more serious matter for Operation ZO's outlying rescue and supply ships. Among these was Roger Keyes's flagship HMS *Warwick*, which spent most of what he later called a 'warm' night lying in the choppy seas some 400 yards off the Zeebrugge lighthouse and thus comfortably within range of the enemy's main six-gun battery. From time to time *Warwick*'s commanding officer, 43-year-old Victor Campbell, a veteran of Robert Scott's Terra Nova expedition, ordered the ship to patrol the immediate area, 'the better to molest the shore guns and to take on board our survivors.' During one such manoeuvre, at around 12.20 a.m., *Warwick* passed out of a bank of smoke flares to suddenly present a seemingly unmissable target to Kapitan Schütte and his men.

The ensuing exchange of fire was 'short but sharp', in Campbell's later description. 'The Mole itself appeared to be a long ring of fire, and everywhere one looked the billowing black clouds reflected a bright red glow from the flames.' An unnamed member of the ship's company told the press:

> We were not 'shadowing' and 'reporting' at Zeebrugge. We were searching and fighting. I could see Admiral Keyes standing on our compass bridge, dressed in full uniform, white muffler round his neck, talking calmly away as the sea exploded all around us – an unpretentious, rather plain figure, ears poking out from under his old cap, very solid and British – completely

unmoved by events, and by his very presence filling one with a wonderful sort of cheer that things would turn out all right.

Meanwhile, the distinctive noise of a pitched land-and-sea battle raging nearby had piqued the interest of the previously captured British officers Seton and Allerton Smith locked in their disused gun emplacement near the lighthouse end of the Mole. A book published in 1919 has the two PoWs then promptly deciding to break down the reinforced steel door of their cell and, having done this, marauding at will up and down the parapet top attacking the various German guard units they encountered there, before dropping some 80 feet into the sea to be rescued by a passing British motor boat. In the book's energetically sustained idiom:

> 'Time for us to be making tracks, old man,' shouted Alec [Seton] to his chum.
> 'Yes, the show's over,' rejoined the other officer, as the pair began to retrace their footsteps. 'Jolly fine stunt – eh, what?'
> For quite 200 yards they fought their way through pungent vapours, hoping to find an exit and thus mingle with the storming-party as the men withdrew to their ships.
> Suddenly they found themselves confronted by a mass of blackened rubble, the stones still warm to the touch. A hasty examination showed that a heavy charge of gun-cotton had blown in the tunnel, completely cutting off escape.
> 'Properly dished!' exclaimed Smith disgustedly. 'We're trapped!'
> 'Tails-up!' exhorted his companion. 'I know of a way. Game for a swim?'

Although none of the other eyewitness accounts mention the presence of two British fifth-columnists making their way down the Mole, wrecking various German installations as they went, the story may not be entirely without substance. Kapitan Schütte later recalled some 'irregularly dressed British troops' throwing grenades and charging down a flight of steps at their startled opponents, the survivors among whom had retreated smartly into the night. A few moments later, Schütte believed that 'machine-gun fire [had] come at us from that general area', although the situation on the Mole was then so confused with 'a hail of bullets, bombs and shells break[ing] out from every part' and 'different skirmishes overlapping and becoming one action' that no one could say for sure if this was the work of the two escapees or not. Most of the attacks on the Mole were hopelessly uncoordinated, in large part because so many of the landing party's officers had already been killed before they could reach shore. The privates and ratings who survived fought ferociously, but as one marine noted, 'There was no real focus. No grids or maps. No chaps with torches throwing light onto your path; just darkness, blood and muck.'

The ear-splitting and sustained roar of the guns continued almost without a pause from 11.57 p.m. until 12.25 a.m., when HMS *Thetis* and the other two blockships – the main thrust of the night's proceedings – made their appearance. In their final minutes the three obsolete cruisers had to pass between the Scylla of the Mole batteries on their starboard side and the Charybdis of the various navigational hazards to port.

We've seen that *Thetis* herself went aground before she could reach the canal mouth where she was due to sink herself. This was not an end to the blockships' problems. As *Thetis*'s commanding officer Ralph Sneyd put it in his report:

> The ship was about 300 yards from the eastern pier head … She had a list to starboard side by the fire from the Mole. This fire still continued, either from guns on the Mole or from craft alongside it, and the ship was also hit several times by guns firing from the shore. One or two machine guns were also firing at the ship. The six-inch gun on the forecastle engaged these guns until our own smoke made it impossible to see.

HMS *Intrepid* and HMS *Iphigenia* then went in past the beached *Thetis* and were met in turn by heavy fire from the Mole batteries. By then *Vindictive* was locked in her own protracted close-range battle with the enemy's entrenched troops, men were seen running the length of the parapet top with upturned cutlasses, and *C3* had spectacularly blown apart the nearby viaduct. 'A stealthy approach was not an option,' *Intrepid*'s commanding officer Lieutenant Bonham Carter later noted with due naval reserve. The entire inner harbour and canal entrance were shrouded by a vast pall of grey smoke which was repeatedly stabbed by the light of exploding star shells. As an added complication, *Iphigenia* soon took a direct hit to her forward steam pipe, and as a result the ship was wreathed in a cloud of blinding white gas. Peering out from the bridge, Lieutenant Billyard-Leake now faced the further challenge of steering a nearly 4,000-ton concrete-filled vessel built in the reign of Queen Victoria into a narrow, heavily fortified channel with only some three feet of visibility in front of him. When the smoke momentarily lifted, 'I found I was heading for the western pier,' he wrote. 'I went full steam astern, and brought the ship in between a dredger and barge, severing the barge from the dredger. I then went ahead starboard and drove the barge up the canal.'

As the strange and violent ballet proceeded in the Zeebrugge harbour basin, the raiders on shore continued to fight their way through to the beaten zone of the heavy gun emplacements. One navy demolition party succeeded in reaching the stone steps of the lighthouse that lay at the far end of the Mole where it jutted out into the North Sea. An unnamed sailor from this group was quoted in the press two weeks later: 'The building was stormed and battered with bombs. The lantern was soon demolished, and afterwards the whole structure was completely wrecked. If there were any Germans in charge [there], then they surely died at their posts.'

Other accounts from those on board the nearby British ships differ as to whether the threat of the lighthouse was ever fully addressed, but agree that the galling fire continued unabated from the heavy guns immediately next to it. Below decks on *Thetis*, Lieutenant-Commander Boddie recalled the moment when his ship passed into the cauldron of the inner harbour:

> When we got near the Vindictive, which had then been secured to the Mole for 20 minutes, we came under heavy attack, and the telegraphs went to 'Full' speed … After pressing on like

this for about 6 minutes, and I estimated we had attained our maximum speed of 16 knots, the starboard engine suddenly came to a grinding stop, with steam and hot water gushing from every pore. A moment later, the port engine did the same ... I telephoned the bridge to report the débâcle, and to suggest that we had run aground.

Working alongside Boddie in the ship's engine room, a seaman named Frank Gale remembered, 'The [Germans] started firing at us as soon as we came round the lighthouse, but all we got down below was splinters, smoke and gas. We put our gas masks on for a little while, but as they hampered our movements we took them off again.' The crew of *Thetis* were among the first to awake to the realities of the Mole defences as they still existed some half an hour after *Vindictive* had landed her first naval and marine storming parties there. Heroically as these men had fought, they had clearly not spiked the main German guns. Indeed, the only relief for the invading blockships came in the form of a spectacular (if ultimately indecisive) own-goal on the defenders' part. An account of the raid published in 1929 quotes a U-boat captain stationed at Zeebrugge as complaining: 'As the blockships came in, the junior commander of the land battery at one side of the entrance thought they were friendly torpedo boats and did not fire on them.' The submariner went on to add that 'only about half our soldiers had wanted to fight', and the particular gunnery officer at fault on this occasion was 'a well-known imbecile'.

The other German battery commanders stationed around the harbour seem to have been made of sterner stuff, and one screaming salvo duly hit *Thetis* full on as she lined up for her final approach to the canal mouth. At that a vivid red flame shot up from her forepart, then came an explosion forward that was followed by a column of billowing black smoke. When this cloud lifted it was seen that *Thetis*'s six-inch gun had been physically wrenched from its mooring, and that its two-man crew was missing. Threading his way forward to assess the damage, one officer saw what he thought was a length of rope lying on the deck, only to realise that it was a severed arm, still covered by a uniform sleeve, 'some of the flesh hanging out loose, and the blood flowing fast'.

✳

To those still on the Mole, it seemed to be a case of conducting a series of increasingly disjointed personal skirmishes – in some cases, more of a punch-up – rather than following any coherent battle plan. Some of the men's jujitsu training proved useful in this part of the operation. Captain Arthur Chater of the 4th Battalion, RMLI, looked on with approval while one of his team disabled a German sentry by kicking him in the testicles. 'After that, all the steam seemed to go out of the poor devil.' Writing home a few days later, Chater would describe in some detail the confused nature of the land operation as a whole. Apart from the question of getting the men ashore in the first place, he had no very high opinion of the 'infernally complicated'

signalling arrangements in force for those still desperately fighting their way towards
the heavy guns at the lighthouse end:

> We discussed the situation [and] decided to organise an attack on the fortified zone along the
> Mole. This entailed attacking a prepared position across some 200 yards of flat pavement devoid
> of any form of cover. Led by Capt. Bamford, the units started to move forward. They were well
> out in the open, when [*Vindictive*'s] siren was heard making what was taken to be the emergency
> recall signal … The signal arranged for this was the sounding of the morse letter 'K' [for Keyes]
> on the ship's siren. Although the siren was blowing, it was not making this sound. We had
> expected to be ashore for one and a quarter hours, but we had been there only 45 minutes.

While Captain Chater doubled back to *Vindictive* to confirm whether his men
were supposed to attack or retire, individual marines doggedly pushed ahead up the
Mole. There was 'no definite and arbitrary plan by that stage,' one unnamed officer
recalled some 20 years later:

> I saw one man running up the parapet-top liberally spraying his portable flamethrower at
> anything in his path. All hell was let loose. Some of the other boys crept up to the deck of a
> German tub tied up on the inner side of the Mole and jumped aboard her. Someone else was
> chucking grenades at a dark shape – a fortified shed of some sort – looming up out of the haze
> in front of us. It was all a series of uncoordinated actions, and there was no time for any of
> the officers to collect their ragged thoughts or the remnants of their units and form them into
> any real plan of attack.

One of the marines in the ad-hoc destroyer boarding party told the press two days
later:

> I belong to what you might call 'the pirate crew' that stormed one of the German ships. The
> first Hun we saw was a sentry on deck. We quickly downed him, and then made a dash for
> the hatchway, knocking the German sailors back much quicker than they could scramble up.
> Before I left I approached our dear old friend, the sentry, and do not know whether he
> was dead or not, but I said, 'Sorry, old chap, but I am a marine myself, so there is no harm
> in taking your helmet.'

It remains arguable whether the various landing parties ever fully achieved their
objectives of silencing the Germans' heavy guns located at the lighthouse end of the
Mole, then of crippling the lighthouse itself, and finally of hoisting a red beacon
in the same vicinity to help lead the three blockships into the harbour. But they
undeniably created a spectacular and sustained diversion. Speaking just two weeks
later, Able Seaman Bernard Devlin, the young Geordie who had volunteered to join
the assault party that clambered off *Daffodil* onto the Mole, cheerfully remembered
the 'total shambles' of the occasion: 'I went [ashore] on my hands and knees and
when I got there was surprised to think how I had escaped injury. Others however
were less fortunate, for I saw a lot shot down. The place was an inferno.'

One of Devlin's section added that the front rank of the German machine gunners
on the Mole had at first seemed to fire 'oddly high' over their attackers' heads, and
that in his opinion this was a deliberate ploy to encourage the raiders to remain

upright in their advance, 'as a few moments later the second rank fired low with a volley that cut our people practically in half.'

While the land action continued, so did the improvised and often frenziedly violent encounters between small groups of opposing troops. During the height of the battle, with 'dozens of men running about, many others dead or dying', only cursory contact with officers – and thus adherence to the master plan – was possible. An unnamed naval rating recalled six years later:

> The parapet was soon pitted with bullet-holes, dead men sprawled here and there, faces blown away, and nearly every one of the casualties lying on his back. A star shell, bursting occasionally from behind the clouds, shone pitilessly down on this sorry land of the dead. And everywhere was the ghastly sound of screaming and sobbing.

In general these were conditions not even those on the Western Front would have envied. William Gough of the navy air service gave some more of the flavour of the carnage on the Mole when he remembered

> crossing the open part of the wall, and, turning, [I] saw three men break from cover behind a wrecked locomotive. Two fell almost immediately, but the third kept running on, firing a pistol as he went. I returned his fire with my revolver and he then seemed to single me out as his particular enemy. Then followed a revolver duel at a gradually decreasing range – and we began at about 30 yards – until when we were absolutely in contact, he went down with a bullet in the throat.

In time Gough made his way back to *Vindictive*, where he saw a marine sergeant standing in an 'awkward pose' near one of the ship's gangways and realised that the man was trying to hide the sight of the remains of one of their comrades who was lying on the deck, the upper part of his body severed from the lower one.

Meanwhile *Vindictive* herself continued to exchange thunderous shellfire with the German shore batteries roughly 1,000 yards to the south. This was an unusual arrangement for a heavily armed cruiser sitting at anchor and whose guns were more often trained on targets that lay up to 20 miles away. After half an hour of near-continuous mutual bombardment, Alfred Carpenter remarked of conditions aboard: 'Shells were still hitting us every few seconds and many casualties were being caused by flying splinters. Large pieces of the funnels and ventilators were being torn out and hurled in all directions. One wondered how much more of this battering the ship could stand.'

Clearly, the sands were running out both for *Vindictive* and the men grimly fighting their way along the Mole. Now all that remained was the matter of whether the blockships could effectively seal up the entrance to the canal. The 'bloody and arduous first phase' of Operation ZO was at an end, Carpenter reflected, but in many ways 'even greater perils to achieving our objectives' lay in wait during the second half of the mission.

CHAPTER 7

Eight VCs Before Dawn

The arrival of the three blockships in the cauldron of Zeebrugge's inner harbour shortly after midnight on 23 April 1918 signalled the defining event of the British raid. By then the opposing land forces had fought each other to a near-standstill, and thanks to the efforts of *C3* the attackers could take credit for having severed the main theatre of battle from the enemy's reserves. Set against this, the heavy guns continued to pound the British ships large and small, and the raiders had already suffered some 400 casualties out of the total 1,600 personnel involved. At the moment HMS *Thetis* and her two sister-ships appeared out of the fog around the end of the harbour Mole and made for the entrance to the canal where they would scuttle themselves, the final outcome of Operation ZO remained in doubt. 'It was a hair-raising affair at that point,' Stuart Bonham Carter, commanding HMS *Intrepid*, later said:

> After a lull, the German batteries opened up on us full force, and the draught of their shells could be felt on the back of one's neck. Sheer hell broke loose. Many was the man among us who, in the thick of battle, felt certain that his next breath would be his last. One of the cutters in the line immediately ahead of us was blown to smithereens. We knew then that we had our work cut out for us.

Not surprisingly, the combined excitement and terror of the whole exercise affected even the most hardened British sailors and marines aboard the three ships. Some crew members prayed out loud as they made their final approach to their destination. Others threw away their playing cards and promised never to gamble again. One 'burly-looking fellow' below decks on *Thetis* publicly vowed to dedicate his life to the Church should he be spared. The ship's chief engine officer, Lieutenant-Commander Boddie, later remembered a 'sensation of nakedness' as they rounded Zeebrugge lighthouse, at which point his teeth had started chattering softly. 'It was interesting to observe the men,' he recorded. 'They showed similar symptoms of nervousness to those I felt, and which I hoped I hadn't shown. They smoked cigarettes hard, almost violently, [and] stoked the fires far more vigorously than was necessary for 7 knots.'

So fast-moving had been the night's events up till then that it may only have been now that the Germans first grasped the true intent of the raid. Watching from his shell-torn perch on *Vindictive*, Capt. Carpenter believed:

> The attacks on the Mole, the blowing-up of the viaduct, the explosions of torpedoes on the inside of the Mole, the smoke, the rapid changes of visibility, and the terrific noise on all sides had combined to leave the enemy in a hopeless state of stupefaction as to our real purpose. We heard afterwards that they believed a forced landing on the coast was in progress.

Thetis took the brunt of the German fire, struggling on to her objective, as we've seen, in a miasma of fog and shellfire, dragging the enemy's boom nets behind her, before finally flaming out some 300 yards short of her goal. There, momentarily, she sat, steam pouring from her holed starboard side, as the German shore batteries continued to use her for target practice. Over the next few agonising minutes *Thetis* presented even more of a sitting duck to the enemy guns than *Vindictive*, which at least had the advantage of lying under the sheltering bulk of the Mole. 'It was not a sustainable position,' Boddie later noted with some restraint. After a 'seeming eternity of being liberally plastered by artillery shot', *Thetis*'s crew somehow succeeded in getting her starboard engine working again. The ship lurched forward like a badly battered but resilient old boxer hearing the bell, ground on for a hundred yards or so to her right, and then finally gave up the fight and settled down into the dredged channel immediately outside the entrance piers of the canal.

Thetis's dying convulsion was made all the more remarkable by the fact that by then there was effectively no one left on the bridge able to steer her. As Lieutenant-Commander Boddie, toiling away in the noise and heat of the engine room, recalled:

> In our predicament, I tried to phone the Bridge, to report the position, and to seek instructions about getting the men away to the boats. There was no response, perhaps the Bridge had been demolished, so I instructed a stoker to make his way [there], along the port side of the ship, find [Commander Ralph] Sneyd, if he was alive, make my report, and get instructions. The messenger did not return.
>
> Ten minutes later I sent another, along the starboard side of the ship. He did not return either. Meanwhile our own smoke had been turned on, and we were now enveloped in dense fog, but still getting some random plastering. At last I came across [Lieutenant George] Belben, who told me the captain was wounded but alive, that Lambert had been gassed by bursting shell, and was bereft of speech, but otherwise uninjured, that one of our two and only [life] boats had been shot to pieces, and that one of the funnels had come down with a crash.

Commander Sneyd was in fact badly wounded in the head and both legs, and suffering from the effects of smoke inhalation, but still actively monitoring the 'extremely uneven' course of events from what remained of his bridge. Reconciled to *Thetis* having now well and truly foundered just short of her mark, his first concern was to blow the ship's charges and leave her at what he deemed an at least 'awkward' angle for the Germans to salvage. When Sneyd peered through the cloud of artificial fog and shellfire eddying around the wheelhouse, however, he found

The foremost firing keys had not been brought to the firing position, the petty officer stationed for that purpose having been killed. Owing to our own smoke and the fumes of a shell which burst under the forecastle, I was unable to find them. The charges were fired with the after firing keys and detonated satisfactorily, the ship sinking very quickly.

According to one of *Thetis*'s stokers who had by then made his way topside, Sneyd had turned to his stricken deputy, Lieutenant Francis Lambert, thanked him for his efforts, and formally announced that he and the other crew members now had his permission to abandon ship. Lambert had found sufficient power of speech to reply, 'If we do have a splash, sir, it's been an honour to serve with you. If only we can put a few more whiz-bangs up them before it's all over.' At that Sneyd and Lambert had stumbled out together to one of the ship's forward rope ladders. A cutter was waiting for them below, the 59 survivors of *Thetis*'s original crew of 72 already aboard it. Among them was Lieutenant-Commander Boddie, who remembered of their escape:

> [Sneyd] attempted to swarm down one of the falls, but was so weak from his wounds that he just dropped into the sea. In helping to drag him out of the water, I got the impression he would have preferred to have been left to drown. Lambert, in the stern of the cutter, had missed this incident, and while the rest of us were itching to get away, had swarmed back on board to search for the captain, which caused a little delay.

The cutter, badly holed by German small-arms fire, and with gas jetting violently from a damaged exhaust, was then rowed furiously down channel towards the exit from the harbour. Just as they were on the verge of finally sinking, the men were pulled aboard *ML 526*, one of the small boats busily patrolling the area. Many of *Thetis*'s surviving crew were covered in oil and chattering with cold, and, as the ship's Australian-born stoker Frank Gale found, even then their problems weren't over:

> We scrambled on board [*ML 526*] and crouched down. We were a bit crowded, as they had half the crew of another ship on board. And in consequence she was a little top heavy. She put on full speed and kept a smoke screen going to cover our tracks, but [the Germans] put up star shells and bombarded us for forty minutes from the great land batteries.

As well as the smoke and the chokingly thick gas, there was the natural swell of the sea. Before long the boat 'reeked of vomit'. Eventually taken aboard the more spacious *ML 286*, the men were each given a clean towel and a tot of rum. One of *Thetis*'s engine room crew later recalled that before being offered these amenities, he had first been asked by his rescuers, 'Are you English or German?' Of the subsequent passage out of Zeebrugge harbour, Lieutenant-Commander Boddie remembered

> The captain [was] in a distressed state of mind. He had been soaked to the skin when he fell into the sea as we left Thetis … The first thing Sneyd did was to pass me a saucepan, in which he had just been sick, saying that Lambert was still suffering from the shell fumes he had inhaled, and that every man on board ought to vomit. I had no difficulty in complying with this order.

Despite managing to collide with another British motor boat while on her way out of the harbour, *ML 286* eventually returned safely to Dover. Four lorries had been laid on there to take *Thetis*'s crew to a nearby barracks, but only three were needed. Sneyd himself survived, full of remorse for not having laid his ship in the proper position, staying on to serve his country with distinction for another 16 years. Lieutenant Hugh Littleton, commanding *ML 526*, was awarded the DSO for his actions at Zeebrugge. The citation read: 'It was solely due to his courage and daring that his boat succeeded in making good her escape with the survivors of the "Thetis".'

Following her sister ship into the inner harbour, the officers and men of HMS *Intrepid* at first enjoyed an eerily quiet passage towards their preassigned blocking position. For them, it might have been a peacetime training exercise in the North Sea. Through his binoculars, Lieutenant Bonham Carter could make out a flickering green light on *Thetis*'s starboard side, which enabled him to pass safely behind her and reach the canal mouth having suffered only superficial damage from the German shore artillery.

This peace was short-lived. Bonham Carter soon observed the heavy fingers of the enemy's ten-inch guns swinging onto him from a range of only 300 yards (or 'about three laps of Tooting Bec lido') and the next few minutes were, in his measured term, 'interesting'. As she neared her mark, *Intrepid* also faced the problem posed by her own artificial fog jetting straight back at her in the wind, with the result that the forepart of the ship was wreathed in blindingly thick grey smoke. Bonham Carter then tried to swing his 300-foot-long vessel by alternately starting and stopping his port and starboard engines across the mouth of the channel – a manoeuvre he later compared to driving a runaway train down a zigzagging downhill track while simultaneously being pelted by gunfire from somewhere above – and succeeded only in beaching her on the silt. By then he had at least inserted his ship into the gap between the piers marking the canal entrance, and in fact was less than half a mile away from the inner lock gates. There was something of a squabble in later years about whether *Intrepid* could have found the strength to go on to ram these, thus truly severing the link between Bruges and the sea. Bonham Carter would not dwell on this particular scenario in his report, which notes only: 'After getting to my position … I waited for the crews to get into the life boats, but finding the ship was coming astern, I had to blow her up before Engineer Sub-Lieut Meikle, ERAs Smith and Farrell, and Stoker PO Smith could get out of the engine room.' All four of these individuals survived the shock first of HMS *Iphigenia* glancing off their port bow in the fog, and then of their ship being blown apart under their feet. Three days later, Stoker Thomas Farrell remarked to the press of this experience:

> I was on board *Intrepid*, [and] as a matter of fact the last man to leave the engine room. We carried a number of mines, and when the engine room blew up I jumped overboard and swam. One of our cutters had already been blown to smithereens, and it was with the help of others and some rafts that we were saved.

Another of *Intrepid*'s engine-room intake, Able Seaman Frederick Hide, also jumped off the ship as she went down and eventually swam towards what he assumed was a British motor launch circling round the wreck site in the fog. As he clambered aboard, however, he realised that his supposed rescuers were Germans, one of whom extended his bayonet and announced in English that he was now their prisoner. 'Go to hell,' Hide replied, and jumped back into the water. 'Everything seemed like slow motion,' he later recorded of the experience of swimming back towards *Intrepid* while under heavy fire, but as the smoke drew in the Germans gave up the chase and he survived the ordeal.

In his report, Bonham Carter tactfully fails to mention that a number of men had effectively served as stowaways under his command, although he notes that 'hav[ing] a crew of 87 rather added to the difficulty of abandoning ship as it had only been drilled with the proper numbers on board, i.e., 54.' Even this was something of an understatement, as none of the 33 supernumerary personnel had at any time practised the correct procedure for an emergency evacuation into enemy waters. It's one of the small miracles of the whole affair that, with the exception of Petty Officer Harold Palliser, who was killed by machine-gun fire while apparently making his way to safety in the motor launch, *Intrepid*'s entire ship's company made it back to Dover without serious injury.

We'll return to the adventure of Bonham Carter's own departure from Zeebrugge, but for now it's worth quoting the account he gave of the raid shortly before his death at the age of 83 some 55 years later:

> As Intrepid closed in she went ahead full steam and got well into the canal and turned into the port side. The Iphigenia came in behind and at first came up on the port side of the Intrepid & partly levered her off the side of the canal. When [I] got Intrepid into position I found she began to go astern, so I did not dare to wait any longer and blew up the ship. [My] Engineer Lieutenant was still in the engine room and came up on deck and used very strong language to me for doing it. The boat which ought to have taken the officers off was used for disembarking the extra crew, and consequently we had only the Carley rafts left. [We] launched one and it had no painter and drifted away, then we launched the other and 3 officers and 4 men got into it and they got away in the dark. By some accident the string which starts the light got pulled and immediately a Hun machine gun, not more than 30 yards away, opened on [us] and it seems impossible that we should have escaped.

Meanwhile HMS *Iphigenia*, the late replacement Lieutenant Edward Billyard-Leake commanding, entered the inner harbour in a Mephistophelean puff of smoke, oily grey clouds of the stuff wafting back over the bridge from a ruptured steam pipe in the bows. 'It was quite a warm business,' the ship's chief stoker later recalled, speaking both literally and metaphorically. After careening off *Intrepid*'s port side, *Iphigenia* came to rest just behind her sister ship, both of them lying diagonally athwart the entrance to the canal without completely blocking it. At that stage, Billyard-Leake remarked in his report: 'I abandoned ship and fired my charges, which all exploded. The ship's company left in one cutter, as the other one was badly damaged. While in the cutter we came under more shrapnel and machine gun fire, which caused some casualties.'

Among these was 20-year-old Sub-Lieutenant Maurice Lloyd, a wealthy estate agent's son from rural Suffolk, who belying his youth had already won the DSC and been wounded in two earlier naval actions. Despite this bravery, his personal fitness reports were far from glowing. 'This young man has a very bad memory, not enough training [and] has done very little time at sea,' an unnamed senior officer had noted of him in February 1917. It was the same sorry tale in July of that year: 'Not suitable officer for Destroyer service as he cannot be trusted to do the simplest thing correctly.' Whatever his other defects, Sub-Lieutenant Lloyd rose magnificently to the occasion at Zeebrugge, where he calmly supervised *Iphigenia*'s aft evacuation before lowering the ship's white ensign and taking this with him into the cutter. A few minutes later, he was one of those hit by a volley of machine-gun fire as the boat proceeded at full speed out of the harbour. Lloyd was eventually lifted off the cutter and taken aboard HMS *Warwick*, where Roger Keyes visited him in the sick bay. Keyes wrote:

> Lloyd had the Iphigenia's white ensign wrapped round his waist, and it was saturated with his blood. I think he knew that his number was up, but was perfectly happy and fearfully proud of having been able to bring away the ensign, which I told him he should keep.

Maurice Lloyd died in hospital the following morning, and was posthumously awarded a bar to his DSC for 'hav[ing] showed great coolness under heavy fire, and by his bravery and devotion setting a fine example to his men'. The planners of Operation ZO, although well aware of the danger posed by the enemy's shore defences to the arriving fleet – something of a preoccupation of Keyes and his senior staff – had gravely underestimated their continued threat to the raid's departing survivors.

When the smoke cleared, HMS *Thetis* lay roughly quarter of a mile adrift of her intended target, wallowing across the main canal approach at an angle that made her a nuisance but hardly an impassable barrier to German sea traffic. There were some dubious reports that a U-boat had later managed to collide with her in the dark and sank with all hands. The other two blocking cruisers were left closer to their mark, lying half-submerged and parallel to one another across the canal mouth itself, although in the event the Germans were soon able to move their submarines up and down a narrow channel they dredged behind them. There must be a suspicion that the blockships, and more particularly *Intrepid*, missed a golden opportunity to reach and ram the lock gates, and thus put the issue of Operation ZO's success beyond doubt, although historians who rebuke Lieutenant Bonham Carter for this oversight perhaps enjoy a more leisurely perspective on events than was available during the confused and sustained fighting on the night.

Nor was Bonham Carter's own ordeal quite over when he ordered his ship's company into the boats. We've seen that some of *Intrepid*'s crew took to a lightweight

Carley raft, where one of them promptly managed to ignite a white distress flare which exposed them to the German machine gunners peering out through the fog from only a few dozen yards away on shore. 'This unfortunately drew their fire on us,' Bonham Carter remarked. 'Two of the officers and the men managed to get out of [the raft] and into a cutter, but I saw there was not room for me and started to swim for it.' The 28-year-old, cricket-playing lieutenant was now alone in the oily water, with bullets rippling all around him, and the wash of blindly passing motor boats repeatedly breaking over his head. 'Not an ideal position,' Bonham Carter was later to admit. Fortunately, the crew of *ML 282*, carrying a motley band of survivors from all three blockships on their way post-haste out of the area, spotting the dark figure bobbing up and down and furiously waving his arms behind them, reversed course back into the heaviest zone of fire immediately around the canal mouth. The boat's commanding officer, 40-year-old Lieutenant Percy Dean, from Blackburn, Lancashire, was another of the heroes of Zeebrugge with an only modest service record up until then. His actions over the next few minutes would win him the VC.

There is some question of whether Bonham Carter had previously tried to come aboard *ML 282* and, after clinging desperately to the boat's stern line, had fallen back into the sea, or if he only now spotted the means of his rescue. One vivid account from 1958 suggests that Lieutenant Dean had doubled back to pick up several survivors from *Intrepid* who were floundering away in the water near the canal mouth. 'Bonham Carter waited until last, was temporarily forgotten, and when Dean put his engines astern under the impression that everyone was aboard, Carter just managed to grasp a trailing rope as *ML 282* shot away' and for the next agonising half-mile was dragged through the seething waters 'like a hooked tarpon' – if true, surely one of the night's most vivid images even within the confines of a harbour where abandoned ships burned and dead men lay floating in the water.

'Just before his arms were about to be hauled out of their sockets,' this account continues, 'Carter was noticed by one of the M.L.'s crew, who immediately jumped to the conclusion that he was a German and picked up a boathook in order to deal with the matter.' The drowning man had forcefully corrected this misapprehension, using some salty language to do so, but had then dropped the line attaching himself to the boat before he could be safely brought aboard. Bonham Carter had next 'watched the M.L. shoot out into the wider areas of the Mole harbour [and] started swimming slowly away towards the eastern pier of the canal entrance', reportedly musing on life's vagaries as he did so.

This may very well be exactly what happened, or it may be that the water-towing incident tended to become more dramatic with each later retelling. In his old age, Bonham Carter himself admitted that he could 'remember very little of what was going on around me' and believed that he had been dragged for 'about forty yards' before letting go of the rope behind *ML 282*. But all sides agree on the central fact that *Intrepid*'s skipper had once again found himself adrift in the smouldering crucible of Zeebrugge harbour, half drowned and flailing his way back to shore, at distinct risk from both the German land gunners and the blockships themselves, where stray shells continued to rain down on the upper decks, smashing through boilers and steam pipes, flinging shards of hot steel into the water.

Lieutenant Dean was by then making his way at full steam directly away from the battle zone, feeling, reasonably enough, that he had done his best for any survivors and now more focused on the navigational challenges that lay ahead of him. Compounding the difficulties of steering his overcrowded launch through the sandbanks and net obstructions between him and the open sea, there was also a 'full armada' of other British motor boats surging around the area, engaged either in rescue or smokescreen activity. As a result, Dean later reported that off his port – or Mole – side he faced a mass of small ships 'as thick as the traffic on Oxford Street', weaving and dodging at top speed through the rain of bullets and other debris falling all around them, and doing so in conditions that ranged from 'heavy grey fog' to the 'full shade of night'. Miraculously, a German star shell burst overhead just at the moment *ML 282* was finally turning away from the blockships, and in that same instant Lieutenant Dean spotted Bonham Carter still struggling away in the water a quarter of a mile behind him. According to his later citation:

> Dean returned, rescued the man, and then proceeded, handling his boat as calmly as if engaged in a practice manoeuvre. Three men were shot down at his side whilst he conned his ship. On clearing the entrance to the canal the steering gear broke down. He manoeuvred his boat by the engines, and avoided complete destruction by steering so close in under the Mole that the guns in the batteries could not [dip] sufficiently to fire on him. The whole of this operation was carried out under a constant machine-gun fire at a few yards range.

Speaking to his hometown newspaper a few days later, Stoker Benjamin Eagleton of *Intrepid* vividly remembered *ML 282*'s subsequent progress out of the harbour:

> As we got away we could see the Germans running about on the Mole with machine guns. Of course all the time they were also firing from the land guns, and shells fell into the water everywhere. There were so many of them that they made the sea like a volcano, and the water boiled all round, the shells being, many of them, filled with poison gas.

Lieutenant Bonham Carter's brother officer Edward Billyard-Leake had meanwhile had a generally more relaxed experience of abandoning ship. After setting the explosive charges aboard *Iphigenia*, Leake, in a full-length leather coat and tin shrapnel helmet, had stepped unhurriedly across the deck of the rapidly sinking cruiser and over the side to join his men in the cutter that eventually brought them to Roger Keyes's flagship *Warwick*. Interviewing the two young blockship commanders on their way home some hours later, Keyes recalled that Billyard-Leake 'might have stepped straight out of a military tailor's shop, very erect and absolutely unperturbed', while Bonham Carter, 'bareheaded and dressed in a dirty wet vest and trousers – as he had been swimming in the canal covered with oil – made a good contrast.'

Keyes himself had been more than a mere observer at Zeebrugge, ordering *Warwick,* under the nominal command of the explorer Victor Campbell, to 'wheel and circle, emerging from her own smokescreens to take occasional pot-shots at the enemy's shore battery, then returning into them or dragging them across some suddenly revealed motor boat'. After satisfying himself that the blockships were in place, Keyes had again ordered *Warwick* to steam into the thick of the fray off the Mole lighthouse, and it was there that she recovered the crew of *ML 282* and three other boats. Designed for a maximum capacity of 62, Lieutenant Dean's launch was then carrying 104 passengers, several of them gravely injured. According to Keyes's biographer, 'when the men first saw *Warwick* bearing down towards them with her Admiral's enormous flag, they all leapt to their feet and started cheering wildly, and very nearly upset the top heavy craft'.

✳

This was not the end of the small boats' contribution to the overall campaign at Zeebrugge. *CMB 22C*, 22-year-old Lieutenant John Annesley commanding, continued to flit around the Mole lighthouse in order to lay a covering smokescreen for the benefit of the departing British ships. All six crew members were successively wounded, but by pooling their resources – 'one man's sound hand held the wheel as he lay beneath it, another's managed the throttle with its possessor propped against the housing', to quote the author Barrie Pitt – they made it safely out of the harbour. There were dozens of similar small craft at work that night, several collisions took place as a result, and in time more than one rescue boat itself needed rescuing. Sub-Lieutenant Leslie Blake, commanding *CMB 7*, later reported that he had taken the opportunity to enter the harbour and fire a torpedo at the German destroyer lying some 400 yards off his starboard bow on the opposite side of the Mole to *Vindictive.* 'After having observed [the] explosion,' he noted evenly,

> I altered course to port so as to escape to eastwards and make smoke screen as ordered … During this time I was heavily fired upon by machine guns on Mole and heavy batteries east of canal. I was also chased by enemy small craft, which opened fire on No. 7 with two machine guns.

Blake and his crew also survived the night's action and were eventually taken under tow back to Dover.

At 12.52 a.m., less than an hour after disembarking from *Vindictive,* the men fighting on the Mole were again on the move back to the ship. Captain Carpenter was responsible for issuing the signal to retire, and later said of his decision to do so:

> I had seen the submarine explosion in the direction of the viaduct, and observed the blockships proceeding shorewards … The main object of storming the Mole had been accomplished. The only reason for remaining alongside any longer was that of continuing the work of demolition

which had been commenced by a party of seamen under the extremely able leadership of Lieutenant Dickinson, RN. Such a reason seemed to me insufficient to warrant waiting alongside until the latest moment allowed by General Orders, viz 01.20 … I therefore ordered the pre-arranged signal to be made for the retirement. All searchlights and sirens having been destroyed in *Vindictive*, I ordered *Daffodil* to sound a succession of K's on her whistle.

As we've seen, the signal itself – a series of spluttering hoots from a ferryboat's pipe which struggled for precedence over the continuing din of battle on the Mole – caused some initial confusion among the marine landing parties. Captain Chater having doubled back to *Vindictive* to confirm the order, the men under his command began to take their leave in piecemeal fashion, several of them lingering to engage particular German machine-gun posts or to personally square accounts with individual enemy forces until the noise from *Daffodil* became an increasingly strident and undeniably urgent high-pitched wail. Some of the raiders still evidently felt dissatisfied with their night's work, which gallantly as they had fought could only be counted a partial strategic success. The enemy's main gun batteries remained intact and their various ships at the quayside were damaged but still afloat. Lieutenant Charles Lamplough, commanding the marines' No. 9 Platoon, could report only, 'During the period we were on the Mole we did what we could to harass a destroyer alongside with such weapons as we had available, and also dealt with a few Germans who came down to the Mole [in] an attempt to interfere with our scaling ladders.'

Twelve years later, when asked whether the land component of Operation ZO was truly a success, Lamplough added,

> My impression was that as far as our objectives went, i.e. the capture of the Battery at the seaward end of the Mole and the damage to material on the Mole, [it] was a failure. [However], we did cause a diversion which we had the satisfaction of knowing gave considerable assistance to the blockships in the carrying out of the main objective of the operation of the blocking of the canal entrance.

The actual retirement from the Mole was a scattered and often desperately confused affair. There were many additional British casualties, and several further cases of outstanding courage under fire. The *Vindictive's* young rating Quinton Murdoch later told his local Scottish newspaper, 'We had to assist with the bringing in of the wounded, and for that purpose had to land on the Mole three times, and fight our way to the injured men. During this time we got it hard.' 'The rats are leaving the sinking ship' was the reaction of one German machine-gunner as small groups of marine or naval personnel were seen to stagger back to safety along the parapet top, the men often dragging a fallen comrade over their shoulders.

Less elevated scenes were apparently reported, too: the marine officer who was found slumped on a low wall, allegedly the worse for drink, or the fire which somehow broke out on the foredeck of *Vindictive*, some of the spectators to this (possibly in a state of shock) 'shouting like schoolboys' until the ship's quartermaster, Petty Officer

Edwin Youlton, bravely stamped out the flames before collapsing with shrapnel wounds from a shell that burst on the deck immediately behind him.

Even after an hour of continuous bombardment and furious hand-to-hand combat, it still came as a shock to some of the crew of *Vindictive* when they looked over the side and saw the small knots of shattered figures, some wearing improvised bandages made up of scarves or handkerchiefs, with grimy faces and dirty clothes, who now hobbled back to the ship. Private Jim Clist of the marines' No. 12 Platoon remembered

> a chap who was a Lewis gunner in my section who came from Yeovil in Somerset. He was called Taylor. He was trying to get a man on his shoulders who was badly wounded. Someone came along and helped him to carry the man aboard. I was told that he also carried my mate Freeman aboard, but he was dead when he got him there. That was the chap who gave me a lock of his hair, which I kept for several months.

The Mole itself by then lay under a pall of acrid grey smoke that lingered from the night's shellfire, through which survivors of the various landing parties loomed up in shadowy groups of two or three. The men on *Vindictive* waiting for their comrades to emerge from the murk had been expecting heavy casualties, but for Captain Carpenter, particularly after the relatively carefree mood of the outward voyage to Zeebrugge, his first contact with the returning troops had a sobering effect. 'It was a shock to me when I recognised men I had seen go over the top only an hour earlier,' he later told a North American audience.

> There was one character I knew, a real practical joker, [who] had changed a great deal even in that time; before me stood a silent man with a tired sunken face. I suppose he was one of the 'lucky' ones. We did our best to get the wounded on board, some on stretchers, some on a friend's back, and taken below. I still remember the queer sense of quiet about it all, broken only by some poor fellow's low moans of pain. Our MO did his best, but men were dying every minute.

Carpenter added in his published memoirs: 'One marine carried a disabled man onto *Vindictive*, placed his charge on the deck, kissed him on both cheeks and was heard to remark, "I wasn't going to leave you, Bill."'

Amid the general confusion of the withdrawal, there were similarly wrenching scenes as members of the original storming crews made their way back on board. The rugby-playing Reverend Charles Peshall, from Oldberrow in Warwickshire, who was then aged 37 and serving as *Vindictive*'s chaplain, repeatedly left the ship in order to rush back into the line of fire to rescue wounded or dying men. Peshall's citation for the DSO notes that he 'did almost superhuman work' that night. One of the naval raiders who had gone ashore to attack the main German battery remembered the 'pitiful chaos' of the reembarkation on *Vindictive* as being one of the bloodiest phases of the entire mission. 'Of fourteen or fifteen landing ladders, only two remained,' he told his local Nottinghamshire paper later that week, and they creaked and bent ominously as 300 or 400 of us scrambled aboard. I found one poor lad lying helplessly on the shore, only a few yards from the gangway, and with a pal's assistance I managed to get him safely back. The scene both on deck and below was too awful to describe, and I am trying to forget it.

Fifteen minutes into the 20 minutes allowed for the retirement process, Alfred Carpenter and his deputy Robert Rosoman were both wounded when a shell struck *Vindictive* a few feet behind where they stood on the foredeck. Rosoman collapsed with shrapnel through both legs, but then insisted on being carried to a chair to resume his duties. Carpenter described his own injury as 'some very slight damage to the shoulder'. He, too, continued at his post, painfully aware that *Vindictive* still remained in acute danger. Four dead men now lay on the floor of the ship's small conning tower, and Carpenter found that the telegraph connecting him to the engine room had been shot away. 'This proved an added inconvenience,' he later told his American audience, in something of a master-class in British understatement. The roles had been 'somewhat reversed' by then, he added, with the British troops defending themselves as they pulled back to the ship, and the German force as the 'attacker and ambusher'.

At 1.11 a.m., a few moments short of the agreed 20-minute notice period for the evacuation, Carpenter signalled across to the waiting ferry *Daffodil* to tow *Vindictive's* bow away from the wall and point her out to sea. As they shoved off, Lieutenant Graham Hewett thought to release the ship's remaining artificial-fog supplies, which partially obscured her from the German guns but also added to the prevailing air of confusion in the immediate area. The 'not young' Corporal George Moyse of the Royal Army Service Corps had to dash headlong back down the Mole and hurl himself into the void behind the departing ship, just managing to cling on to the stern rail by his fingertips. In his haste he at first failed to realise that he had been shot while somewhere in midair. Carpenter wrote that by that stage 'practically all the storming parties had returned' and that it was imperative that the ship now slip its moorings without further ado. A persistent legend insists that the last group of sailors to retire from the Mole had hoisted a Union Jack before they left, although this particular detail has proved impossible to corroborate.

Other accounts suggest that the honour of being the last British serviceman to successfully leave the Mole belonged to 23-year-old Private William Hopewell, the man who had volunteered for the mission in the first place largely in order to avenge the deaths of his two brothers on the Western Front. He had spent the previous hour picking his way up and down the parapet top between *Vindictive's* temporary berth and the German gun batteries. When Hopewell heard the recall signal from *Daffodil* he doubled back, firing his Lewis gun at two enemy soldiers crouching at the door of a low-lying shed on his left, then turning to his right in order to cross a narrow roadway that separated him from *Vindictive*. He then ran stooping in the dark down the rain-slicked seaward side of the Mole, where to his surprise he saw a marine private who was marching robotically up and down between the ship and a nearby bollard or small lamppost, turning smartly about at each end as if on parade duty, steadily muttering away to himself amid the roar of the battle. Hopewell watched as another private emerged from the smoke to gently lead the man by the arm back to safety. Following this there seemed to be no British personnel left in the immediate vicinity.

Taking the same route as the two marines before him, Hopewell groped his way forward to the spot where he believed the wall's edge met the sea until he suddenly found his foot on the top rung of a ladder leading down to *Vindictive*'s midsection. Both the ship's bow and stern ends were invisible to him in the low-lying film of smoke. As Hopewell took his first tentative step down the rickety gangway, another burst of shrapnel swept the quayside, knocking his own gun from his hand. Still uninjured, he hurried down the ramp onto the port side of the ship, which was a shambles of tangled equipment and metalwork, among which men lay on wooden pallets or propped up on empty flour sacks, a row of sandbags crudely marking out the improvised dressing station where the dead or grievously wounded waited to be taken below. This was the scene on *Vindictive*'s deck as she left Zeebrugge.

Recommending him for the Conspicuous Gallantry Medal, Hopewell's commanding officer wrote:

> … after the proper Nos. 1 and 2 of his Lewis gun section had become casualties in the ship, he took the Lewis gun ashore and into the action. He kept the gun going throughout the operation, and was almost the final man to retire, bringing his gun out with him, until it was rendered useless by a direct hit from a shell.

Although Private Hopewell was among the last – if not the last – of the landing parties to return safely to *Vindictive*, that was not quite an end to the British presence on the Mole. Thanks to the confused signalling arrangements, 13 servicemen were left behind and forced to watch their only means of escape set sail into the night without them. Sergeant Harry Wright of the marines' No. 10 Platoon later wrote that after attacking the German destroyer tied up on the inner side of the sea wall, he and his comrades 'were 200 yards from Vindictive when she moved off. We were now stranded, and left to the mercy of the Germans. It seemed cruelly hard to know we had come through that terrible experience unscathed, and now were left behind through no fault of our own.'

Quickly assessing the situation, Wright and his fellow stragglers from 10 Platoon decided that their best bet was to lie down next to one another on top of the wall and play dead. Some two hours later, a German patrol cautiously approached the inert men sprawled among the rubble and debris of the Mole.

'They began to search us,' Wright later wrote, 'but first one man moved and then another. The Germans' nerves being highly strung, they jumped back, shouting and gesticulating, and made ready with their bayonets. We had not relinquished our rifles, and so prepared to fight to a finish.'

In the end, however, Wright and his comrades elected to surrender. Recalling this incident some years later, he added the detail that the German officer taking them into custody 'said to us in quite good English, "The game is up, lads." Seeing we still hesitated, he continued: "Play the game, and we will play the game with you. Lay down your arms and put your hands up. We will not harm you."'

Just a day later, Wright and his brothers-in-arms had the novel experience of being paraded on top of the Mole while Kaiser Wilhelm appeared before them to personally inspect the damage they had inflicted on his military hardware. By all accounts, the German emperor took a generous view of the proceedings and commended the British troops for their efforts. When the Kaiser then offered to shake hands with the marines' commanding officer Captain John Palmer, however, Palmer remained rigidly to attention and ignored the outstretched hand. The British prisoners were repatriated at intervals in November and December 1918, having spent some seven months in captivity. They were generally well treated, although at least three of the men, including Palmer, later succumbed to illness possibly caused by their experience. One PoW's family in the north of England, despite their own poverty, had meanwhile tried to raise a ransom in order to pay the Germans to release their son, collecting what their local paper called 'a penny here and a shilling there' from concerned citizens. Their efforts came to nothing, and Sergeant Harry Wright was left to note ruefully:

I was for five weeks a Prisoner of War at Brandenburg *after* the Armistice, and during that time became friendly with a German petty officer. It was astonishing to learn the full facts, from the enemy's point of view, as to what really happened at Zeebrugge. He told me the German Navy thought quite highly of our raid.

'What a massacre,' wrote one marine, who preferred anonymity, of his own breakout from Zeebrugge on board the overcrowded *Iris*. 'The plan may have looked good to our lords and masters when they studied it over their tea and biscuits in the War Building, but their knowledge of conditions on the day as I saw them must have been practically nil.' *Iris* was repeatedly hit at close range as she left the harbour, and the scene below decks soon became one that more resembled a slaughterhouse than a corporation ferry that until recently had been busily carrying passengers across the Mersey. A lone army surgeon, Captain Frank Pocock, RAMC, worked without respite at a lamp-lit amputation table amid the moans of those piled up nearby on pallets or bare planks awaiting his attention until the moment *Iris* finally reached Dover some 13 hours later. He was awarded the DSO for his efforts. But for the steady rattle of machine guns during the ship's departure it was a scene that could have been the aftermath of some Cromwellian bloodbath. One man below decks long remembered the sight of a 'soft-faced lad laid out for surgery … so pale and thin in a uniform far too large for him. His leg was missing below the knee'.

Although Frank Brock himself had fallen early on in the furious hand-to-hand combat on the Mole, the remaining stores of his patented 'artificial fog' provided at least some degree of cover as *Vindictive* and her two consorts moved off into the night. The Australian-born Warrant Officer William Edgar later spoke of an 'unforgettable scene of labour' below decks on *Iris*, the engine-room crew desperately stoking what remained of her boilers, 'officers and men both stripped to the waist, working like ants, and immediately above us the terrible noise of explosives ripping apart the bridge, and everything bathed in a ghastly pale-blue glow.'

Edgar's own citation for the DSO mentions that

> It was due to this officer that the ship was kept going during the action under very heavy fire, and though holed several times, succeeded in returning to base … He showed great bravery when the ship was under attack by coming up onto the upper deck, and with the help of a [rating] turned on the fog apparatus.

The smoke cylinders were also deployed on board *Vindictive* in the first critical moments of her exodus, and, if anything, proved all too effective. 'In less than a minute, all previous fog records were beaten beyond comparison,' Captain Carpenter wrote. Brock's protégé Lieutenant Graham Hewett said of the same procedure, 'The [smokescreen], combined with the exceptional handling of the ship, undeniably saved us from further gunfire, the fog being so thick aboard it was impossible to see more than two or three feet even when flare rockets were put up.'

The official Admiralty report gives some idea of *Vindictive*'s overall state during the withdrawal when it speaks of the already semi-derelict cruiser presenting 'a great black shape, with funnels gapped and leaning out of the true, flying a vast streamer of flame as her stokers worked her up – her, the almost wreck – to a final display of 17 knots'. The speed was necessary, *Vindictive*'s gunnery officer Lieutenant Hilton Young added, because

> We still had a race against time before us – to get out of range of the big guns ashore before we were revealed to them by the dawn that was about to break … With flames pouring from her battered funnels and burdened with triumph, death, and pain, the Vindictive sped away from Zeebrugge into the North Sea.

Air Mechanic Frank Donovan, one of the last men to scramble back on board the ship before she left the Mole, only now came to appreciate the full magnitude of what they had all been through. Donovan was a tough, wiry man, regarded as a fearless fighter, who had run ashore waving a cutlass when his portable flamethrower was shot from his back. He was also a 20-year-old school leaver experiencing real action for the first time. 'It wasn't until I went along the deck during the return voyage, and I saw the awful mess of splintered steel, blood, oil and shattered bodies that I realised the horror of it,' Donovan told an interviewer. Shortly afterwards, the *Daily Record* quoted an unnamed marine officer as remarking of the scene: 'When we got back on board, *Vindictive* was a terrible sight. The upper decks were slippery with blood.' At one end of the ship, 'the deck was literally covered with corpses. There was no daylight between them. All of their features were smashed and grey. Only the white arm-bands gleamed in the dark'.

There were numerous cases of outstanding individual heroism when it came to getting the bulk of the British task force safely back to home port. *Vindictive*'s second-in-command Lieutenant-Commander Rosoman, who had been wounded in both legs, remained uncomplainingly at his post, declining all offers to go below, for the next six hours. On board *Iris*, the teenaged Able Seaman Lake set about clearing both the enemy and 'friendly' unexploded ordnance lying around the ship by picking the shells up with his bare hands and tossing them overboard, following which he relieved the mortally wounded Lieutenant George Spencer at the wheel. At breakfast time on 23 April Lake was still there, 'blackened, dead-tired, but unyielding'. Petty Officer James Cownie similarly took the helm of *Daffodil*, steering the ferry through the barrage of German fire on both flanks as she slipped from harbour into the night. Below decks on the same vessel, Harry Adams added a human touch when he later wrote:

> We worked our smoke boxes in the initial [escape], and that helped a good deal. My own personal feelings were, well, so far so good, but if we were to get a nasty one, I intended to have a swim for it. So I duly stripped off to the skin – midnight – middle of April – and a long swim it would have been. Ugh! But we seemed to dodge the shells.

During the bitter closing duel of the raid, in which Adams would ultimately be spared the ordeal of having to swim for it, the Germans inflicted at least one major blow on the departing task force. This came when the British M-class destroyer *North Star* lost her way in the smoke and steamed headlong back into the harbour instead of away from it. Realising his mistake, the captain of the *North Star* turned his ship about and made at full speed for the open sea, but was caught by the enemy's searchlights as he passed the Mole lighthouse. A slaughter ensued. Both the Mole batteries and the shore artillery pummelled the destroyer's exposed port side, demolishing first her aft funnel, then her bridge, and finally her engine room. This caused a massive explosion, which was at once followed by the unearthly noise of a high-pitched whistling from the nearby HMS *Phoebe* (with the rescued crew of *C3* on board), whose siren apparatus had been hit by shrapnel and become stuck in the 'on' position as a result. As this eerie soundtrack played, the entire 270-foot-long *North Star* lifted up as if punched from below. Her bows disappeared, her stern for a moment continued to sail on, and as *Phoebe* raced in to the rescue, peppered by hot falling debris, *North Star*'s propellers were seen to be still turning, threshing away as the shell of the crippled ship began to list alarmingly to starboard.

Air Mechanic Sidney Hesse was on watch on *Phoebe* and remembered coming alongside *North Star* while she was sinking, 'because her boats were full of holes. We took about 75 of her crew off … It was then that I was nearly killed. I was talking to three fellows – they were stokers who came up from a manhole down below and asked how the battle was going. I'd never been in action before, and I said that it didn't look too good to me. Just then a shell hit the funnel where I was standing, and blew bits all over the place. It knocked me senseless, and killed the three fellows I was talking to. A piece of the funnel stuck into my lifebelt, but I wasn't hurt.'

Just as *Phoebe* finally drew away from the doomed destroyer, a lone figure appeared on *North Star*'s now precariously angled stern section, took a run-up and launched himself towards the outstretched arms frantically beckoning to him from the rescue ship. Silhouetted for a split-second by the flash of another exploding shell, the unidentified man never landed on *Phoebe*'s deck. He was one of the 18 crew members who died at their post.

By 2.20 a.m., the last of the surviving British ships had rounded the Zeebrugge lighthouse and begun their race for home before the dawn exposed them to the long-range German artillery. *Vindictive* kept up the fight to the end. The badly wounded Lieutenant Hilton Young remained at the ship's forward port six-inch gun and remembered the moment when 'The din in firing had [finally] ceased, and all but the guns' crew were below, the decks were empty, and there was nothing to hear now but the wash of the waves alongside.'

For several more minutes, Lieutenant Young strained his ears as a 'faint popping' sound seemed to follow the ship from somewhere in the direction of the harbour. Then even this muted salvo faded into the night:

> So by the biggest wonder of that day of wonders, we repassed the batteries not only unsunk but unhit. Confused by our smokescreen and flurried, no doubt, by what had been happening on the Mole, the Germans dropped behind us every shot they fired, in a furious and harmless bombardment in our wake.

For some of the men on *Vindictive* there was nothing more to do after that but play cards and treat themselves to the ship's remaining stocks of rum during the seven-hour return voyage. To others, the scene remained one of unmitigated horror, with conditions below decks that resembled some floating charnel house, strewn with equipment and dead bodies, buried among which an occasional pitiful voice cried for help. Staff Surgeon McCutcheon worked unrelieved through the night, eventually covered up to his shoulders in blood. 'Most of the cases,' he noted clinically, 'had multiple wounds of an extensive nature, accompanied by severe hemorrhage, which had been caused by shell, shrapnel, high explosive, or what appeared to be explosive bullet.'

Elsewhere, the story of the return passage was one that combined anguish, endurance and eventual relief, much like an echo of the action itself. The uninjured survivors were able to relax or reflect on their fates, casualties were dealt with – *Iris*, in particular, was effectively a seaborne hospital, whose signalman, shot through both legs, was hoisted up by two comrades in order to flash out an emergency call for additional medical help to come aboard – and temporary damage to the ship patched up. Below decks on *Daffodil*, Harry Adams 'knelt naked – [I] rested my head on one of that old ferry's seats that had carried millions of passengers and thanked God'. He had been lightly wounded in the arm by a shell splinter.

As they sailed across the North Sea, *Daffodil's* commanding officer Lieutenant Campbell, who received shrapnel in the eye during the evacuation, came out on a deck still slick with blood to tell his crew: 'Don't you think we're lucky, lads, to be alive? If we'd stopped another five minutes I'm afraid we would have all been dead men.' Later in the journey, the body of one marine private was sewn up in a hammock, ready for burial at sea, only for Campbell to change his mind at the last moment and decide that the man should instead be brought back with them and given a 'proper grave' in England.

At about 5.30 a.m., roughly 25 miles off the coast of Dover, Roger Keyes's flagship HMS *Warwick* swept up out of the early-morning haze to briefly sail alongside *Vindictive*. One of the latter's officers remembered that *Warwick* had hoisted a series of flags, which 'bleary eyed, we read as "Magnificent – Operations successful"'. Private Philip Hodgson of the marines' 12 Platoon added that 'for some seconds only a few yards separated the ships, long enough for Sir Roger using a megaphone to shout, "Well done Vindictive".' It was only then that some of the returning men felt themselves to be completely safe. *Warwick* then sped ahead in order to land her wounded as quickly as possible. About an hour and a quarter later, a shout went up on *Vindictive's* deck, and through a patch of fog the crew could see what one of them called 'the finest sight of my life ... There, just ahead, we could make out the cliffs of Dover surmounted by the Castle, and could appreciate to the full the quiet beauty of the scene.'

There are conflicting accounts about the men's reception once they disembarked at their home port. The harbour itself was *en fête*, flag-strewn and adorned by a municipal brass band that struck up 'Rule, Britannia' and other patriotic airs as *Vindictive* came alongside. *Daffodil* and *Iris* followed in short order. There were tables at the quayside with cups of tea, sandwiches and cigarettes. A young woman was seen to be rapidly walking up and down the nearby piers, apparently anxious for news of her husband. Keyes himself soon appeared in order to congratulate all ranks and assure them that the whole mission had been a glorious success. A junior officer in turn asked the men if they were downhearted, and the reply came back 'like the roar of the guns at Zeebrugge – *No!*' A Press Association reporter who went aboard *Vindictive* noted that the scene was one of 'inexplicable confusion ... The decks were hampered with litter, including everything from a big shell to a sailor's cap riddled with bullets. The steel armouring was bent and twisted into amazing shapes. Shot and shell had riddled the vents until they had become like sieves'. Amidst this scene of 'utter ruin and spoil', the good-luck horseshoe Keyes's wife Eva had presented the ship's company just 24 hours earlier was found to still be nailed in place on *Vindictive*'s middle funnel, the only one of the three funnels to escape undamaged.

Set against this warm welcome, Harry Adams, as quoted by the author Paul Kendall, remembered a generally more muted atmosphere among the raid's survivors, who were quickly herded aboard the monitor *Sir John Moore* for a roll call, 'and a more motley crew you'd never see in a life time. Every man ghostly white – some half-clad, some only with shorts and a bit of rag round their neck – some still limping with minor wounds but all washed out and done up'. Several other ships appeared at intervals throughout the late morning and early afternoon, by which time the brass band had gone home. Reaching port on board *ML 286*, HMS *Thetis*'s stoker Frank Gale remembered that 'the crowds cheered us as we marched through the streets', up until the moment the men entered a railway waiting room where they were greeted by the 'very British' sign: 'ALL RETURNING FORCES ARE REMINDED THAT THEY ARE STILL SUBJECT TO KING'S REGULATIONS.'

Apart from the living, or the walking wounded, Gale adds that there was also the 'gruesome matter' of bringing out the dead. Although the Press Association visitor fails to mention it, *Vindictive*'s Private James Feeney described the returning cruiser as 'a shambles … We had all the bodies collected up together lying on the decks and tables at one end'. The ship's engine-room officer Lieutenant-Commander William Bury, emphasising the terrible aptness of his surname, remembered that 'When we got alongside, [my] first job was to help remove the dead, who were laid out in rows in Dover market awaiting funeral.' Later that same afternoon, an emotional Bury was at the bar of the town's Burlington Hotel, where he was said to have made an 'unnecessarily rude' remark to the waitress. The young woman evidently gave as good as she got, 'sending the officer scurrying with a flea in his ear'.

James Feeney gave another sombre account of *Vindictive*'s homecoming when he went on to tell the Royal Marines newspaper *Globe & Laurel*,

> The [ship's] company entrained at Dover Priory, and [went] to Deal. There was not many to meet us. Motors took down the wounded to hospital. We made no sound when marching through the town. We attempted three times to sing 'Take me back to dear Old Blighty', but we could never finish it.

Another marine added that the full enormity of what the men had just been through struck them only when they were safely back in the relative peace and quiet of their barracks hut: 'Then the reaction set in. There were 24 men in the room originally and now there were only 11. After eating my first meal in over 24 hours and after a good soak in a warm bath, I turned in and in spite of the recent excitement was soon asleep.'

✳

Total British losses in the Zeebrugge raid are still the subject of debate and range from 475 to slightly more than 600, out of a total complement of 1,600, depending on whether the lightly wounded and the PoWs are included. There were approximately 225 deaths. This means that roughly eight men became casualties for every minute *Vindictive* spent at the Mole. The figures are doubly significant because the British war office went on to publish 'final and corrected numerical data' showing a total of 573,507 UK servicemen killed in action from 4 August 1914 to 30 April 1919, in addition to 1,643,469 individuals described as 'wounded or otherwise impaired' out of some 6.2 million total enlistments. By averaging the above sets of statistics, it's possible to say that the chance of a front-line British serviceman losing his life or being injured in the course of some four years' combat in the war as a whole was roughly 9.3 per cent and 26.5 per cent respectively. The corresponding figures for Operation ZO are 14 per cent and between 16.5 to 23.5 per cent. A man setting sail on the British task force in the early afternoon of 22 April 1918 had about one chance in three of being a casualty less than 12 hours later. The official Admiralty files show four closely typed pages of fatalities, and conclude with the stark note: 'Eight unrecognisable Naval ratings.'

There were also those suffering from today's post-traumatic stress syndrome, among them Harry Adams: 'As soon as the lights were out that first night,' he wrote, 'tired and beaten as I was, I lived that raid over and over again; and for about three weeks afterwards I was terrified of sleeping in the dark – some of the hateful night would reappear so vividly – and my nerves seemed all gone.'

Admirals Beatty and Keyes had had high hopes for the subsidiary St. George's Day attack which called for the British task force under the command of the stocky and tough (though, in civilian life, quiet and nature-loving) Commodore Hubert Lynes to sink two obsolete cruisers in the canal mouth at Ostend, roughly 15 miles downshore of Zeebrugge, which they described as the 'single best-trained unit' of the combined operation. They were therefore somewhat surprised and dismayed when the 33-strong armada, reinforced by a detachment of three French destroyers and four motor launches, foundered due to navigational problems largely brought about by the local German commander's initiative in moving a critical marker buoy to a position more than a mile east to the one shown on British charts. 'Their lordships will share our disappointment at the defeat of our plans by the legitimate ruse of the enemy,' Keyes was left to conclude in his official report to the Admiralty.

Lieutenant Francis Harrison and his four-man crew on *CMB 19* were the first to reach the displaced marker. Rather than credit the Germans for having had the foresight to deliberately complicate the approach to their harbour by an enemy force by luring them onto a decoy path, Harrison apparently assumed that in the dark he had simply taken the wrong course, and so, after circling around for some minutes, he dropped a calcium flare on the water in order to show the rest of the

Anglo-French flotilla steaming up behind him where he thought they should line up for their attack. *CMB 19* then proceeded further south to locate the all-important canal entrance, but as she did so the small launch came under heavy machine-gun fire from the shore. At the same time, powerful searchlights were suddenly trained on the boat from the harbour pier only some 300 yards away, making it all but impossible for Lieutenant Harrison to see his way forward. He probably did not even notice the silhouettes of six heavy guns, affectionately dubbed by their operators Ludendorff, Hindenburg, Irene, Friedrich, Preussen and Eylau, now also rapidly locking onto him, and might not have cared; he was trying to outrun danger. The subsequent 'volcanic roar' of the German artillery opening up at the retreating boat signalled the end of the element of surprise for the approaching convoy. 'Now we're for it,' one of the crew muttered in the brief lull between rounds.

Harrison pushed forward on his throttle and blasted straight ahead at full speed, desperately heading for cover as the incendiary shells crashed down to either side of him. Only when *CMB 19* reached the comparative safety of the far side of the harbour's outlying sandbank was it found that their young motor mechanic, a soccer-loving Londoner named Roy Alexander, lay sprawled across the aft-deck with blood pouring from his chest. Despite the seriousness of his injuries, Alexander remained fully alert, 'talking away inconsequentially' to his shipmates, who could only utter a few reassuring platitudes about the prospect of his being fit to play in the next year's football season while using a torn shirt to hurriedly bind up his wounds.

Meanwhile a squadron of motor launches under the overall command of 55-year-old Captain Ion Hamilton Benn, a longtime member of the naval reserve and the current Conservative MP for Greenwich, surged forward in an attempt to lay smoke at the harbour entrance and thus cloak the arrival of the blockships *Brilliant* and *Sirius*. As it did so, the wind abruptly changed direction, sweeping the clouds of grey, acidic-tasting artificial fog back into the face of the approaching cruisers. Undeterred, *Brilliant* drove blindly on towards her supposed target, taking heavy artillery fire as she neared land, before lurching aground on the sand a mile and a half from the canal gates. A few moments later, *Sirius* in turn emerged from the fog only to find *Brilliant* lying dead in the water immediately in front of her. None of the British ships involved at Ostend had practised the drill for an emergency turnaround as part of their preparations for the raid. By then *Sirius* had already been hit by at least 15 shells from the land batteries, and was struggling to maintain her course and speed. With no time to manoeuvre, she ploughed into *Brilliant*'s port quarter, forming one grotesquely conjoined wreck that continued to provide target practice for the German gunners over the course of the next 50 minutes.

A few days later, 23-year-old Lieutenant Edward Berthon, DSC, sat down to write of these 'interesting moments' on the bridge of HMS *Sirius*:

We were coming up to the time limit for the Stroom Bank buoy but could not see it, when all of a sudden the whole heavens were lit up by star shells bursting above the clouds and dropping below them, and several batteries opened out on us … Blue devils (8 blue shells tied together with wire) came hurtling through the air making an infernal noise and heavy stuff hit us on the forecastle.

Somehow or other as if gripped by some power which came from up above I was quite myself, tho' we were being hit hard and regularly. The whole world was filled with light, one heavy shell hit us on the port quarter, another on the starboard side, and a fire began in the sick bay.

I knew precious little of what was going on as I had my hands and mind full with managing the ship and keeping close to Brilliant; the Huns had put up such a smoke barrage round them that no CMB or precious few could see them. We certainly could not see anything. Hell had been let loose, every machine gun, every big gun was firing at the two blockships. It was just like day between us and the coast and star shells burst continually above us. One shell took off the top third of the foremost funnel. One could feel it. Suddenly Brilliant and us closed on each other. Order – 'Full speed astern, hard a'starboard' – but we were too late. We smashed into her port side and tore a huge hole in her there.

As German shells continued to pound the wrecks, the combined crews were ordered to abandon ship and take to the nearest available motor launch. *Sirius* and *Brilliant* were then scuttled where they lay. The mass evacuation proved remarkably orderly under the circumstances, and as at Zeebrugge there were several instances of outstanding individual bravery. The operation as a whole might have fared better had it relied for its success solely on the personal initiative of some of its rank and file members.

Born in London in 1885, the bespectacled Lieutenant Rowland Bourke, RNVR, had been bullied at school there because of what he called his 'nasal' voice and generally anemic appearance. One contemporary said that as a 12-year-old Bourke had had the look of a 'prematurely hatched bird'. He 'wasn't exactly a character straight from Conrad or the Jolly Jack Tar on a packet of "Players Please",' a naval colleague added. Belying these characteristics, Bourke had gone on to immigrate to western Canada as a teenager and to work there successively as a farmhand, cattle-punch and Klondike gold-miner among other equally bracing pursuits. Rejected by all three arms of the Canadian forces when he tried to enlist on the outbreak of World War I, Bourke returned to England at his own expense and was eventually admitted to the Naval Reserve. When the time came he volunteered his motor launch *276* to accompany the Ostend raid.

In the pre-midnight gloom of 22 April 1918 Bourke ate a 'heart-starting' meal of 'cold eggs of some species, beans, ship's biscuits and a stiff brandy', studied his charts, briefed his men, and then on seeing the first of the star shells 'slapping the sky a silvery-white hue to our southward', pointed his 75-foot, Canadian-built petrol-fuelled boat towards the stricken blockships, which peering through his thick glasses he could make out immediately ahead, 'illuminated like a ghastly Bonfire Night pyre' wedged together at an ungainly angle in the sand. As Bourke turned to speak to him, the man just behind him in the boat received a bullet in the chest and collapsed.

Over the next 35 minutes, Bourke came alongside four times to pick up survivors from *Brilliant*, taking artillery and long-range machine-gun fire throughout the protracted ordeal, before returning a fifth and final time to tow the crippled *ML 532* out of the harbour. Over the previous two years he had trained for many hundreds of hours in simulated rescue and recovery exercises, but this was his first time in action. Lieutenant Bourke eventually took 47 British officers and men on board his small craft before heading safely back into the North Sea. At the first opportunity following his return to Dover, he arranged an interview with Admiral Keyes, saluted him, presented his boat's log, and formally asked that he be considered for any future such operations Keyes might have in mind. This 'very characteristic' request was granted. For showing 'the greatest coolness and skill in handling his motor-launch', 32-year-old Lieutenant Bourke, once thought too puny to fight, was meanwhile awarded the Distinguished Service Order.

The Ostend raid left behind the hulks of two 30-year-old British cruisers, which provided the Germans with desultory target practice over the coming days, but proved quite useless in their objective of blocking sea traffic in and out of the vital port of Bruges. It remains uncertain how many personnel died in the attempt, the Admiralty generally preferring to combine the casualties suffered in the two distinct halves of Operation ZO into a single list. A distant impression, from the Eylau battery on the fringes of Ostend itself, was given by a German gunnery officer, Lieutenant Georg Jünger:

> The enemy cruisers went up in smoke, and in the searchlights we could see the tiny figures sliding down the ropes and into their rescue boats. Sometimes they missed and fell into the waves. The British sailors were having a hard time, and although my own troop desisted from firing, some of the other shore [units] pounded the wrecks until a vivid red flame shot up from the sea into the black night.

At the height of the mêlée, 27-year-old Lieutenant-Commander Keith Hoare, an heir to the family banking firm, took his launch *ML 283* alongside and rescued a further 50 men from *Sirius* and *Brilliant*. A hastily conducted roll call held on the edge of the harbour's danger zone revealed that *Sirius*'s 14-man engine-room crew was still unaccounted for. Two motor launches made their way back to the wreck site, but found no one in the water there. Hauntingly, one of the rescuers later recalled that he and his shipmates had heard a voice calling faintly out from somewhere below decks on HMS *Brilliant*. Later that night, *Sirius*'s missing stokers were found a dozen miles out to sea, exhausted but safe, rowing their way back to England.

Reflecting on his night's activities, Lieutenant Edward Berthon wrote:

> We reached Dunkirk at 3 a.m., [where] the CMB Mess put us up. A very bloody sight.

That evening I was very sick. Sent a wire. The next day went over to Dover in monitor General Crawford and was very kindly treated. Rang up home.

We had failed to block Ostend and had grounded 1,800 yards East due to the Stroom Bank buoy having been moved by the Germans, proving that they knew we were coming.

One gave God all thanks for having brought us out. The seamen were magnificent throughout, simply splendid. One felt very proud to belong to Sirius with those men in her.

CHAPTER 8

Aftermath

'Dear Admiral Keyes,' wrote 70-year-old Randall Davidson, the archbishop of Canterbury, late on 23 April 1918,

> The news which tonight's paper gives us is of the sort which makes a man 'hold his breath' in admiration of the magnificent courage and skill involved in such an enterprise … I should like, on St. George's Day, to say to you and to your brave men how intensely we appreciate the heroism of such deeds, and how proud we are of those who are thus adding lustre to the long and varied records of English seamanship and Naval prowess.

The prelate's testimonial, which Keyes kept in his desk drawer for the remainder of his life, was only one example, if among the most effusively phrased, of the popular British reaction to the day's events at Zeebrugge and Ostend. Much of the early press coverage was also fulsome, and some of it positively euphoric. The poet and historian Henry Newbolt wrote,

> The double attack of St. George's Day achieved not only a diminution of the enemy's strength, but an increase of our own. All over the world we hear it hailed as a great feat of arms, and a proof of mastery; our hearts are stronger for being so vividly reminded that our seamen are what they have always been – the greatest fighting men alive.

In the more measured words of the London *Globe*, 'The position at Zeebrugge is eminently satisfactory; the German vessels there now appear completely immobile.' Other papers explored the human drama of the affair, and perhaps fuelled what could be called the *Boy's Own* view of events as a result. 'IN THE JAWS OF DEATH. SMASHING UP ZEEBRUGGE MOLE – ENSANGUINED HERO'S STORY' ran the headline in the London *Evening News*.

Although the Germans naturally played down the strategic importance of the main raid, as we've seen it was still enough to bring Kaiser Wilhelm on a hurriedly arranged visit to personally assess the damage. Several bodies of British servicemen were still lying on the Zeebrugge Mole while the kaiser walked up and down the parapet with his silver-topped swagger stick inspecting the scene. Identification was not always possible. 'How soon a fighting force can become litter on a battlefield,' the German emperor remarked. Whatever the different views of it on either side of the North Sea, Operation ZO marked not only a significant propaganda opportunity for both belligerents, but also the mutual recognition that the Germans would be at least temporarily forced to curtail their raiding operations from the Flanders coast, if not to abandon altogether their remaining hopes of a full-scale seaborne invasion of the British mainland.

✳

'It was a queer feeling on our return to Dover' one of *Vindictive*'s enlisted men told a reporter from the *Daily Express* 20 years later. 'You felt that you did not belong, it was a sort of lost feeling.' Thirty-one-year-old Leading Deckhand James Smith, the churchgoing baker who still lived at his parents' home in Burnley, agreed that it was 'odd' to be sailing home aboard *ML 262*, its deck still wet with blood, to a reception like that for a Cup Final team: 'The working parties at the piers were standing on the piles, and as the boat passed the officers and men cheered for all they were worth, and the inhabitants lined up on the shore swelled the great chorus accompanied by the sound of ships' hooters and bells.'

Watching the surviving Royal Marines march through Deal town centre, the Press Association correspondent agreed there had been a 'rousing welcome' for the men. 'They presented a striking appearance,' he added. 'Their faces were black and greasy and they were plastered from head to foot with mud and blood. There were stirring scenes as they passed along the streets to their barracks. Relatives and friends mingled with the men in the ranks.'

One of the marine privates aboard *Iris* as she limped into Dover harbour later claimed to have seen an 'immaculately clad' Admiral Keyes, a red rose in his buttonhole, waiting for them on the jetty 'waving a telegram in his hand and saying, "I have been knighted by His Majesty the King."' Other contemporary accounts cast some doubt on this train of events, pointing out that Keyes had first learned of his award only later in the afternoon or early evening of 23 April. If the marine's memory was fragile, however, the story was sturdy and found its way into the subsequent Zeebrugge literature. It's known that Keyes and his wife Eva gave a dinner that night at their home on Dover's Marine Parade for some of the returning men, and that the brandy 'flowed evenly between all ranks' – another example, perhaps, of how the intensity of war can forge a spirit of mutual comradeship lacking in peacetime. Keyes himself noted of the occasion:

> My wife had prepared every bed in the house and we put up as [many] as it would hold … Billyard-Leake had a wound in his leg, which he did not want reported, as he did not want to be sent to hospital and was going on leave next morning. Harold Campbell [the officer who had taken a shrapnel splinter direct to the eye as he steered *Daffodil* out of Zeebrugge] had also not gone to hospital, but promised he would go to an oculist in London next morning. We heard later that he had been kept in a dark room for three weeks.

There were altogether more sombre scenes as the dead were laid out in their rows in Dover market, and the wounded helped on to lorries to be driven the 45 miles to Chatham hospital. 'This gruesome parade was our first job when we got back,' recalled *Vindictive*'s Lieutenant-Commander Bury, who had soon gone on from there to his ill-tempered encounter with the barmaid in the Burlington Hotel. The first funeral took place two days later, when Captain Henry Halahan, felled by shell and machine-gun fire while he stood waiting to lead his men onto the Zeebrugge Mole, was committed for burial at sea off the coast of Deal. He was the pipe-smoking family man from Surrey who had written to assure Keyes when volunteering for the raid that he 'willingly accepted' the risk of not coming back. Halahan's early death in the battle, wrote a colleague, 'had a shattering effect, like a gun-burst, upon us'.

There were to be some 220 further funerals, at land or sea, over the course of the next few weeks, months and even years as some of the survivors of the raid gradually succumbed to their wounds. Twenty-one-year-old Able Seaman John Helman, a retired army colour sergeant's son from Guernsey, had asked to serve on board *Daffodil* during the Zeebrugge landing. 'Don't tell my mother I am going there,' he wrote to a relative on 21 April 1918. 'The Captain says we are undertaking a terrible thing, and I may never see her again.' Despite being successively shot and subjected to chlorine gas poisoning during the ferry's withdrawal from the Mole, Seaman Helman had remained at his post on the forward mess deck. A companion named William Mudge later told Helman's mother, 'Jack picked up one of his wounded chums, and when he tried to carry him below he noticed that the head had been blown off the body.'

John Helman died at his home in Guernsey of an unspecified lung condition on 28 February 1920, nearly two years after his return from Zeebrugge. He was twenty-three. The British authorities were sometimes less conscientious in their arrangements than the Germans, who recovered several bodies from the waters off Zeebrugge and buried them with full military honours. The *Guernsey Star* account of Helman's funeral is headlined 'An Unfortunate Blunder' and goes on to report:

> The Seaman was one of those brave lads who volunteered to take part, at the risk of almost certain death, in the Zeebrugge expedition. He came back with his life but has since expired after a long and painful illness due to the effects of gassing ... His parents, trusting the promise of someone in authority that full military or naval honours should be accorded to the dead sailor, made no arrangements whatever for a private service ... The parents and relatives justly feel enraged. Their boy, a dearly loved son, was accorded hardly a decent burial and their resentment and sorrow run deep. So far as we have been able to ascertain, this much regretted error appears to have been due to the miscarriage of an order. Captain Crowley, CRO, had made arrangements whereby a gun carriage and a party of soldiers would have been present, but although the funeral was delayed for a considerable time they did not arrive.

Naturally, the British press of the time dwelt more on the raid's morale-boosting effects on a war-weary nation than on the individual tragedies of its survivors. So did many of the newspapers in the Allied or nonaligned world. The front-page splash in the *Chicago Tribune* of 26 April 1918 was typical of the American reaction. It was headed 'British Action in Belgium Full Success – Germany Locked in For Weeks, Naval Official Says.' The story described how Operation ZO had in one swoop 'completely bottled up the Germans' Flanders flotilla', although set against this the paper also quoted in smaller print the kaiser's official statement on the affair insisting that his ships 'have in no way been impeded by the British foolishness'. A thousand miles south of Zeebrugge, the Algerian *Al-balagh al-jazairi*, or *Daily Messenger*, thought the raid a 'glittering deed [which] has brought to an end the cowardly and contemptible submarine menace ... the proud triumph of English gentlemen hardened in fire and flame'.

Ironically, not all of those more closely acquainted with the full facts of Operation ZO shared the widespread sense of relief and satisfaction at its apparent outcome. Admiral Keyes, while publicly praising the undoubted courage of his men, privately expressed his frustration that the planned follow-up bombing of the interned German ships at Bruges was quietly abandoned owing to a 'complete bloody breakdown' in British inter-service liaison. In particular, Keyes had 'no very high opinion' of the newly organised Royal Air Force. 'The formation of this service,' he wrote to the Admiralty on 28 May 1918,

> has, up to the present, resulted most detrimentally as regards cooperation with the naval forces under my command ... I am very strongly of opinion that the present situation is thoroughly unsatisfactory ... the General Officer commanding the R.A.F. ... does not seem to understand the elements of the naval requirements on the Flanders shore or the great importance of its bearing on the general conduct of the war.

In Whitehall, the war cabinet also took a nuanced view of the events of St. George's Day on the Belgian coast. Rear Admiral George Hope, the deputy First Sea Lord, told the special meeting held in Downing Street on the morning of 24 April: 'The Vindictive was received with heavy fire, and suffered many casualties before getting alongside the Mole ... We are still assessing these ... About 500 men were landed at Zeebrugge, and our total losses are about 400 from the whole force engaged.' The following day, Hope's superior Sir Rosslyn Wemyss told the prime minister that 'Official reports [had] not yet been received, but information was available that ... the Marines had done a great deal of damage, and that the sum result was that Zeebrugge had been effectively blocked, but that Ostend had not.' Twenty-four hours later, Wemyss was back to announce that aerial photographs taken of the area 'were much marked by clouds and indistinct, [but] that the steel pile viaduct as struck by submarine C3 is breached for 100 to 120 feet clear [the true figure was about 80 feet], though a temporary bridge has been placed across the gap.' Two weeks later, it was Admiral Hope's turn to again tell ministers: 'On the basis of photographs taken yesterday, there [is] no apparent change in the lock gates at Zeebrugge.' On 10 June, seven weeks after the completion of Operation ZO, Hope told the cabinet that British destroyers were now bombarding the Flanders coast with 'satisfactory results' and that their objectives were the German 'salvage craft and other assemblage of vessels gathered round our three block-ships.'

While the admirals and politicians still debated what to make of the results of Operation ZO, a second attempt was launched to block Ostend harbour. This took place in the early hours of 10 May 1918, just 17 days after the original attack. As a result, there was little chance to properly repair HMS *Vindictive*, which – incredibly, by today's health and safety standards – was thought fit to return to the Belgian coast and, laden with 200 tons of concrete, to now serve as the raid's sacrificial blockship. The dockyard labourers at Dover did their best for the battered old cruiser in the short time available, but the folly of the decision to send her back into action was soon exposed when *Vindictive* found herself under the German guns at Ostend and struggling desperately to stay afloat long enough to effect a critical turn that would have allowed her to successfully reach the canal head. Churning white foam, flames shooting vertically from her stricken forward funnel, the heavily patched-up cruiser, until recently serving out her retirement as a school ship for young cadets, could do no more than lurch forward until she pitched against one of the harbour's outer piers at an angle of approximately 25 degrees and came to an abrupt stop there. It was later established that *Vindictive*'s port screw had been damaged when she scraped against the sea wall at Zeebrugge, and, in the careful words of the Admiralty report, 'insufficient attention had been paid to that particular defect in her structure'.

The Royal Flying Corps and Royal Air Force had between them sent up eleven reconnaissance flights over the Belgian coast in the week 24–30 April, and worked hand in glove with the codebreakers of the Admiralty's Room 40 – still the preserve of academics, bankers, lawyers, authors and actors as much as of career servicemen – to determine the optimum date on which to launch the new raid, which was at first officially designated VO, until for obscure reasons, possibly connected to the names of its two principal ships, this became Operation VS. First planned for as early as 27 April, in the event spring gales delayed matters for another fortnight. On the Sunday afternoon of 5 May, *Vindictive* went out for a shakedown cruise carrying her new cargo of 3,375 bags of cement and other assorted rubble packed into her forward storage holds and two bunkers built around the base of the conning tower. According to the naval historian Barrie Pitt, 'the cruiser was taken out and "swung" by Lieutenant Sir John Alleyne, navigating officer of the monitor *Lord Clive*. A cursory glance below decks was sufficient to reveal her transformation into a blockship.' There were few other structural or technical preparations.

Many of the surviving crews of Operation ZO again offered their services on the new expedition. It was led as before by Hubert Lynes, and 33-year-old Alfred Godsal, an unmarried man from Windsor who had risen through the ranks after joining the navy 20 years earlier, commanded *Vindictive*. A similarly modified cruiser, the 1890-vintage HMS *Sappho*, entrusted to Lieutenant Henry Hardy and manned by an all-volunteer crew of 52, accompanied the raid as a second blockship. Admiral Keyes himself was again present in the destroyer *Warwick*. Keyes and Lynes both spent the afternoon of 9 May as guests of the king and queen of Belgium at their seaside exile in La Panne, located some 25 miles west of Ostend in the tiny sliver of their country not occupied by the Germans.

Keyes wrote in his account of the day:

> During lunch there was a good deal of talk about wild birds, and amongst other things we discussed was the flighting of wild geese. The queen was very anxious to know when I meant to attack the coast again …
>
> After lunch, the king took me out to the sand dunes, opposite the villa, and very shyly gave me the Star of a Grand Officer of the Order of Leopold, and said very nice things about our exploit [at Zeebrugge].
>
> We all went for a walk along the shore afterwards, and I noticed a gentle wind blowing in from seaward. It was the first possible day of the new sailing period. I told Lynes we must get back at once, and we motored full speed to Dunkirk, where I sent off the warning signal, and returned with all dispatch in *Warwick* to Dover. When saying goodbye to the queen, I said: "The wild geese will fly tonight, Ma'am", and she wished me luck.

No one was more taken aback by what happened that night than Keyes. He had counted on the Germans being too preoccupied with clearing the damage at Zeebrugge to seriously think that anyone might be rash enough to launch a second seaborne assault in the same general area only days later. After reaching Dover at seven in the evening of the 9th, Keyes briefly went aboard each of the 13 ships and five supporting motor launches that would again set sail for the Belgian coast just two hours later. He found morale 'uniformly excellent' among the men, although he later admitted to having been uneasy following his tour of *Vindictive*.

'Godsal,' Keyes told his wife Eva, 'looked serene and happy, as if he had not a care in the world. But I felt quite sure, and I'm certain he did too, that we would not meet again in this world.'

Things first went awry a minute before midnight, when *Sappho* blew a boiler and had to drop out of the task force roughly 15 miles short of its objective. Ninety minutes later, *Vindictive* successfully found the entrance to the harbour, hitting thick fog as she did so. As noted, the Germans were fully alive to the possibility of this new attack on their canal network, and the night soon presented terrifying, strobelike conditions of pitch darkness alternating with blinding flashes of artillery fire. To add to the mêlée, seven Handley Page bombers from the RAF's 214 Squadron circled overhead pounding the shore defences. As *Vindictive* then struggled to turn to starboard to line up for her final approach, Commander Godsal stepped outside the conning tower to give orders for the blocking position. Three seconds later, a German shell hit the cruiser full on exactly where he stood. Godsal's body was either swept overboard or simply pulverised in the explosion; in either case, he was never seen again.

With smoke pouring from her shattered hull, *Vindictive* reeled up at a drunken angle against the harbour's outer pier, her guns still banging incessantly and a forest of towering waterspouts in turn billowing up all around her from the close-range artillery fire. Godsal's second-in-command, Lieutenant Victor Crutchley, set the explosive charges and ordered all hands to abandon ship. Crutchley received the VC for the calm way in which he had then walked around the decks, torch in hand, searching for any surviving crew members. His citation also mentions that once embarked on the rescue launch *ML 254*,

> This officer took command when the boat's commanding officer sank exhausted from his wounds, the deputy having been killed. The vessel was full of wounded and very seriously damaged by shellfire, the forepart being flooded. With indomitable energy and by dint of baling with buckets, and shifting weight aft, Lieutenant Crutchley and the unwounded kept her afloat, but the leaks could not be kept under and she was in a sinking condition with her forecastle nearly awash, when picked up by HMS *Warwick*.

There were several other scenes of individual drama as the little ships lunged around the inferno of the inner harbour hunting for survivors. The reedy-voiced sometime cowboy Lieutenant Rowland Bourke added to his recent glory by repeatedly steering *ML 276* back into the firing line between the beached *Vindictive* and the German shore batteries. 'Finding no one,' in the words of his own VC citation, 'he withdrew, but hearing cries from the water he again entered the harbour and after a prolonged search eventually found Lieutenant Sir John Alleyne and two ratings all badly wounded in the water, clinging to an upended skiff, and rescued them.' During this period, *ML 276* was hit 55 times, once by a six-inch shell which killed two of her crew and wounded a third. Thirty-two-year-old Lieutenant-Commander Geoffrey Drummond had been the original commanding officer of *ML 254*, and ignored what he called the 'footling discomfort' of a leg shattered in three places by a shell splinter long enough to successfully bring his boat alongside *Vindictive* to take off 40 survivors and only then to relinquish command with the words, 'I should get us away now, Number Two, as we're in rather a warm spot here.' He, too, received the VC for his contribution to the second Ostend operation.

Even then, the night's misfortunes weren't quite over. At 3.45 a.m., Keyes gave the order for HMS *Warwick* to turn about and set course for home. Fifteen minutes later, *Warwick* hit a mine, destroying the aft part of the ship. It appeared that she might sink then and there, but with one accompanying destroyer towing her, a second lashed alongside to keep her afloat and the German navy nowhere to be seen, she made harbour again just before sunset that evening. The British task force as a whole had suffered some 52 casualties, of whom 12 were known to be dead, in the course of Operation VS. Ostend was not blocked.

It is less easy to say whether the original Zeebrugge raid was a glorious success that, as Churchill wrote, 'may well rank as the finest feat of arms' of the war, or rather, as a modern critic puts it, 'further proof of the great British talent for failure.' The debate began even before the ships had returned to port and continues to exercise military historians and others a century later. All parties acknowledge the prodigious gallantry of the raiders, but for some the amateurish preparations for the mission seem to distil the national propensity for 'muddling through' rather than taking the more patient, bricklaying approach traditionally preferred by the Germans to such matters.

With hindsight, it seems fair to say that Admiral Keyes and senior members of his staff made certain mistakes in the six weeks or so in which they actively put together Operation ZO. Some of the men's training was haphazard at best, and even by the standards of the day the casualty arrangements were almost willfully inadequate. Keyes himself may once have been an archetype of British derring-do, stoicism and fortitude against the odds, but as such things became unfashionable he increasingly fell into modern biographical disrepute. 'He was an obsessive,' one author notes, 'who made decisions based on a schoolboyish taste for adventure and the sort of irregular, neo-commando operations embodied by Zeebrugge' – a sort of Horatio Hornblower figure, in other words, with an excessive love of action which almost certainly stemmed from some sort of inferiority complex.

Set against this harsh critique was Winston Churchill's dictum on mourning Keyes's death some 30 years later. 'Only mediocrity is always at its best,' he said, an epitaph Churchill himself might be thought to have merited. Britain's wartime prime minister went on to remind an audience at the naval college in Dartmouth,

> Many of the late admiral's qualities of self-confidence and unflinching devotion to God, country and rank once allowed a small European island to create and maintain an empire that benignly governed roughly one third of the world's population and completely dominated its seas. These are not small achievements.

This was a relatively mild encomium compared to the wide-reaching outpouring of joy with which British audiences first received word of the Zeebrugge raid, in its way the match of the peal of church bells and roar of cannon fire that had greeted news of the relief of Mafeking 18 years earlier. Modern readers need only think of the popular reaction to an especially high-profile royal wedding combined with the more raucously sustained celebration of victory in the World Cup, if such a thing can be imagined, to get some of the flavour. We've already touched on the prevalent tone of the press coverage of the time. The *Daily Telegraph* was full of praise for what it called 'An Immortal Deed', and the *Illustrated London News* was similarly convinced that 'Our Senior Service has scored a glorious success in Flanders', before going on to publish the somewhat grainy aerial photographs that seemed to prove the point. To the *Aberdeen Evening Express*, 'All that was romantic and adventurous in the traditions of the British Navy lived again – it [was] the rebirth of the spirit of Nelson and Drake.' A stirring Pathé news film was hurriedly released under the title *Hearts of Oak*. The manager of the small cinema specially built above the forecourt of London's Victoria station timed the 'crescendo of hand-clapping and foot-banging' that followed one early-evening performance, and found that the hands of his pocket watch reached just under two minutes. It may be the longest sustained applause ever to greet a current-affairs news short shown outside of the totalitarian world.

When Admiral Keyes came to write his official account of the two raids, prepared in May 1918 but published in the *London Gazette* only on 19 February 1919, by which time the war itself was over, he was similarly enthusiastic:

> The main results achieved have proved greater than I expected when the fleet returned to port on the morning of the 23rd April. Aerial observation and photographs up to the present date show clearly that even the lighter craft in Bruges ship-canal and docks have so far been unable to find an exit … Although doubtless in time the enemy will succeed in opening a way out, it seems likely that this important section of his raiding and commerce-destroying forces must inevitably be seriously hampered for a considerable period.

In his prologue, Keyes boldly told the Admiralty: 'As will be seen from the subsequent narrative, our operations were completely successful in attaining their first and most important object. The entrance to the Bruges ship-canal was blocked.'

Writing some six months after the event, the prolific author of children's (and military) literature Percy Westerman concluded: 'From 23 April 1918 the Belgian ports were useless to the enemy both as torpedo-boat and submarine bases – the Dover Patrol had closed and secured the Gateway of the Channel.' Summarising the raids in the third volume of his war memoir *The World Crisis*, published in 1927, Churchill added, 'Zeebrugge was completely blocked for about three weeks and was dangerous to U-boats for a period of two months. Although the Germans by strenuous efforts partially cleared the entrance after some weeks, no operations of any importance were ever again carried out by the Flanders destroyers.' Thirty years later, the historian Barrie Pitt saw the whole thing as one of those slightly illogical but plucky enterprises that are part of the British military tradition. 'The Zeebrugge raid,' he wrote, 'was a disaster for the Germans, and one out of all proportion to its true weight, for there is nothing so well-calculated to upset a balanced and powerful attack as a sudden threat to the flank: this is the ankle-tap by which the judo expert floors and defeats his heavyweight opponent.'

All of these commentators paid due tribute to the British victims at Zeebrugge and Ostend, while noting that by the standards of 1914–18 the human cost of the three separate missions had been comparatively modest. Crass though it is to use the word 'light' in connection to casualties, the argument went, it might fairly be applied on a relative basis here. In May 1944, 81-year-old David Lloyd George told the deputy chief of staff of the Second Army (and future Tory cabinet minister) Selwyn Lloyd that Britain had suffered 'roughly 200 men dead' in the combined Flanders operations and 'won a considerable publicity victory'.

Lloyd George was only one of many people, if better qualified than most, who came to view the Zeebrugge raid as the latest in a distinguished line of intrepid British military projects, and that, like all the best such ventures, it succeeded as much on the psychological as the tactical level. In his slightly florid words: 'The endeavour occurred at the exact moment that the nation most needed a balm for her soul.'

As we've seen, the original St. George's Day operation took place at the height of the German spring offensive, and followed within just 24 hours of the successful enemy attack on the Kemmelberg heights, near Ypres, part of a sustained drive to cut off the British forces in Flanders from their supply line, 'and [thus] render our troops fit to fight only on a more sparing basis', in General Haig's careful term. The British public had been particularly hungry for some crumb of good news around the last week of April 1918, in other words, and Zeebrugge gave it to them. As a result of the triumphant way it was reported, the raid not only provided a much-needed boost to national morale, but also went some way to retrieving the Royal Navy's reputation in the eyes of those for whom the service had performed only fitfully up to its full potential during the previous four years.

Apart from that, there was the hard fact that Germany's smaller coastal U-boats were again able to pass through the canal head at Zeebrugge within just three days (rather than Churchill's three weeks) of the raid, and that their destroyers could do so less than a month later. Korvettenkapitan Eric Schülze, the senior intelligence officer for the enemy's marine divisions in Flanders, wrote in 1927, by which time he presumably had no reason to lie about the matter:

> Our submarine *UB 15* went out at Zeebrugge on the night of April 25. It is true that for a certain time after the attack the passage by the blockships was impossible except at high tide, but this was of no importance as it sufficed to wait a few hours in order to be able to get in again.

In his official report on the Zeebrugge raid, Admiral Alfred von Tirpitz, former secretary of state for the German navy, agreed that the plan to block the canal had failed, but nonetheless paid tribute to the fighting spirit involved. 'During the night of April 22,' he wrote, 'an enterprise of the British naval forces against our Flanders bases, conceived on a large scale and planned regardless of sacrifice, was frustrated.

> According to the statements of prisoners, a detachment of four companies of the Royal Marines was to occupy the Mole at Zeebrugge by a *coup de main* in order to destroy all the structures, guns, and war material on it. Only about forty men actually landed. These fell into our hands, some alive, some dead. On the narrow high wall of the Mole both parties fought with the utmost fierceness.
>
> Beyond damage caused by a torpedo [*sic*] hit, our harbour-works and coast batteries are quite unimpaired. Of our naval forces only one boat suffered damage of the lightest character. Our casualties are small.

Although Tirpitz's reaction was perhaps only natural from an enemy combatant who had by then spent 53 years closely associated with the kaiser's forces, it was not a verdict confined to the German side. Admiral 'Jackie' Fisher, the Royal Navy's own eminence grise, and a man sometimes called the second most significant figure in British maritime history after Nelson, had not been a fan of Operation ZO from the start, writing in his memoirs that he 'demurred to any attempt to attack Zeebrugge without the cooperation of the army along the coast'.

One author quotes Fisher as having added after the fact: 'No such folly was ever devised by fools as that at Zeebrugge … For sailors to go on shore and attack forts, which Nelson said no sailor but a lunatic would do, is not only silly – it is murder and it is criminal.'

These were not the only words critical of the planning and execution of Operation ZO to emanate from within the senior ranks of the Royal Navy. Admiral Keyes's own contemporary at college (where he formed a dislike of him that time would in no way eradicate) and later his staff intelligence officer, Captain Herbert Grant, went on to write an unpublished book called *The Immortal Folly of Zeebrugge*. In it he quotes Keyes as having said of HMS *Intrepid*'s failure to ram the lock gates once given the chance to do so: 'Bonham Carter ought to have used his common sense; he is as brave as a lion but has no brains. I ought to have had Billyard-Leake in the Intrepid.'

Even Alfred Carpenter, the man who heroically kept *Vindictive*'s nose pinned against the Zeebrugge Mole for more than an hour under withering German fire, wasn't immune from criticism when he later embarked on a lecture tour of North America, bringing certain souvenirs of the raid with him. 'The captain was wonderful, if not exactly a soul of modesty, and there was some talk afterwards that he might have been a little less flashy about waving his shot-up cap around,' the *New York Herald* reported.

On their return to Dover on 23 April, *Vindictive*'s crew had discovered that a half-ton block of concrete from the Mole had wedged itself between a fender and a ledge on the ship's port side, and in time this more substantial relic of the mission made its way to London's Imperial War Museum. Carpenter himself took some pride in the fact that, in his own words, 'The loss of German lives [and] the damage sustained during the action were by no means negligible,' although against this he allowed,

> Some of the photographs [of Zeebrugge], taken at high tide, appeared to show sufficient space through which vessels could pass on either side of our ships. But … as long as the canal remained blocked, German submarines, detailed for operating against Allied commerce in the English Channel were, for the most part, compelled to do so from the Heligoland Bight. This increased the length of voyage, and consequently reduced the duration of their stay in such waters. Our splendid fellows did not die in vain.

Strategically, then, the attacks of April and May 1918 could only be counted a mixed success, the Allied shipping losses for that summer effectively acknowledging that the more rosy conclusions of Keyes's report of February 1919 had already been proved wrong. Lowell Thomas's otherwise admiring account of Operation ZO, *Raiders of the Deep*, written in 1928, quotes a local U-boat commander who called the raid 'a brilliant adventure on the part of the British', but added that in coldly material terms,

'It did not block the Flanders base. The sunken ships did not cover the entrance thoroughly ... We immediately began to dredge a passage at one side of the canal, and in three days it was deep enough for a torpedo boat to pass through at high tide.'

The Germans continued to make use of their advance Flanders bases almost until the end of the war. In May 1918 the Allies lost a total of 196 ships to U-boat activity, and even with the most up-to-date signals intelligence available from Room 40 this figure fell only to 187 in August. But then events on the Western Front, along with mounting civil unrest in Berlin and elsewhere, took a hand. On 17 October, Ostend and, on 19 October, Zeebrugge were evacuated by the Germans after four years of occupation. The departing crews were forced to blow up four U-boats and five destroyers that could not be made seaworthy in time. When the imperial fleet was ordered to assemble at Wilhelmshaven on 29 October for one climactic battle with the British, mutiny broke out in varying degrees, from insubordination to acts of sabotage, and then merged with spontaneous workers' risings elsewhere. On the evening of 10 November, the red flag of revolution was flying over German naval headquarters at Kiel. The following morning, the war ended.

While the Germans had initially proclaimed a great victory at Jutland, so, two years later, the British hailed a triumph in the Nelson tradition at Zeebrugge. In both cases the facts would scarcely seem to justify these laurels. For all that, it's hard to seriously disagree with the naval historian Richard Hough when he wrote:

> Zeebrugge was a courageous and thrilling exploit deserving its place in history, not for its tangible results, which the Admiralty really believed for a time were considerable, but for its inspiration. And example and inspiration were sorely needed in April 1918 ... The [raid] confirmed peoples' faith in the Navy in the most glorious manner and gave back to the Admiralty the reputation for high quality which it deserved in spite of the Zeebrugge failure.

Retrospective 'insight' into military matters can be deeply misleading. At the time, the British readily accepted the Zeebrugge operation as an audacious coup on the part of their maritime forces, and this belief in itself becomes an important factor in our modern judgement of the raid. While some of the men involved returned home on St. George's Day convinced that they had failed to achieve their objectives, few if any of them were left in any doubt that their efforts had captured the public's imagination – the jubilant headlines, municipal celebrations, spontaneous street parties and wholesale issuing of honours and awards can have allowed no other verdict. Even in later years, as Alfred Carpenter (who lived long enough to serve in the Home Guard during World War II) acknowledged: 'If [Zeebrugge] was increasingly judged a failure, it was as one of those "honourable" failures, like Dunkirk, that rather endear themselves to the British.'

Notions of patriotism may indeed have 'taken a battering', as Carpenter said, later in the twentieth century. But no amount of revisionism could detract from his achievements. By any standards, it was a remarkable feat of arms to have landed men, as he did, from an imperfectly moored ship rocking up and down in a heavy swell onto a defended sea wall in the dead of night, quite apart from the raid's other touchy elements. To the end of his life, Carpenter believed it to be a 'flawed but brazen episode' in British naval history.

Vindictive's Leading Stoker Henry Baker perhaps put it best when he told his local Folkestone paper shortly after returning from Zeebrugge:

> You reporters ask sometimes what the Navy is doing? Where is the Navy? Is it asleep? Well, the Zeebrugge job is one answer to that and sundry questions. You can take it from me that those people who ask 'What is the Navy doing?' are not doing our branch of the service a good turn or the nation either. Take it from me – the Navy is always doing.

Keyes, for his part, bristled at any suggestion that at least the Zeebrugge part of the three operations had been anything but a famous success, which criticisms, to him, stemmed from 'armchair sailors, rather than those who actually know something about fighting a sea battle'. He was duly generous when it came time to submit his list of recommended awards and decorations for those who took part in the raids. The process began as early as 11 a.m. on 23 April, at which point HMS *Warwick* had been back at home base for all of three hours, when Buckingham Palace announced that, in response to a telephoned request from Fleet House, Lieutenant Keith Wright, gravely injured in *ML 282*'s rescue of survivors from the Zeebrugge blockships, and Sub-Lieutenant Maurice Lloyd, who lay dying of wounds sustained on abandoning HMS *Iphigenia* respectively be awarded the DSC and a bar to the one already possessed, both with immediate effect. Lloyd succumbed to his injuries only hours later, but Wright lived to wear his decoration. Later that same afternoon, the king appointed Keyes himself a knight commander, prompting Admiral William 'W.W.' Fisher (not to be confused with 'Jackie' Fisher), the director of the Admiralty's anti-submarine division, to write to him: 'You have earned the gratitude of the whole Navy. We feel vindicated. We can put our heads up again.'

In all there were to be 29 DSCs, 21 DSOs, 143 medals for Distinguished Service, 16 for Conspicuous Gallantry and 283 names mentioned in dispatches, along with no fewer than eight Victoria Crosses for the men who fought at Zeebrugge, meaning that roughly one in three participants (the same ratio as those who were wounded or killed) received an official honour. Even the ferries *Iris* and *Daffodil* were each given the prefix *Royal* on command of the king. Keyes secured a further seven DSOs, three bars to the Order, two bars to the DSC, 59 medals for Distinguished Service, two for Conspicuous Gallantry, 57 mentions in dispatches, a CMG and three VCs for the Ostend contingent. It was an impressive tally, even allowing for the numerous acts of valour and self-sacrifice involved, and, some critics carped, perhaps all a bit of a lottery – literally so in certain cases, where Keyes invoked Rule 13 of the Royal Warrant of 1856, which allows an individual military formation to select one of their own for decoration by means of a ballot.

Keyes seemed to dispense even with this convention when coming to recognise the exceptional bravery of the 4th Battalion, RMLI, who had landed at Zeebrugge on board HMS *Vindictive*. 'Slips of paper were issued; the troops were told to break off for a few minutes to consult before writing a name on their paper and handing it in,' Captain Arthur Chater recalled. 'The CO and I left Capt. Bamford in charge to collect the voting slips and add up the result. Half an hour later he arrived at the office looking rather sheepish. He handed the CO a list showing himself as [having] received the greatest number of votes.'

When Keyes arrived to inspect the unit the next morning, Chater continued: 'The CO and I met him at the side of the parade ground. He then told us that we were to receive not one, but two Victoria Crosses, and asked who was to receive the second one. After a moment's consultation with me, the CO said Sergeant Finch.'

The Ostend VCs were awarded to Lieutenant-Commander Geoffrey Drummond and Lieutenant-Commander Rowland Bourke for rescue work in their respective motor launches, and to Lieutenant Victor Crutchley, the second-in-command of *Vindictive*. Similarly honoured for Zeebrugge were *Vindictive*'s original commanding officer, Captain Alfred Carpenter; Lieutenant Percy Dean, who repeatedly took his launch back into the firing line to search for survivors; the two intrepid marines, Captain Edward Bamford and Sergeant Norman Finch; Lieutenant Richard Sandford of submarine *C3*; and 19-year-old Able Seaman Albert McKenzie, who had advanced up the Mole, gun blazing, while most of the officers and men in his immediate party fell dead at his feet. In March 1919, Keyes also proposed Lieutenant-Commander Arthur Harrison of *Vindictive* and Lieutenant-Commander George Bradford of *Iris* for the VC. These were posthumous awards, as both men had been killed in the attempt to land on the Mole or shortly thereafter.

Keyes himself was in no doubt about the scale of what had been achieved at Zeebrugge, and was said by Winston Churchill to have been 'puce with rage' when civil servants at first questioned some of the names on his draft submission for awards, apparently in the belief that the list was simply too long. Churchill added that the crisis had been resolved only when the admiral went on to successfully press his case 'while strolling side by side with His Majesty the King down a seafront promenade in liberated France'. The celebration banquets that duly marked the main investiture ceremony held in July 1918 provided a brief but welcome respite from the provisions of the Rationing Order announced the previous winter.

By all accounts Keyes duly appreciated the public acclaim, as well as the £10,000 voted to him by parliament, that he came to enjoy in postwar Britain. Although his was in some ways a shy and retiring character, he expected a proper degree of respect both for his own office and for the men who had fought for him in the Belgian raids. In that spirit, Keyes had gone to London's Prince's Theatre in late November 1918 for the royal premiere of *Jolly Jack Tar*, an entertainment depicting famous episodes in British naval history, although in the event a heavy lighting bridge had crashed down onto the stage in mid-performance, bringing the night to an abrupt end before the climactic scene portraying the storming of the Mole at Zeebrugge. A more solemn occasion followed in April 1919, when Keyes went back to the Flanders coast to take part in commemorations marking the first anniversary of the raids. Funds for a memorial to the Dover Patrol were being collected at the time, and among the subscriptions was a cheque for £1,000 from the king of the Belgians, along with a handwritten note:

> Dear Admiral
>   The Queen and I would be glad to see our names associated with the manifestations of gratitude and respect towards the splendid sailors whose skill and heroism largely prevented the enemy from making efficient use of his naval base on the Flemish coast.

Although generally self-effacing, Keyes could be stubborn when it came to holding out for his favoured projects, a man who, once having made up his mind, rarely allowed that there might be different perspectives of equal or greater validity on the matter under discussion. *The Navy* magazine seemed to hint at this quality when it later wrote of him:

> All meteors produce friction as they proceed on their way, and [Keyes] had his detractors and, it must be admitted, his limitations. He sometimes spoilt his case by overstating it. But no one can deny that what mistakes he made were born of a genuine keenness and an absolute belief in what he advocated. No obstacle was for him impassable. His giant spirit would never admit such a thing.

While on a visit to Australia, Keyes once infuriated his hosts by commenting on repairs being undertaken at a local shipyard: 'At an [American] base they work 24 hours a day, as all sailors and soldiers have to be prepared to do … instead of as in this country where labour and the number of hours worked is controlled by someone of whom I have no knowledge.' Some critics thought Keyes snobbish, and that as the years advanced he became more adept as a polo player than as a naval strategist. In February 1936 Admiral Sir Reginald Bacon, perhaps still embittered by his removal from the Dover Patrol nearly 20 years earlier, wrote to a friend:

> Of course, R.K. had no brain worth talking about. I warned the Admiralty that [Operation ZO] could never block the Zeebrugge channels … I have never served with Keyes, [and] I see no reason why he should have hated me except that he must have known that he was supplanting me under false pretences.

Keyes retired from the navy in 1934, aged 62, and entered parliament that same year as Conservative MP for Portsmouth North. He was one of the relatively few politicians who then clearly identified the growing peril of Nazi Germany – 'a true sage, who [had] in him the stuff of legend,' according to the young John F. Kennedy. Although no great orator, Keyes's speeches condemning disarmament and appeasement commanded widespread respect coming from what *The Times* called 'our greatest sea captain since Nelson', a comparison Keyes himself was thought not to actively reject. He became Britain's first director of Combined Operations in June 1940, but fell out of official favour after complaining of the way in which ministers consistently failed to accede to his proposals for more aggressive use of the nation's commando forces. There was to be a ghastly irony to this when in November 1941 Keyes's 24-year-old elder son Geoffrey lost his life in a special-operations raid designed to capture or kill General Erwin Rommel at his headquarters in Libya. Rommel is said to have laid his own Iron Cross on the young man's coffin as it was buried with full military honours in a local Catholic cemetery.

This tragedy, although stoically borne, certainly precipitated the terminal events of Roger Keyes's life. Raised to the peerage in 1943, he devoted himself to a series of fighting speeches until the autumn of 1944 when he suffered severe smoke inhalation while standing as an observer on the deck of the USS *Appalachian* as she engaged the Japanese in waters off the Philippine island of Leyte. He never fully recovered. Keyes died at his English home in December 1945, aged 73, and was laid to rest alongside 65 of his men in the Zeebrugge corner of St. James's cemetery in Dover.

In April 1918, Keyes had acted as swiftly in announcing promotions as he had in bestowing medals on those who fought in the Flanders raids. Among them was 30-year-old Lieutenant-Commander Francis Sandford, whose picket boat, in the words of the official report, had 'made a voyage of 170 miles to and from the Belgian coast in unpleasant conditions, and which picked up men in the face of almost insurmountable difficulties, due to enemy action, weather and tide'. One of those Sandford rescued in this way was his younger brother Richard, recently evacuated from the floating time bomb that was submarine *C3*. Frank Sandford rose to the rank of captain, and in 1925 became the Admiralty's assistant director of plans. This cyclopean scholar-warrior with an Oxford history degree remarked genially that he had somehow 'managed to get paid for [his] staff work in Whitehall' while still finding time to read a good deal and maintain his usual hectic social life. Francis Sandford died of blood poisoning while staying at a Swiss resort hotel in February 1926; he was thirty-seven.

Richard Sandford was sufficiently recovered from his Zeebrugge injuries to accompany his comrades to London to receive his VC at an investiture held outdoors at Buckingham Palace on 31 July 1918. One newspaper reported: 'Great enthusiasm was displayed when the Flanders contingent went forward, and every man of the party was loudly cheered on mounting the dais and coming to a halt in front of His Majesty.'

Officially declared fit for duty six weeks later, Sandford was given command of the submarine *G 11*, based at Middlesborough. He fell ill after only a few days there, and was taken to Eston Hospital in North Yorkshire. On 22 November, while under the temporary command of another officer, *G 11* lost her bearings and ran aground on rocks off the coast of Northumberland, two of her crew drowning during the evacuation. Richard Sandford died the following morning of what was probably typhoid fever, just 12 days after the armistice and 20 days since his fellow Zeebrugge veteran Albert McKenzie had succumbed to influenza. In the brief period since their investiture, both men, along with the mission's other VCs, had earned the right to be addressed as 'Sir' by all ranks. Richard Sandford was just 27 at the time of his death.

Captain Carpenter of the *Vindictive* lived until 1955, 35 years after the wreck of his ship was raised from Ostend harbour and its midsection broken up for scrap. *Intrepid's* commanding officer Stuart Bonham Carter, the man who arguably could have settled the outcome of Operation ZO in a few seconds by ramming the lock gates at Zeebrugge, saw further service in the Second World War and died aged eighty-three. Commander Ralph Sneyd and Lieutenant Victor Crutchley both enjoyed long and distinguished naval careers in the years following the twin raids, the latter being one of their last survivors when he died in 1986 at the age of ninety-two. Having been born at a time when the Royal Navy still employed steam-powered sloops, Crutchley had lived long enough to see an age when humanity could be effectively wiped out by the touch of a button, a development he regarded as 'both fantastic and retrograde, and in general not one to be admired'. The bespectacled Lieutenant Rowland Bourke meanwhile went back to his adopted home and eventually retired from the Royal Canadian Navy with the rank of commander in 1950, eight years before his death at the age of seventy-two.

In late April 1918, 27-year-old Sgt. Norman Finch, VC, returned to his barracks in Eastney, near Portsmouth, where:

> A band was heard approaching, and finally came in sight up the long avenue, heralding a much-beflagged motor-car drawn by a number of Marines. Sgt. Finch sprang out, and was warmly welcomed by Brigadier-General Gunningham-Campbell, who shook hands with him, to the accompaniment of a tremendous cheer from the serried ranks of his comrades.

Finch's later life had been 'less noisy', he remarked mildly at the time he and the author's family had been neighbours in Portsmouth, where, trim and moustachioed, he sometimes strolled around in a neat three-piece suit with his medal discreetly tucked to one side of his waistcoat. Sergeant Finch died in March 1966, aged seventy-five.

Lieutenant Sir John Alleyne, despite being successively gassed, shot and half-drowned when taking his leave of HMS *Vindictive* as she ran aground at Ostend, lived to be ninety-four. Even this was eclipsed by the record of Captain Ion Hamilton Benn, who, already middle-aged when he came to command a motor launch in the Zeebrugge and second Ostend raids, remained active in business and politics right up to the time of his death in 1961, aged ninety-eight. His sometime fellow MP Lieutenant Edward Hilton Young lost his right arm while manning a forward port gun on *Vindictive* at Zeebrugge, but went on to serve first as the 1931–35 National

Government's minister of health, and later as a distinguished financial journalist, along the way marrying the sculptor Kathleen Bruce, widow of Captain Scott of the Antarctic. In one of his last letters, written at the time he was advising the Treasury on technical matters of shares and securities, Young noted matter-of-factly that at one point he had 'supped full of the horrors of life' but had learned to 'move ahead with something approximating joy in one's soul.' He was 81 at the time of his death in 1960.

Not all of the survivors of Operations ZO and VS fared quite as well as these individuals did in the years ahead. One able seaman who served on *Vindictive* at Zeebrugge was later found wedged in the skylight of a shop in Bakewell, Derbyshire, which he had evidently meant to burgle, and in time was sent to an asylum for what would likely have been only rudimentary treatment of his wartime shell-shock. Several of the sailors and marines returning from Flanders fell on hard times after leaving the service. One of the crew of the blockship *Intrepid* was later obliged to sell his service medal in order to raise funds, and even then found himself being sued by his local council for non-payment of rent. In April 1926, Lieutenant Lionel Chappell, who somehow fittingly commanded a rescue boat at Zeebrugge, launched a public appeal on behalf of distressed veterans of the raid. 'It is a sad thought that after eight years these gallant fellows are practically destitute through lack of employment,' he told the press, adding that 'at least fifty' of the survivors were 'very acutely embarrassed financially.'

Perhaps the cruellest fate of all was reserved for the men of the Belgian operations who survived the carnage but never quite recovered in mind or body. We've noted the lonely death and pitiful funeral of Able Seaman John Helman, who succumbed to the lingering effects of the gas poisoning he suffered at Zeebrugge. Several of Helman's comrades-in-arms who, like him, had been promised a 'Land fit for Heroes' after the war, also struggled with the long-term consequences of combat-related illness or injury. Lieutenant Cecil Dickinson had led one of the first demolition parties to land on the Mole in the early moments of Operation ZO, and after returning to his ship an hour later actually caught a glimpse of Helman 'and others of my men bravely assisting the wounded on the mess deck'. Dickinson himself returned to England, where he received the DSO for his efforts but died following an abdominal operation in February 1928, at the age of thirty-five. Some of those familiar with his case believed that he had never quite recovered after the events of ten years earlier. Geoffrey Drummond, the man whose leg had been shattered by a shell splinter during the second Ostend raid, and who won the VC for his rescue work that night, later fell to the ground when his injured knee gave way while he was carrying a sack of coal to a friend's house in Rotherhithe, east London. Drummond hit his head on the concrete pavement, suffered a concussion, and died at the age of fifty-five.

Just six weeks after Lieutenant Dickinson's death, his fellow Zeebrugge veteran Sergeant-Major Charles Thatcher, RMLI, succumbed to the wounds he suffered during the assault on the Mole. Thatcher had been shot in the leg, which was later amputated, while standing exposed to German fire holding a scaling ladder in place to allow his men to scramble back on board *Vindictive*. His headstone reads: 'Died March 14th 1928 in his 46th year from effects of wounds received at Zeebrugge.'

These were not the last fatalities associated with the Belgian raids. On Christmas Day 1936, the *Sevenoaks Chronicle* reported:

> In the Battle of Zeebrugge in 1918, Marine Alexander Thomas Bailey Pepper, serving on the *Vindictive*, was seriously wounded in the head by shrapnel. These wounds led to his ultimate death, last Saturday, 18 years after the naval epic.
>
> Mrs. Nellie Pepper, a widow, told [authorities] that the dead man was her son, aged 38, who had followed no occupation since the war. He was an ex-marine and on the *Vindictive* when he received severe head wounds for which he received £2 a week. His general health had suffered greatly as a result of the war service. He always complained of head pains. Early on Saturday he began to have fits to which he was subjected and after the fourth he expired. She sent for assistance.

On a quiet breakwater outside Ostend harbour, the recovered bow end of HMS *Vindictive*, neatly restored and painted, stands today as a bulky if, to some, oddly bland and impersonal reminder of the events on the Flanders coast in 1918.

Able Seaman Wilfred Wainwright afterwards wrote of his experience on *Vindictive* as she came alongside at Zeebrugge:

> Every gun in the ship that could bear now gave tongue and the night was made hideous by the nerve-racking shatter of the pom-poms, the deep bell-like boom of the howitzers and trench mortars, and all-pervading rattle of musketry and machine-gun fire. It was hell with a vengeance.
>
> Up into the night went one huge yell, all the pent-up feeling of the years of war and hatred and the lust for killing, and the seamen's storming party landed, followed by the Royal Marines.

Such was the reality behind this smooth and serene monument.

Sources and Chapter Notes

The following pages show at least the newspaper reports, other published works, or primary archive material used in the preparation of the book. I should particularly acknowledge and thank Charles Keyes, Colin McKenzie and Daniel Sandford, each of whose ancestor played a leading role in the Zeebrugge Raid, and also Paul Kendall's excellent book *Voices from the Past*, as cited in the bibliography, which collects a number of first-hand tales about the mission. In a very few cases I was given access to a diary entry or a letter detailing some of the events of April–May 1918 with the request that I not publish the name of the writer. A brief account of my own family connection to the story described here appears in the acknowledgements at the front of the book.

Chapter 1

Some of the account of the ill-fated Operation EC1 is taken from the log of the submarine HMS *K6*, held by the UK National Archives, Document no. ADM 173/6170 1243369. For further information on the disaster I also consulted Edward C. Whitman's story, *'K' for Katastrophe*, published in *Undersea Warfare* magazine, Issue no. 49, Winter 2013. Other sources used in this chapter included Cecil Aspinall-Oglander, *Roger Keyes*, and Robert K. Massie, *Castles of Steel*, both as cited in the bibliography. Stephen Prince's *The Blocking of Zeebrugge*, also cited, gives a concise but vivid account of some of the origins and prelude to the raid.

Among other published reports, I also consulted *The Cambridge Independent News*, *Daily Mail*, *Dover Express*, *Globe & Laurel*, *Portsmouth Evening News*, *The Times* and *Western Daily Press*. The Royal Marines Museum and the National Museum of the Royal Navy each contains a small but valuable archive on the events depicted. The relevant cabinet papers touching (albeit briefly) on the tragedy of Operation EC1 are available through the UK National Archives. The official political discussion of the affair was limited to a two-sentence report read out to ministers at Downing Street on 2 February 1918. It would be a further 84 years before a commemorative plaque was erected near the scene of the catastrophe that needlessly resulted in 104 British casualties.

Chapter 2

For an account of Adm Keyes's visit to the Zeebrugge Mole in October 1914, see Cecil Aspinall-Oglander, *Roger Keyes*, as noted in the bibliography. For the American naval historian Arthur Marder's report of the kaiser's reaction to the Battle of Jutland, see Robert Massie, *Castles of Steel*, p. 659. The subsequent German decision to implement unrestricted U-boat warfare is described in Richard Hough's book *The Great War at Sea 1914–1918* (Oxford: Oxford University Press, 1983), p. 302. Adm Jellicoe's views on the war situation of April 1917 appear in A. Temple Patterson's *The Jellicoe Papers* (two volumes, Arundel: Pegasaurus Books, 1966–68), vol. 2, p. 161 – emphasis in the original text. Jellicoe's memorandum to the cabinet of 29 June 1917 is held in the cabinet papers of the UK

National Archives. The same individual's remarks in a memo to the prime minister of 1 July 1917 are also in the National Archives, file G.T. 1273. Jellicoe's further comments about the Admiralty 'desir[ing] to take up eight coasting steamers ...' are part of the National Archives file CAB 42/25/4. For the remarks of the Home Front volunteer Ernest Cooper, see *People at War 1914–1918*, ed. Michael Moynihan (Newton Abbot: David & Charles, 1973), p. 204. For the account of Winston Churchill at Rosyth, see Churchill's 'My Spy-Story' in *Thoughts and Adventures* (New York: Norton, 1932), a typically stirring if perhaps also impressionistic tale of what actually happened.

It is a pleasure to again acknowledge, as any Zeebrugge author should, Paul Kendall's book *Voices from the Past*, and also both Deborah Lake's very fine *The Zeebrugge and Ostend Raids 1918* and Barrie Pitt's vivid *Zeebrugge*, all as cited in the bibliography.

I also consulted the archives of the *Daily Mail*, *Illustrated London News*, *Liverpool Chronicle*, *The Times* and *Western Mail*, all of which published accounts of the war at sea leading up to the events of April–May 1918.

Chapter 3

For the account of Adm Keyes's encounter with the palm reader at Aberdour House, see Cecil Aspinall-Oglander, *Roger Keyes*, as previously cited. Pte James Feeney's views on HMS *Hindustan* are included in Paul Kendall's *Voices from the Past*, and also in Philip Warner's *The Zeebrugge Raid* (Barnsley: Pen and Sword, 2008). Lt- Cdr Ronald Boddie's story about the volunteers for the raid can be read in the Imperial War Museum, Department of Documents, no. 96/47/1.

Barrie Pitt's description beginning 'Keyes, his blood up, exploded to the Admiralty ...' appears on p. 43 of that author's book *Zeebrugge*, as cited in the bibliography. Adm Wemyss's words, 'At a meeting of the Naval Lords ...' appear in Lady Wester Wemyss's book *The Life & Letters of Lord Wester Wemyss*, also as cited in the bibliography. The line of Cdr Patrick Edwards, RNVR, insisting, 'I went off to my cabin that night, but I could not sleep. How lucky I was to be in [the Zeebrugge raid]' appear in Roger Keyes's book, *The Naval Memoirs of Admiral of the Fleet Sir Roger Keyes 1916–1918* (London: Thornton Butterworth, 1935), p. 222.

I am grateful to Daniel Sandford, to my great-uncle V. Adm Edward Renouf, CB, CVO, and also to my late father Rear-Adm Sefton Sandford, CB, for details of Francis and Richard Sandford and their various exploits.

Lt-Cdr Boddie's only mixed account of morale on board HMS *Hindustan* before the Zeebrugge raid can be found in the Imperial War Museum, Department of Documents, no. 96/47/1. For Sgt Harry Wright's impression of the heavily modified HMS *Vindictive*, see the Royal Marines Museum Archive (Eastney, Hants), file 10/2/W. Lt F. J. Hore's account of the training regimen for the raid was published in *Globe & Laurel*, 1918. Capt Alfred Carpenter's description of the indomitable Frank Brock appears in Carpenter's book *The Blocking of Zeebrugge*, as cited in the bibliography, p. 122.

Harry Adams's own views on the training routine are part of the 'Private Papers of Petty Officer Harry Adams', as quoted in Paul Kendall's book *Voices from the Past*, p. 28. The letter from Eng-Cdr W. A. Bury, RN, was written on 25 June 1918 and as far as can be reasonably established is in public domain. Pte Ernest Tracey's account recalling Winston Churchill's words, 'You are going on a daring and arduous stunt ...' are included in Paul Kendall's *Voices from the Past*, p. 33. For the lines of L-Cpl George Calverley beginning 'I was standing in the supernumerary rank ...' see Imperial War Museum Department of Documents, file 02/30/1. The medical preparations for the raid are quoted in S/Surgeon James McCutcheon's report held in the Zeebrugge file in the UK National Archives, no. ADM 137/3894.

I'm also grateful to the staff of the British Newspaper Archive, Hampshire Record Office, the UK Maritime Archives and Library, University of Leeds Library Special Collections and Wirral Archives Service for their Zeebrugge material used in this chapter.

Chapter 4

For the character sketch of Wing Cdr Frank Brock, see Cecil Oglander-Aspinall, *Roger Keyes*, p. 228. The highly pertinent thought beginning 'To risk [Brock's] capture or death was short-sighted ...' appears in Deborah Lake, *The Zeebrugge and Ostend Raids 1918*, p. 60. The line by Sir Douglas Brownrigg about imposing an embargo on any parliamentary debate of the Zeebrugge raid appears in Brownrigg's *Indiscretions of the Naval Censor* (London: Cassell, 1920), p. 94.

The testimonial to Adm Keyes's personal humility and concern for the men who served under him similarly appears in Cecil Oglander-Aspinall, *Roger Keyes*, p. 248. The account by Lt-Cdr Boddie of Keyes 'giv[ing] the assembled officers a full explanation of the intended operation' forms part of file 96/47/1, Imperial War Museum's Department of Documents. Norbert McCrory's memory of the same training phase is held by the Australian War Memorial (AWM), DRL/429, file 12/11/4812: Papers of Stoker N. McCrory. The comments by Air Mechanic Henry Groothius about the ordeal of drilling with the 5th Battalion, Middlesex Regiment, are courtesy of The Liddle Collection, University of Leeds Library Special Collections, file WW1/RNMN/037.

Capt Alfred Carpenter's line beginning 'In spite of the almost incredible difficulties and tremendous risk involved, the number of applications ...' appears in Carpenter's book *The Blocking of Zeebrugge*, p. 94. The memory of William O'Hara that 'While at Chatham, no leave was given ...' forms part of the 'Private Papers of Petty Officer William O'Hara', as quoted in Paul Kendall, *Voices from the Past*, p. 35, cited in the bibliography. For the description of the crew of *ML 4452*, see p. 17, Percy F. Westerman, *The Thick of the Fray at Zeebrugge*, a short but lively account of the whole operation sustained by some energetic period idiom along the lines of 'Beastly rotten chaps, these Boche' and, emphasising this fact: '"Englisch offizier-pig!" the Hun captain shouted. "You der hospitality of Zherman U-boat must make. We you take prisoner."'

The comments of Sgt Harry Wright beginning 'We were issued with a Lewis gun and a flame-thrower ...' are held in the Royal Marines Museum, Eastney, archive file 10/2/W. For the account of HMS *Botha* being 'towed back to Dunkirk, with the French destroyers forming a protective screen ...' see Barrie Pitt, *Zeebrugge*, p. 55. The description of Alfred Carpenter as 'still a comparatively junior commander ...' appears in Cecil Aspinall-Oglander, *Roger Keyes*, p. 231. The memory of Kapitan Eric Schülze that 'We found a map giving us first hand information ...' and the words of the directive addressed to the Royal Marine units training at Deal ('Officers [are] to imbue their commands with the idea of carrying the operation through with the bayonet') appear in Deborah Lake, *The Zeebrugge and Ostend Raids 1918*, pp. 90 and 59 respectively.

For details of the first casualties of the Zeebrugge raid, suffered when a Stokes shell exploded prematurely during a training exercise at Deal, see Royal Marines Museum Archive, Eastney, Lt-Col Bertram Elliot report of 2 April 1918. For Capt Alfred Carpenter's admission 'We felt pretty sure of being able to recognise any portion of [the Zeebrugge Mole] immediately. In that we were over-confident ...' see that author's book *The Blocking of Zeebrugge*, p. 195. The author Deborah Lake's view that '[Even] the choice of [the codeword] Operation ZO ... underlines the essentially amateur approach that runs like a thread through the planning' and her conclusion that 'Nobody considered specialist navigators necessary [on] the venture ... that neglect cost dearly' appear in her book *The Zeebrugge and Ostend Raids 1918*, pp. 51 and 173 respectively. Private 'Beau' Tracey's memory of experiencing 'a certain degree of pride to be able to [see] that massive Admiral's flag' appears in Paul Kendall, *Voices from the Past*, p. 70. The description of the modified HMS *Vindictive* resembling 'a tipsy cake' comes in Alfred Carpenter, *The Blocking of Zeebrugge*, p. 124. For Adm Keyes's pre-sailing battle order of 7 April 1918, see Sir Roger Keyes, *The Naval Memoirs of Admiral of the Fleet Sir Roger Keyes 1916–1918* (London: Thornton Butterworth, 1935), p. 249.

For the account of the 'near mutiny' aboard HMS *Intrepid*, see Carpenter, *The Blocking of Zeebrugge*, p. 131. Adm Keyes's comments about the need to 'guard against [German detection] which would have meant the certain failure of the expedition ...' appear in his report on the Zeebrugge operation held by the UK National Archives, file ADM 137/3894.The memory of Sgt Harry Wright marching through Deal while en route to his ship for Zeebrugge is held in the Royal Marines Museum archive file 10/2/W. For the account of the security breach that led to a hearing before Southend magistrates concerned with the Defence of the Realm Act, see the report published in *Essex Newsman*, 15–16 June 1918. Capt Carpenter's line beginning 'This officer ordered one of [his] men to sit on the hole,' appears in Carpenter's *The Blocking of Zeebrugge*, p. 159. The same author's memory, 'The tenor [was] "We must push on to-night" …' appears in *The Blocking of Zeebrugge*, p. 164. Capt Arthur Chater's account beginning 'The Admiralty now became apprehensive …' is held in the Imperial War Museum, Department of Documents, file 74/101/1. The account by PO Harry Adams regarding 'General quarters, general evolutions …. etc' forms part of the 'Private Papers of Petty Officer Harry Adams', as quoted in Paul Kendall, *Voices from the Past*, p. 65. The line of the poet and naval historian Henry Newbolt insisting, 'Some of the crew lost control and behaved like madmen …' appears in that author's *Submarine and Anti-Submarine*, as cited in the bibliography, p. 189. The line by Capt Wilfred Tomkinson beginning 'There's one thing about it …' appears in Deborah Lake, *The Zeebrugge and Ostend Raids 1918*, p. 98. The line beginning 'From their respective decks the crews of [*CMB 35A's*] sister-ships watched her drop behind …' appears in Barrie Pitt, *Zeebrugge*, p. 88. For the views of Lt Richard Sandford as he approached his target at Zeebrugge, see UK National Archives, Lt R. D. Sandford, VC, official report, file ADM 137/3894.

Chapter 5

Pte James Feeney's words beginning 'At 7 p.m. I can count 57 vessels …' appear in *Globe & Laurel* 1919. Capt Alfred Carpenter's comment that 'These [men] could handle the vessel and its engines during the passage overseas …' appears in Carpenter's book *The Blocking of Zeebrugge*, p. 91. The words of Capt Ralph Collins beginning 'I regret to [say] that the excess personnel …' form part of his official report on the Zeebrugge operation, held by the UK National Archives, file ADM 137/3894. Capt Carpenter's remark, 'The visibility at this time can hardly have amounted to a yard' appear in *The Blocking of Zeebrugge*, p. 189.

The account by Harry Adams of running into Frank Brock's smokescreen at Zeebrugge forms part of the 'Private Papers of Petty Officer Harry Adams', as quoted in Paul Kendall, *Voices from the Past*, p. 78. The views of Stoker Henry Bindall of submarine *C3* are quoted in Deborah Lake, *The Zeebrugge and Ostend Raids 1918*, p. 125. The comments of Capt Arthur Chater concerning the rum ration are included in the Imperial War Museum Department of Documents, file 74/101/1. Capt Carpenter's account beginning 'We took up our action stations …' appears in his *The Blocking of Zeebrugge*, p. 188. His line 'We were one minute late on scheduled time …' appears in *The Blocking of Zeebrugge*, pp. 194-5.

Sgt Harry Wright's line, 'Then the silence was broken by a terrific report …' is included in the Royal Marines Museum archive, Eastney, file 10/2/W. For Capt Carpenter's account beginning 'We got pretty near shore before they saw us …' see the UK National Archives, Capt A. Carpenter, VC, report, file ADM 137/3894. Carpenter's factual comment noting drily, '*Vindictive* [was] a sitting duck …' appears in *The Blocking of Zeebrugge*, p. 191. For the graphic account by Lt Edward Hilton Young of the effects of the explosion on board HMS *Vindictive*, see Sir John Hammerton, *The Great War: I Was There* (London: Amalgamated Press, 1938), p. 1648. Lt Arthur Lougher's memory beginning 'The noise was deafening …' was published in the *South Wales Daily News*, 30 April 1918, and thus has the merit of being fresh in the interviewee's mind. For the account of L-Cpl George Calverley on *Vindictive*'s final approach to the Zeebrugge Mole, see Imperial War Museum, Department of Documents, file 02/30/1.

Sgt Harry Wright's memory of waiting to transfer from *Vindictive* onto the Zeebrugge Mole, 'We were packed tight in five ranks …' appears in Deborah Lake, *The Zeebrugge and Ostend Raids 1918*, pp. 105-106. Pte Jack Finney's remarks beginning 'We were all layed down at that time …' form part of Pte Arthur Burnell papers, as quoted in Paul Kendall, *Voices from the Past*, p. 88. For the account by the Royal Navy rating 'We were fitted with special grapnels …' see the report published in *Dumfries & Galloway Standard*, 4 May 1918. Leading Seaman Dowell's account beginning 'A derrick had been rigged out …' was even fresher than this, appearing in *The Daily Chronicle* of 27 April 1918. For Capt Carpenter's account stating,'The two foremost brows reached the wall …' see UK National Archives, report of Capt A. Carpenter, VC, file ADM 137/3894. The letter by Eng-Cdr. W. A. Bury was dated 25 June 1918, is in public domain and was first quoted in *Dover During the Dark Days* by A. 'Dug-Out' (London: John Lane, The Bodley Head, 1919). For the account of Leading Seaman William Childs storming the Zeebrugge Mole, see Philip Warner, *The Zeebrugge Raid* (Barnsley: Pen & Sword, 2008), p. 93.

Capt Alfred Carpenter's lines 'This change of arrangement …' and 'At the top of the foremost ladder …' appear in his book *The Blocking of Zeebrugge*, p. 202. The remarks of Lt Stuart Bonham Carter beginning 'When *Thetis* came within sight of the Mole …' are part of his unpublished Zeebrugge memoir, courtesy of Hampshire Record Office. I am also grateful to my late great-uncle V. Adm Edward 'Sonny' Renouf, CB, CVO, who once generously put his memories of many of these individuals and events at my disposal.

Chapter 6

The account by PO William O'Hara beginning 'We managed to get a line to him which he grasped …' forms part of the 'Private Papers of Petty Officer William O'Hara', as quoted by Paul Kendall, *Voices from the Past*, p. 114. For AB Charles Pooley's account, 'It was hell while it lasted …' see the report published in the *Western Mail*, 27 April 1918. The words of Air Mech Frank Donovan and of Pte Jim Clist both similarly appear in Paul Kendall, *Voices from the Past*, pp. 151-2 and pp. 152-3 respectively. For the account of the unnamed Royal Marines officer beginning 'We formed up and forced our way ashore …' see the report published in the *Daily Record*, 25 April 1918. The account by the supremely brave 19-year-old AB Albert McKenzie is part of his oral report of the Zeebrugge operation; I should particularly thank Colin McKenzie for certain information on this gallant individual. For the account by AB Bernard Devlin, who clambered onto the Zeebrugge Mole from HMS *Daffodil*, see the report in *Thomson's Weekly News*, 4 May 1918.

For Sub-Lt Chevallier's remarks, 'The *Vindictive* [was] being shelled all the time …' see the UK National Archives, Sub-Lt Felix Chevallier report, file ADM 137/3894. For Capt Alfred Carpenter's account beginning 'Every available space on the mess deck was occupied by casualties …' see that author's book *The Blocking of Zeebrugge*, p. 209. Albert McKenzie's account of the probable death of Frank Brock appears in Deborah Lake, *The Zeebrugge and Ostend Raids 1918*, p. 114. The further report beginning 'Without any arms, Brock rushed among the German gun crew …' appeared in the *Coventry Evening Telegraph*, among other newspapers, on 30 April 1918. For the words of Lt Richard Sandford, see the UK National Archives, Lt. R. D. Sandford, VC, report, contained in file ADM 137/3894. I'm also grateful to the late V. Adm Edward Renouf, RN, for his personal views and memories of the event. For an almost immediate report on the action by submarine *C3* and the subsequent fate of its crew, see the account of Stoker Henry Bindall as published in the *Daily Mail* of 24 April 1918. Lt Richard Sandford's account beginning 'The charge exploded when the skiff was only 200–300 yards from the viaduct …' also appears in his official report on the Zeebrugge raid, UK National Archives, file ADM 137/3894.

For Capt Alfred Carpenter's memory of '… a terrific explosion seen away to the westward' see Carpenter's book *The Blocking of Zeebrugge*, p. 207. The reaction of PO Harry Adams to the same climactic event is quoted by Paul Kendall, *Voices from the Past*, p. 122. For some of the legendary affair of the German bicyclist or bicyclists who allegedly rode headlong to their doom by pedalling into the gap blown by Sandford and *C3* in the Zeebrugge viaduct, see Barrie Pitt, *Zeebrugge*, p. 114. Lt Sandford's remark that 'I set the fuse myself and I think the thing was done all right …' was given to reporters as he lay in hospital recovering from his wounds on the afternoon of 23 April 1918, and duly appeared in the following morning's *Daily Mail*. An account of the rescue work carried out by Lt-Cdr Francis Sandford ('Ten minutes after the explosion, the picket-boat arrived …') appears in Barrie Pitt, *Zeebrugge*, p. 115.

The line by Midshipman David Morris remembering 'We had a terrible fight …' is quoted by Paul Kendall, *Voices from the Past*, p. 157. The dying words of Lt-Cdr James Dawbarn Young were published in an account of his life and career that appeared in *St. Albans and District Congregational* magazine, June 1918. For the report stating 'An explosion was heard, but Commanding Officer states that he could not see the effect …' see Lt A. Welman note in the UK National Archives, file ADM 137/3894. For the line beginning 'The destroyer apparently observed *CMB 5* in light of star shell …' see Sub-Lt C. Outhwaite note, also in UK National Archives, file ADM 137/3894. Capt Alfred Carpenter's account stating 'Valentine Gibbs, Iris's captain, was mortally wounded …' appears in that author's book *The Blocking of Zeebrugge*, p. 221. The 1970s account by L-Cpl George Calverley of the horrors he encountered on board HMS *Iris* ('I said to one of my section, "Well Cornforth, the worst is over …"') is held by The Imperial War Museum, Department of Documents, file 02/30/1.

For the account of HMS *Vindictive* alongside the Zeebrugge Mole beginning 'It was soon found necessary to utilize the ward room … for the disposal of the wounded' see the report of S/Surgeon J. McCutcheon, UK National Archives, file ADM 137/3894. Capt Alfred Carpenter's memory of shouting out 'about everything going splendidly …' appears in his book *The Blocking of Zeebrugge*, p. 210. For the lively report beginning 'Time for us to be making tracks, old man …' see Percy Westerman, *The Thick of the Fray at Zeebrugge*, p. 37. For the account by Cdr Ralph Sneyd beginning 'The ship was about 300 yards from the eastern pier …' see that officer's official report included in the UK National Archives, file ADM 137/3894. For the account of the unnamed naval rating beginning 'The building was stormed and battered with bombs …' see *Thomson's Weekly News* dated 4 May 1918. For Lt-Cdr Ronald Boddie's memory, 'When we got near the *Vindictive* … we came under heavy attack,' see Boddie's account held in the Imperial War Museum Department of Documents, file 96/47/1. The account of the U-boat commander complaining 'As the blockships came in, the junior commander of the land battery … thought they were friendly' appears in Lowell Thomas, *Raiders of the Deep* (London: William Heinemann, 1929), p. 250. Capt Arthur Chater's account beginning 'We discussed the situation …' is contained in the Imperial War Museum, Department of Documents, file 74/101/1.

AB Devlin's account of storming the Zeebrugge Mole ('I went [ashore] on my hands and knees …') was published in *Thomson's Weekly News*, 4 May 1918. For Air Mech William Gough's account, see Imperial War Museum, Department of Documents, file 91/11/1. Capt Alfred Carpenter's lines beginning 'Shells were still hitting us every few seconds …' appear in his book *The Blocking of Zeebrugge*, p. 211.

Chapter 7

The memory of Lt-Cdr Ronald Boddie of HMS *Thetis* is contained in the Imperial War Museum, Department of Documents, file 96/47/1. For Cdr Sneyd's account beginning 'The foremost firing keys had not been brought to the firing position …' see Cdr R. Sneyd report held in the UK National Archives, file ADM 137/3894. Chief Engine Room Artificer Frank Gale's account beginning 'We scrambled on board …' was first published in *Downham Market Gazette*, 4 May 1918, and later widely reprinted. For the report of Lt Stuart Bonham Carter beginning 'After getting to my position … I waited for the crews to get into the life boats', see that officer's report included in the UK National Archives, file ADM 137/3894; I'm also grateful to the staff of Hampshire Record Office for access to Lt Bonham Carter's unpublished account of the operation. Stoker Thomas Farrell's account beginning 'I was on board *Intrepid*, [and] as a matter of fact the last man to leave …' first appeared in the *Chatham, Rochester & Gillingham News*, 27 April 1918. Lt Bonham Carter's subsequent remarks beginning 'As *Intrepid* closed in she went ahead full steam …' were provided by Hampshire Record Office, file no. 94 M 72/F333.

For the memory of Lt Edward Billyard-Leake stating 'I then abandoned ship and fired my charges …' see that officer's official report held by the UK National Archives, file ADM 137/3894. Adm Keyes's account beginning 'Lloyd had the Iphigenia's white ensign wrapped round his waist,' appears in Sir Roger Keyes, *The Naval Memoirs of Admiral of the Fleet Sir Roger Keyes 1916–1918*, p. 291. The account of Lt Percy Dean, VC, doubling back to pick up survivors from HMS *Intrepid* appears in Barrie Pitt, *Zeebrugge*, p. 141. Stoker Benjamin Eagleton's account, 'As we got away we could see the Germans running about on the Mole with machine guns …' appeared in his hometown newspaper the *Southend Standard* on 2 May 1918. Adm Keyes's comments on the contrasting appearance of Lt Bonham Carter and Lt Billyard-Leake following their rescue at Zeebrugge appear in Keyes's *Naval Memoirs*, p. 291.

The account of Adm Keyes's own direct role at Zeebrugge, beginning '[to] wheel and circle, emerging from her own smokescreens …' appears in Barrie Pitt, *Zeebrugge*, p. 145. The line noting 'When the men saw *Warwick* bearing down towards them …' appears in Cecil Aspinall-Oglander, *Roger Keyes*, p. 246. Capt Alfred Carpenter's account, 'I had seen the submarine explosion in the direction of the viaduct …' forms part of the report of Capt A. Carpenter, VC, held by the UK National Archives, file ADM 137/3894. The comment by Lt Charles Lamplough of 9 Platoon, Royal Marines, beginning 'During the period we were on the Mole …' appears in Deborah Lake, *The Zeebrugge and Ostend Raids 1918*, p. 123. Lt Lamplough's subsequent remark, 'My impression of the operation after the attack was, that as far as our objectives were concerned … the operation was a failure', appears in a collection of Adm Roger Keyes's papers and correspondence held by the UK National Archives, file CAB 45/268. The account by AB Quinton Murdoch ('We had to assist with the bringing in of the wounded …') first appeared in his hometown newspaper the *Dumfries & Galloway Standard*, 4 May 1918. Capt Alfred Carpenter's lines beginning 'One marine carried a disabled man onto *Vindictive* …' appear in Carpenter's book *The Blocking of Zeebrugge*, p. 254.

The comment by the naval rating who remembered the 'pitiful chaos' of the reembarkation on *Vindictive* ('Of 14 or 15 landing ladders only two remained') first appeared in the *Nottingham Journal* of 30 April 1918. The report on Private William Hopewell ('After the proper Nos. 1 and 2 of his Lewis gun Section had become casualties …') forms part of the report by Maj B. Weller, held by the UK National Archives, file ADM 137/3894. The account by Sgt Harry Wright of watching *Vindictive* leave her berth on the Zeebrugge Mole without him ('It seemed cruelly hard to know we had come through unscathed, and now were left behind through no fault of our own') is held in the Royal Marines Museum archive, Eastney, file 10/2/W. Sgt Wright's subsequent remark, 'I was for five weeks a Prisoner of War at Brandenburg *after* the Armistice …' is held by the same archive, file 11/12/5(5). For WO William Edgar's citation for the DSO, see *The London Gazette*, 23 July 1918. Capt Alfred Carpenter's lines beginning 'In less than a minute all previous fog records were beaten …' appear in his book *The Blocking of Zeebrugge*, p. 257.

The account by Frank Brock's protégé Lt Graham Hewett of *Vindictive*'s retirement from the Zeebrugge Mole appears in that officer's report held by the UK National Archives, file ADM 137/3894. For Lt Hilton Young's lines 'We still had a race against time before us – to get out of range of the big guns', see Sir John Hammerton, *The Great War: I Was There*, p. 1651. The account stating 'At breakfast time [Able Seaman] Lake was still there …' appears in Barrie Pitt, *Zeebrugge*, p. 128. The remark of PO Harry Adams ('We worked our smoke boxes …') forms part of the 'Private Papers of Petty Officer Harry Adams', as quoted by Paul Kendall, *Voices from the Past*, p. 216. The words of Air Mech Sidney Hesse beginning 'because her boats were full of holes. We took about 75 of her crew off …' appear in *Cross and Cockade International Journal*, Volume 32, no. 2, 2001. For the account by Lt Edward Hilton Young beginning 'The din in firing had [finally] ceased …', again see Sir John Hammerton's book *The Great War: I Was There*, p. 1651. Pte Philip Hodgson's memory 'for some seconds, only a few yards separated the ships …' is part of his account held in the Royal Marines Museum archive, Eastney, file 7/17/2. For the line recalling 'The finest sight of my life … There, just ahead, we could make out the cliffs of Dover', see Imperial War Museum, Department of Documents (note by Air Mech William Gough), file 91/11/1. For Lt Harold Campbell's words 'Don't you think we're lucky, lads …?' see *Thomson's Weekly News*, 4 May 1918.

The remarks by Pte James Feeney about 'all the bodies collected up together' on board HMS *Vindictive* appear in *Globe & Laurel*, 1919. The lines by the returning Royal Marine remembering 'Then the reaction set in …' are held in the Imperial War Museum, Department of Documents, file 02/30/1. For the comments of Lt Edward Berthon on the Ostend operation, 'We were coming up to the time limit …' see that officer's report held by the Brotherton Library, University of Leeds.

Chapter 8

The remarks by the archbishop of Canterbury beginning 'Dear Admiral Keyes … The news which tonight's paper gives us …' appear in Cecil Aspinall-Oglander, *Roger Keyes*, p. 464. Henry Newbolt's remarks beginning 'The double attack of St. George's Day achieved not only …' appear in that author's book *Submarine and Anti-Submarine*, p. 191. The account beginning 'The working parties at the piers were standing on the piles …' first appeared in the *Burnley News*, 1 May 1918.

For the Press Association correspondent's description of the returning troops, 'They presented a striking appearance …' see the *Derbyshire Daily Telegraph*, 24 April 1918, among other subsequent reprints. Adm Keyes's memory beginning 'My wife had prepared every bed in the house …' appears in Sir Roger Keyes, *The Naval Memoirs of Admiral of the Fleet Sir Roger Keyes 1916-1918*, pp. 299-300. Keyes's less fulsome remarks beginning 'The formation of this service …' are quoted in Cecil Aspinall-Oglander, *Roger Keyes*, p. 247.

The successive reports to the prime minister and cabinet on the results of the Zeebrugge and Ostend operations are held by the UK National Archives, Cabinet Papers of 24 April 1918, 25 April 1918, 8 May 1918 and 10 June 1918.

For the lines beginning 'The ship was taken out and "swung" by Lt Sir John Alleyne …' see Barrie Pitt, *Zeebrugge*, p. 179. Adm Keyes's final memory of Cdr Alfred Godsal ('[He] looked serene and happy …') appears in Cecil Aspinall-Oglander, *Roger Keyes*, p. 252. Keyes's perhaps optimistic conclusion about the success of the Zeebrugge raid, beginning 'The main results achieved have proved greater …' appears in his official report held by the UK National Archives, file ADM 137/3894. The equally effusive appraisal beginning 'From that day [23 April 1918], the Belgian ports were useless to the enemy …' appears in Percy Westerman's book *The Thick of the Fray at Zeebrugge*, p. 48. Winston Churchill's more measured assessment appears in his book *The World Crisis 1911–1918*, Vol. 3 (London: Thornton Butterworth, 1927), p. 1242. Barrie Pitt's remark beginning 'The Zeebrugge raid was a disaster for the Germans …' appears in that author's *Zeebrugge*, p. 205. Selwyn Lloyd MP told the then schoolboy author the story of Lloyd George's own considered account of the Belgian coastal raids in an interview at the House of Commons in November 1972. The view of the senior German intelligence officer for the marine divisions in Flanders appears in Col G.M. Stinglhamber, *The Story of Zeebrugge*, p. 34.

For the view on Operation ZO by Adm Sir John Fisher, at least as circulated by Capt Herbert Grant, RN ('No such folly was ever devised …'), see Deborah Lake, *The Zeebrugge and Ostend Raids*

1918, p. 191. Capt Grant is also quoted in his unpublished book *The Immortal Folly of Zeebrugge* by Deborah Lake, p. 139. The U-boat commander insisting '[The raid] did not block the Flanders base …' is quoted in Lowell Thomas's book *Raiders of the Deep*, p. 250. For the views of the respected naval historian Richard Hough beginning 'Zeebrugge was a courageous and thrilling exploit …' see that author's book *The Great War at Sea 1914–1918* (Oxford: Oxford University Press, 1983), p. 316. Adm William Fisher's remark that 'You have earned the gratitude of the whole Navy' appears in Cecil Aspinall-Oglander, *Roger Keyes*, p. 463. For an account of the honours conferred in particular on Capt Edward Bamford and Sgt Norman Finch, see Imperial War Museum, Department of Documents, file 74/101/1. For the assessment of Sir Roger Keyes as a 'meteor', see the tribute to him by V. Adm Sir James Pipon, KBE, *The Navy* magazine, February 1946. For an account of the investiture held at Buckingham Palace on 31 July 1918, see the *Liverpool Daily Post*, 1 August 1918, among several other similar reports. The account of the valiant Sgt Norman Finch, VC, returning to barracks in Eastney first appeared in *Globe & Laurel*, 1918.

Bibliography

Aspinall-Oglander, Cecil, *Roger Keyes* (London: Hogarth Press, 1951)

Bacon, Admiral Sir Reginald, *The Dover Patrol* (London: Hutchinson, 1919)

Carpenter, Capt Alfred, *The Blocking of Zeebrugge* (Boston, Houghton Mifflin Co., 1922)

Coleman, E. C., *No Pyrrhic Victories: The 1918 Raids on Zeebrugge and Ostend* (Stroud: The History Press, 2014)

Compton-Hall, Richard, *Submarines and The War at Sea 1914–1918* (London: Macmillan, 1991)

Cook, Sir Edward, *The Press in War Time* (London: Macmillan, 1920)

Ewing, Alfred W., *The Man of Room 40* (London: Hutchinson, 1939)

Fullerton, Alexander, *60 Minutes for St. George* (London: Pan Books, 1978)

Keeble, Howard, *The Zeebrugge Affair* (New York: George H. Doran, 1918)

Kendall, Paul, *Voices from the Past: The Zeebrugge Raid 1918* (Barnsley: Frontline Books, 2016)

Lake, Deborah, *The Zeebrugge and Ostend Raids 1918* (Barnsley: Pen & Sword Books, 2002)

Liddle, Peter, *The Sailor's War* (London: Blandford Publishing, 1985)

Massie, Robert K., *Castles of Steel* (New York: Random House, 2003)

Maxwell, Gordon S., *The Naval Front* (London: A & C Black, 1920)

Newbolt, Henry, *Submarine and Anti-Submarine* (London: Longmans, 1918)

Pitt, Barrie, *Zeebrugge* (London: Cassell, 1958)

Prince, Stephen, *The Blocking of Zeebrugge* (London: Bloomsbury, 2010)

Stinglhamber, Col. G. M., *The Story of Zeebrugge* (Zeebrugge: The Zeebrugge Museum, 1935)

Tucker, Spencer C., *The Great War 1914–18* (Bloomington: Indiana University Press, 1998)

Wemyss, Lady Wester, *The Life & Letters of Lord Wester Wemyss* (London: Eyre & Spottiswoode, 1935)

Westerman, Percy F., *The Thick of the Fray at Zeebrugge* (London: Blackie & Son Ltd., 1918)

Index